IT'S GOOD TO BE ALIVE

IT'S
GOOD
TO BE
ALIVE

Roy Campanella

LITTLE, BROWN AND COMPANY
BOSTON · TORONTO

Illustrations occur between pages 214 and 215

TO MY WIFE, RUTHE
AND THE CHILDREN

This book was written during a period of convalescence, at a time when I was fighting to get well. I needed a helping hand in its preparation. I was fortunate in that I had two — Joe Reichler of the Associated Press and Dave Camerer of the Columbia Broadcasting System. To them, my sincere thanks.

ROY CAMPANELLA

Salt Spray
Glen Cove, New York
July 25, 1959

IT'S GOOD TO BE ALIVE

ONE

MY MIND IS SO FULL OF THOUGHTS AS I SIT in my wheel chair and get ready to dictate the story of my life . . . a life that has been so eventful, so exciting, so wonderful . . . a life that was almost taken away from me but which God spared . . . a life such as few people have been fortunate enough to live.

Where shall I start? How do I begin? There is so much to tell. Shall I begin with the automobile accident? When I recovered consciousness in the car and discovered that I was paralyzed? Shall I start with the time I came out of the anesthesia after they cut a hole in my windpipe to allow me to breathe?

Shall I open with the time I presented a baseball to a little boy in the hospital with me; and, after I had apologized for not being physically able to autograph it for him, he said simply, "That's all right, Mr. Campanella, I can't see."

Then there was the World Series day in Yankee Stadium when I slumped in my wheel chair and cried unashamedly as the huge crowd stood on its feet and cheered me for five full minutes.

Baseball has been my life ever since I was old enough to throw one, so perhaps I should start from the day I played my first professional game; or when I joined the Brooklyn Dodgers organization; or when I hit the first of my 242 major league home runs; or when I won the first of my three Most Valuable Player awards.

3

Perhaps the proper beginning would be the day I left Rusk Institute to begin a new life, my life in a wheel chair as a quadriplegic? There are so many starting points, so many new phases, so many milestones, it's hard to decide just where to begin.

What stands out most in my mind of all that has happened since the fateful morning of January 28, 1958, when the world turned upside down for me, was something that happened at Holman Stadium in Vero Beach, Florida, nearly fourteen months after my accident.

From where I was sitting in my wheel chair, I could see this little crippled old lady struggling up the steep ramp. She wore steel braces on both legs. Slowly she made her way up with the aid of a wooden crutch under her right arm. Her left arm hung loosely at her side, paralyzed. Her snow-white head was tilted slightly to the left.

Her attendant, a middle-aged man, walked slowly alongside, ever on the alert to grab her should she stumble or fall. Once or twice he tried to assist her, but she shrugged him off. She finally made the top of the ramp where I was sitting. She was gasping and out of breath. She opened her mouth to speak; but no words came. She stood there looking at me in the chair. Her eyes, sorrowed by years of suffering, looked down on my paralyzed body. She slowly lifted them to my face. Reaching out an old, thinned right arm, she took my limp hand in hers.

"Mr. Campanella," she finally managed to say, "I came a long, long way to see you. More than a thousand miles. I just had to see you and thank you, for you gave me the courage and the will to go on when everything seemed hopeless." Her voice trailed off. She was all spent from the excitement, the long trip, the steep climb, the deep emotion. She was very old, and she must have weighed all of eighty-five or ninety pounds. Who was she? Why had she made this long

4

trip? Had she really come just to see me? I wanted to say something to her as she stood there looking down at me, barely able to stand up and refusing to support herself on the arm of her attendant. Then I saw she was ready to speak again.

"Oh, I'm so glad I came," she said earnestly. "You see, I was a patient in the same hospital with you in New York. At the same time. I had a stroke and my entire left side became paralyzed. I couldn't even talk. They didn't give me much hope. As for me, I didn't care whether I made it or not. Then you were brought in. The people at the hospital said you had no chance to live. Crushed vertebrae. A broken neck.

"But you did live. The doctors marveled at your courage. They were thrilled with your faith. They set you up as the example, the inspiration. You became a symbol.

"I don't know exactly when I stopped giving up. All I know is that one day I decided that I just didn't want to stop yet. I was determined to get back on my feet. It was you who gave me the courage, the will to live."

I sat there without saying a word. I just couldn't find any. I've never been accused of being the quiet, shy type. I'm a firm believer in free speech. But that was one time when my tongue was stuck in my mouth. It was most embarrassing. I wanted to thank her. I wanted to ask her name; find out where she was from; learn whether she had any children. But all I could think of was that this wonderful little crippled old lady had come down the length of the United States just to say hello to me — me, Roy Campanella, a Negro ballplayer who happened to have an accident that ended his career and maybe put him for the rest of his life in a wheel chair.

I thought about that a long time after she left. I thought about this little old lady. I thought about the hundreds, no,

5

thousands of people, strangers, who had come to see me since I arrived at this Dodgers spring training camp. Men and women who had come to shake my hand, to encourage me and wish me well; boys and girls who had come just to look at me and ask for my autograph and who turned away, some disappointed, some embarrassed, when I apologized for not being able to hold a pen or pencil. I thought of the hundreds of thousands of letters and telegrams I had received while in the hospital, from people in all walks of life, from people all over the world — from President Eisenhower down.

The Dodgers and Reds were playing an exhibition game. As a rule no one watches a game with more interest and more concentration than I do. But at this moment the game could have been miles away. I was sitting in back of the last row of the grandstand, behind home plate. My two attendants, Jimmy Williamson and Danny Mackey, were standing on each side of me, to protect me from foul balls. I had been flown down from my home in Glen Cove, Long Island, only a week before to begin my duties as special coach of all the pitchers and catchers in the Dodger organization.

Being there with my old buddies, with Pee Wee and Duke and Gil and Carl and Clem and my protégé Johnny Roseboro, and being back with the game I love so much was a wonderful thing for me both physically and mentally. Only a year before, when I was lying flat on my back in Glen Cove Community Hospital, fighting for my life, I didn't dare dream that I would ever be back on a baseball field where I had made my living for twenty years, where I had grown from a scared boy into a confident man, where I had learned that on a ballfield it doesn't matter what you are or who you are, but how you're hitting, or fielding, or pitching. It's what you do on that baseball diamond that counts. Nothing else.

I'm a lucky guy. I've got so much to be thankful for. Don't

feel sorry for me. Please. I'm on my way back, and I'm going to make it.

Some people may think the Lord turned his back on me because of the accident. That's not so. I consider myself very lucky that I was able to play ball for twenty years, half of them in the big leagues. And even when I had the accident I was lucky. How many people have similar accidents and are killed? I could have been burned up in that automobile, and I could have died in the hospital after I got pneumonia. The car turned over on me and the engine was running for I don't know how long. The gasoline could easily have leaked out and caught fire, and I couldn't have done anything about it. I tried to turn off the ignition with my left hand. I couldn't move my arm. I couldn't move anything. That's when I knew my whole body was paralyzed.

I have made a great deal of progress. I'm going to make more. There was a time when I couldn't move my arms or my head, when I couldn't sit up. For many months after the accident I couldn't use my hands at all. I couldn't eat or drink by myself. Now I can do all those things. Each day I feel stronger and every day I try something new.

It doesn't take too much fight if you have the courage and the faith. All of us want to live and I'm one of them. And I hope to continue to live and maybe to help some others in the same condition who may have given up just a little.

My last year as a ballplayer was 1957. That was the year Walter O'Malley, owner of the Dodgers, decided to move them out of Brooklyn to Los Angeles. I first began hearing rumors of the switch in February of that year when spring training began at Vero Beach. I remember it was on the eve of Washington's Birthday. The Dodgers pitchers and catchers had been down early and working out before the others arrived. And it was that evening that Mr. O'Malley made a

7

startling announcement. Ever since baseball has been played there have been player swaps and deals. But this was no player deal. This was a franchise deal! Mr. O'Malley and Phil Wrigley, Jr., owner of the Chicago Cubs, had exchanged minor league clubs. The Cubs got the Dodgers' Fort Worth club in the Texas League in exchange for Chicago's Los Angeles club of the Pacific Coast League. The deal included the ball parks. That meant that the Dodgers now had Wrigley Field in Los Angeles and a foothold on the Coast if and when.

I should have figured it out right then. Why would Mr. O'Malley make such a deal unless he intended to move? Looking back, it's so obvious. But somehow I didn't see it then. Maybe because I didn't want to see it. I had spent nine of my happiest years in Brooklyn. That's where I wanted to finish my playing career. I got my wish all right, but in a much different way.

Not everybody was as innocent as me, though. The people on the West Coast got the idea pretty quick. The newsprint was hardly dry on those Los Angeles papers when the politicians came swarming in on us at Vero Beach. They arrived in camp like conquerors, looking us over the way a guy does a piece of property knowing he's about to own it. Always looking for an angle, the photographers rigged up a Dodgers cap with the letters *L A* on it and asked me to pose with the Los Angeles mayor, Norris Poulson, wearing the cap. I went along with it but to me it was a big joke. The Dodgers leave Ebbets Field? Maybe. But the Dodgers leave Brooklyn? Never.

After we shook hands, Mayor Poulson put one arm around me and said: "Campy, next year you'll no longer be a Brooklyn Bum; you'll be a Los Angeles Bum."

"That'll sure be the day," I grinned.

At the time I wasn't thinking about where I'd be playing

"next year." I was more concerned with this year. I was coming off a bad season and was looking to make a good comeback. In '56 I'd played the entire season with two bad hands. The left one had been operated on in '54 and the right one during the winter of '56. Some people thought that after '56 I'd had it.

One big reason why I was looking to a good year was because the pain had left my hands. The numbness was still there but the pain had gone, and I could grip a bat again and had been strengthening my hands by swinging a loaded bat in the cellar of my store. And finally, this was the odd year. This was '57, and I had won the National League's Most Valuable Player award three times, all in odd years — 1951, 1953 and 1955. If ballplayers are superstitious, this at least was a happy hunch.

For ballplayers, spring training is a time for tuning up, getting set for the season ahead. Each man has to prepare himself, and of course I was thinking most about my hands and my ability to play as well as I had in my good years. Pee Wee Reese was worried about his legs and his back, being the oldest player on the team. Carl Erskine was trying to come back from arm trouble. Duke Snider had a bad knee and was hoping he could get through the season without undergoing surgery. Don Newcombe had his usual sore arm in the spring. Each of us, especially the veterans, had a personal problem.

But we had a mutual concern: the possibility of this being our last year as the Brooklyn Dodgers. As time wore on, we began to think more and more about moving to Los Angeles, and we talked about it almost every day in the clubhouse and on the bench. Some were for it; some didn't care much either way; and others, like myself, didn't like it. We all had personal reasons for the way we felt.

Gil Hodges was like me. He wanted no part of the West

Coast. "I just don't want to move," he said. Gil had lived in Indiana until he got to the big leagues. "I live in Brooklyn," he said. "I'm not just a Dodger ballplayer. Brooklyn is my home. I don't want to have to sell my house, take my kids out of school, leave old friends and all that."

Snider felt the opposite. "I guess it's better for me if we shift. I got an avocado ranch up there in the valley not too far from L. A.," he said.

Reese didn't want to go. He wanted to finish his career in Brooklyn. I guess he played there longer than any other player in history. And nobody was more popular in Brooklyn than Pee Wee. He asked me how I felt about moving.

"Man," I said, "I don't like it nohow. I got my business in New York. I got my home in Glen Cove. Yes, and my youngsters are in good schools. Then there's my boat. Jersey City is as far West as I wanna go."

The Dodgers had played eight games in Jersey City the year before, in '56, because Mr. O'Malley was trying to prove his point to New York City officials that the Dodgers were too big for Ebbets Field. We had simply outgrown the old park. We needed a much bigger field, with bigger and better parking areas. Now, we had another eight games scheduled for Jersey City in '57. I kinda looked forward to those games. Not because I loved hitting in that prairie-sized park. Heck, no. It's just that I would take my boat from the dock near my home in the morning and have an enjoyable cruise down Long Island Sound, into the East River and then on into the Hudson River, and tie up at Jersey City. All our games there were played at night, and so it gave me a day on the water. Oh, how I enjoyed those trips.

The rumored shift to California was only a minor annoyance compared to what was really worrying me. My hands. They weren't right. I knew it in spring training just

10

as soon as I began to bear down. The old breaks and the old and new operations all started hurting at once. At thirty-five, plus, my hands felt more like eighty-five. I wore a kid glove on my mitt hand to help ease the impact on catching a fast ball. Foul tips hurt the bare hand.

As that '57 season wore on, the daily pounding made the hands worse. Occasionally I hit the ball hard, but I knew I wasn't myself at the plate. Manager Walter Alston knew it too. He had to bench me. I was really hurtin'. I didn't like to ride the bench, but the rest did help some. That season I managed to catch a hundred games for the ninth consecutive year. I hit only .242, and the thirteen homers were a very little bit for old Campy. My spirits hit a new low in August, and to make it worse it was in that month that I found out for sure we were going to Los Angeles. The only thing that could save us was a miracle — like New York City giving us a new ball park, strictly a thousand-to-one shot.

Even though most of us older players were having a bad year, our young pitchers such as Johnny Podres and Don Drysdale were very strong. We managed to stay in the pennant race until August as part of a five-team dogfight. It was strictly dog-eat-dog and the fans loved it. Then everybody but Milwaukee started losing all at once — St. Louis, Cincinnati, Philadelphia and Brooklyn. Just like that, the race cracked wide open. The Braves won the flag in a breeze and the Cardinals beat us out for second place. Milwaukee clinched on September 23, and we just played out the schedule for those last half-dozen games.

The Giants had announced early in August that they were quitting New York for San Francisco, so we felt pretty sure, that last week of the season, that we were locking up Ebbets Field. Mr. O'Malley hadn't announced our move officially, but the rumors were too strong. When I went behind the bat in the windup game in Ebbets Field, I knew it was good-

11

bye to that cozy park. It was Thursday, September 28, 1957 and the few fans on hand for the wake waved goodbye after the final out.

We finished the season that weekend in Philadelphia. I drove down and took Roy, Jr., then eight, with me. Tony, two years younger, was slated to go too, but at the last minute he stayed home with his mother. Whenever we played in Philadelphia in all my years in the National League I stayed with my parents rather than with the team at the Warwick Hotel.

With nothing at stake, I ordinarily would not have had to catch any of those last three games. But I needed one more to give me a league record of catching a hundred games nine years in a row. Ballplayers don't usually watch such things too closely. But I was proud of it. The reporters with the club reminded me of it. They told Alston, too.

So the manager had me catch the first game of the Sunday double-header. I knew it was my last game as a Brooklyn player, but had no idea it would be my last game ever. I caught three innings and that completed exactly twenty years in organized professional baseball, ten years in Negro ball and ten in the National League. And my son Roy, Jr., sitting in a box seat behind home plate, saw me catch my last game of baseball.

I drove to New York after the game. I didn't return to my parents' house, because Roy had to get back home and into bed so as to be fresh for school the next morning.

I saw every game of the World Series at Yankee Stadium. The Braves and Yankees had a day off for travel from Milwaukee to New York after the fifth game. On that day, when there was no game, O'Malley announced he was transferring the club from Brooklyn to Los Angeles. It was finally official. Here it was, the move I kept hoping and hoping wouldn't ever happen to us.

12

It meant that we now had to decide on the things we had talked about in spring training: whether to move our families West and pull out of New York altogether or to just rent in California and remain Eastern people.

My wife Ruthe and I had talked it over at times during the summer, hoping we never would be forced to decide, but being sensible enough to realize it might be forced on us. I had to decide whether to sell the business, the house, real estate I own in Harlem, and the boat.

We were very happy in the house, a large, rambling ranch house on Long Island Sound with our own dock. It was wonderful for the children. We knew what we had here. We didn't know what we would get there. And we didn't feel it was right to uproot the children.

My liquor store was doing well, and I saw no sense in selling it. It was the best investment I ever made. I remember when I first mentioned the liquor business, Branch Rickey was dead set against it. Mr. Rickey is a very religious man. He preaches from the pulpit and is a non-drinker. His only vice is smoking expensive cigars. He didn't think that liquor and baseball were a good mix and felt that people might get the wrong idea if a ballplayer sold whiskey.

"Campy," he said, "why don't you invest your money in a sporting goods store or something else where there will be no taint?"

I told him: "Mr. Rickey, you're a white man. Maybe you don't understand the problem a colored man has going into business. How many businesses do you think are open to colored men, outside of entertainment? My people drink. They'll make better customers for whiskey than for sporting goods."

I convinced Mr. Rickey. It was the only time I ever out-talked him. I had no trouble with Mr. O'Malley. He was all for it, and he loaned me the money to get started. So, like I say, I decided to hold onto the store; but the boat was something else.

"I sure hate to sell the *Princess,* Campy," Ruthe said. "But think of the problems it would create. There's no sense shipping it to California. We don't even know where we're going to live. We'd have no place to keep it there and no chance to use it."

I knew she was right.

I decided to get my last licks in enjoying the boat on a one-week fishing cruise in the Atlantic in the nice weather in October.

In many ways that was the most interesting vacation I ever had. I hired a captain and crew of two plus a guide to smell out the fish and bait up the rods. We were after tuna, sail and marlin.

We picked the professionals up at Montauk, way down at the tip end of Long Island. "We" included some fellas — old friends of mine, who didn't get seasick, liked to fish, eat, laugh, and enjoyed drinking beer and tossing the cans in the Atlantic. Once we pulled the hook at Montauk we didn't stop until we were nearly fifty miles out to sea.

As self-appointed cook, I was in charge of the galley. I'd remembered to bring along some frozen meat — pork chops, steaks, and two pheasants. These provisions were brought along just in case. Actually, we expected to eat fish practically every meal. Fish that we caught and boated.

But as things turned out, it's a good thing I brought along that meat. If we'd had to depend on what we caught, we'd have starved. During those first two days out to sea, we never even raised a tuna or sail, much less a marlin. But we did tie into two blue sharks. Each weighed close to 400 pounds. The one I caught took me nearly one and one-half hours to boat. Man, rasslin' with that fish straightened me up! I thought I was in good shape following a full season and all. But that

14

old shark really dragged me out! When I boated him he snapped at me and just missed my toe. We kicked him overboard and cut the other one loose.

On the third and fourth day, we didn't see even a fin. About sundown, I called our home in Glen Cove on the ship-to-shore phone.

"Ruthe," I said, "we're not too lucky out here. We're comin' home."

And that's what we did. I knew that was about the last time I'd be aboard the *Princess*. She would be put up for sale that winter.

It costs cash to maintain a yacht, plenty of it. But for the pleasure she gave my family and me, it was worth it. Some of the nicest times I've ever known have been aboard that boat. One day maybe, when I'm able to do more and get around even better than now, I'll get another boat. There will probably be a lot less of her, but she'll be all boat and something that maybe I can pilot again.

I didn't sell the boat right away. It wasn't until the following June, while I was still in the hospital, that it was sold at auction for $20,000, which was just enough to pay off the notes. I had paid $36,000 for it in 1955 and must have put in about $12,000 in improvements, so I took a pretty good bath.

I got my first look at L. A. in November of 1957. The city threw a welcoming luncheon to celebrate coming into the major leagues. Reese, Snider, Hodges and I were invited. Hodges and I caught a plane from New York together. Reese flew in from Louisville, Kentucky, and Duke drove up from his ranch. While we were there I spent a few days looking for a house to lease but couldn't find what I wanted.

I didn't run into racial or social problems. It was just that it wasn't easy to find the right place for a large family with small children.

After enjoying Christmas at home, I returned to the Coast

15

in January to resume house-hunting and also to appear on a TV spectacular in a salute to Miss Ethel Barrymore. Bing Crosby, Frank Sinatra, Laraine Day, Lauren Bacall, Orson Welles, Joseph Cotten, Hoagy Carmichael were among the theater people on it. Leo Durocher, Braves manager Fred Haney, and Casey Stengel were there too. I presented Miss Barrymore with a season pass for the Dodgers home games, and to her nephew I presented an autographed ball, signed by the whole team. I had to rehearse for a week and spent the free time looking for a place to live.

I was fortunate to find a family in L. A. who would lease me their home all furnished. It was a lovely place in Lincoln Park. I told them that I had young children, and Mrs. Wood said that was all right as she was sure they wouldn't break anything. I phoned Ruthe in Glen Cove, and she was pleased. But I wanted her to actually see it herself. I wouldn't sign the lease until she saw it, so I arranged to come back with her the first Sunday in February.

I'm glad that I didn't know then what would happen to me before Ruthe and I could keep that date.

TWO

'LL NEVER FORGET JANUARY 28, 1958. THAT WAS the date the world turned around for me.

On Sunday night, the 26th, I attended the Baseball Writers Dinner at the Waldorf-Astoria in New York [City]. I usually go to this affair, which includes a show that kids people and events in baseball. I was sitting at one of the Dodger tables, with Gil Hodges, Don Drysdale, and Sandy Koufax, when I was interrupted by Harry Wismer, the radio man.

Harry had a TV show on Monday night after the television of the fights at St. Nicholas Arena. He said the Harlem Branch of the YMCA had told him to call me. They had a fund-raising drive on and felt I could help them by appearing on TV. He asked me to appear the next night.

I had been close to the kids at the "Y," working with them in the winters in the gym, and wanted to help. I told Harry I'd go on with him, and we set up the date.

The show was to go on around 10:45 P.M., depending on the length of the fight. I told Wismer to call me at the store before four in the afternoon to make the final arrangements.

Monday was a raw, wintry day. When I walked out of the house to my car around 9:30 in the morning, the wind was howling off the Sound. I got into my 1958 Chevrolet station wagon after waving goodbye to Ruthe and the kids and telling them to watch me on TV that night.

It had snowed a few days before and the roads were icy and treacherous, particularly Eastland Drive and Dosoris Lane, near where I live. Dosoris Lane leads into Glen Cove Road, which in turn leads to Northern State Parkway and on into New York.

When I got into the city, I didn't go straight to my store, which is at Seventh Avenue and 134th Street. Instead, I headed for the Curry Chevrolet service department at 136th and Broadway, a couple of blocks from the store.

The wagon wasn't running right. The motor needed adjustment and the radio was out of whack. These were minor things, but I figured I might as well take it in early in the week and get them fixed. They were busy and said I couldn't get the car back that day. "I want to do a good job for you, Campy," the service manager said. "No sense rushing it. We couldn't get it done in one day and have it the way I'd like it."

I agreed to leave it and rented a 1957 Chevy sedan so I

17

could get around during the day and get home that night. I got to the store around 11 A.M. Cynthia Mason, my secretary, had been away on a two-week vacation; and there were many points to go over, as I had been filling in for her.

Wismer called me before noon and said everything was all set and that I should be at the studios on 67th Street off Central Park West at 10 P.M. I agreed. I told him I'd go out to dinner and be there afterwards. But at nine o'clock after I returned from dinner, Harry called back.

"Campy," he said, "why don't we call off this thing tonight and do it next Monday? That will give me a chance to publicize your appearance, and we should get a larger audience next week. It will mean more money for the 'Y.' "

"Okay, Harry," I said.

Louis Johnson, my clerk, was alone at the time; so I stayed there with him. I usually left the store at four in the afternoon to beat the traffic leaving the city at night, but I had been delayed so long by now that I stayed on.

Johnson and I shifted some stock, and it got so late that I decided to stay until closing and check out the cash register ribbons. We closed the store at midnight, but there was still work to be done. We set up the burglar traps and cleaned up the store.

I counted the receipts and closed the safe, and by the time we had finished, it was about 1:30 in the morning of January 28th. I always have been careful to clean up the store — no empty boxes, no trash on the floor — and to put the plastic covers on the cash registers. I left before two and walked to the car.

How does a man know when he is taking the last steps of his life? I haven't taken one since.

I was tired and it was cold and late. But I drove carefully, as I usually do. I've always been a careful driver and never have been a fast driver. I had never had an accident. The roads in the city had been cleared up from the snowstorms but those in the suburban areas had not been cleaned fully, and they had slippery patches of ice and snow.

I managed the main highways without any trouble and made a left turn into Dosoris Lane, passing the school my children go to. I went down Dosoris Lane and came to this S-curve, which is a couple of miles from my home.

There were big ice patches on the road. They looked like white spots. I could see them clearly. I wasn't going fast, I don't think more than 30 or 35 miles an hour, though I wasn't looking at the speedometer. I followed the road around the bend in the S and was headed for the right side of the road as I came out of the bend. Then I suddenly lost control. The car wouldn't behave. I tried to steer it away from the side of the road. The brakes didn't hold. The surface was sandy and icy. I fought the wheel. The brakes were useless.

I tried furiously to swerve and felt a chill in my spine when I saw I couldn't. I saw this telephone pole right where I was heading. If this had been my own station wagon, which is three hundred pounds heavier and had snow tires, I might have gotten it out of the skid. I managed to turn it away from hitting the pole dead center, but not enough to miss it altogether.

I just did hit it, the right front fender crashing against it. The car bounced off and turned completely over, landing on its right side. I felt the car turning over and the force of it tore my hands from the wheel. The collision knocked me forward and down onto the floor on the passenger's side of the front seat.

I guess my neck hit the dashboard as I plunged. Anyway, my body jackknifed, and I was wedged in under the dash and on the floor. I never thought I was that small to fit into such a small space.

19

I've gone through the accident a hundred times in my mind. I can still see that pole. You know, it was just about a year later that we went over the same road when Ruthe was driving and I saw patches of ice in exactly the same place. A shudder shot through me at the memory of that night.

"Please, Ruthe," I cautioned her, "take it easy here. This is where it happened."

I guess I never really blacked out for a while, because I remember thinking that the car might catch fire. I was pinned down there under the dashboard with the car overturned. I could feel no pain. In fact, I couldn't feel a thing. But I knew the motor was running. I tried to reach up to turn off the ignition, but I couldn't reach the key. I couldn't move my arms.

That's when the terrible thought came to me: "I'm paralyzed."

I was terrified. I cried out, "O Lord, have mercy on me."

I couldn't move anything.

I don't know how long I lay there, but it seemed long to me. The next thing I knew, a light was shining through the window of the car.

"Why, it's Campy," the fellow with the searchlight said.

"Yes, it's me," I groaned. "Please help me. Help me, somebody. I can't move."

The man with the light was a police officer. Patrolman Frank Poepplein. I recognized his voice. He used to wave to me in town at times and stop and talk. "Okay, Campy," he said. "Just take it easy. We'll get you out."

"Turn off the ignition," I pleaded. "The car will catch fire."

Moments later I must have blacked out for good. I found out later that the sound of the crash woke up people in houses along the road. I've read since that a doctor crawled into the car and gave me a shot with a needle. But I don't remember that at all. As a matter of fact, I don't even remember being taken out of the car. Ruthe told me later that Poepplein had worked his way into the car and held me rigid while a wrecker got it back on its wheels. It took twenty minutes to free me. They had to use crowbars to get me loose. They laid me face down and rushed me to Glen Cove Community Hospital in a Nassau County police ambulance.

In the meantime, Patrolman Poepplein went to my home. Ruthe was waked up by the bell. It was now nearly four o'clock.

"I hate to come with bad news like this, Mrs. Campanella," he said, nervously. "But your husband has had an auto accident and is on the way to the hospital. I'll be glad to take you there."

They arrived at the hospital about 4:30 A.M. By that time, I already had been wheeled into the X-ray room. There were two doctors there: Dr. Gilbert Taylor and Dr. Charles W. Hayden. Dr. Taylor was holding my head.

"I don't want to alarm you, Mrs. Campanella," Dr. Taylor said. "But your husband is in a state of shock. I'm afraid he's paralyzed. He can't move his legs."

Dr. Robert Sengstaken, chief of neurosurgery at the hospital, had already been called. When he arrived, he examined the X-ray pictures. Interns on duty had read the wet plates which indicated damage to the upper part of my spine. He confirmed this. The X-rays showed that two vertebrae had slipped and overlapped each other.

"He has a fracture and dislocation of vertebrae five and six," Dr. Sengstaken said. "He's paralyzed from just below the shoulders to the toes. He can't push his arms out or grasp, but he can pull his arms in if they're held out for him.

"We've got to operate immediately. We haven't a moment

21

to lose. The quicker it's done, the better. The pressure on his spinal cord must be relieved quickly."

Dr. Sengstaken said he had to have Ruthe's permission before he could operate. She said she was willing to go along with whatever the doctors thought best.

"Perhaps it would be a good idea to call the club," Dr. Hayden suggested.

Ruthe thought that Mr. O'Malley was on his way from his home in Amityville, Long Island, to Los Angeles, so she called Buzzy Bavasi, the Dodgers' Vice President, at his home in Scarsdale. It turned out that it was Bavasi who had left for Los Angeles, but Mrs. Bavasi gave Ruthe the number for Bavasi in L. A., and Dr. Hayden got on the phone and explained the situation to him.

It was close to seven o'clock when Dr. Sengstaken gathered his operating team of three doctors and six nurses. They took me up to the operating room on the elevator. Ruthe walked along beside me. I was on my stomach, face down, but I knew she was there.

When we reached the door of the operating room, Dr. Sengstaken drew her aside.

"Mrs. Campanella, please go home. There's nothing you can do here now. I assure you that you can help your husband more by getting a few hours sleep. Your children need you, too. We'll keep in touch with you. I promise that we'll call you as soon as the operation is over."

Ruthe didn't want to leave but she realized the doctor was right. As she turned to go, I said, "Honey, it hurts."

THREE

MY NECK WAS BROKEN. MY SPINAL CORD WAS all but severed.

The doctors began to fight to save my life. It now was a race against time. They had to relieve the pressure on my spinal cord to save me. I was a sick man — but I didn't know how sick. They wheeled me into the operating room; and, although my face was down, I was aware of the glare of the bright lights overhead.

"Doc, what's happened to me?" I cried.

That's all I remember. Right then, they gave me the anesthesia.

The operation lasted over four hours. It wasn't until three days later that I learned what had been done.

The first thing they did was bore two small holes in the top of my skull, one on each side. Into these holes a spring device was hooked. From the extension arms of the springs, clamps were attached and hooked on to the edge of the operating table beyond my head. Weights were hung from the clamps. This is what they call Crutchfield tongs. The traction kept my head steady and my neck under tension during the operation.

Dr. Sengstaken then made his first incision. He cut into the back of my neck, clearing away tissue and muscle. After probing farther and laying aside deeper layers of muscle, the injured area was exposed.

He examined the exposed area. Just as he thought: a clear fracture and dislocation of the vertebrae. That could be repaired. In medical terms, they call it a laminectomy. This is surgery which straightens out damaged vertebrae and relieves pressure on the spinal cord.

The real worry was whether there was any serious damage to the spinal cord itself. If there was, it could prove fatal, or result in permanent paralysis. That depended on the type and extent of the injury.

Dr. Sengstaken saw no visible damage to the spinal cord itself. There was a clear fracture and dislocation of the fifth and sixth cervical vertebrae. There are twenty-four separate vertebrae in the body. Had the third and fourth cervicals, which are an inch higher, been damaged, there would have been no need to operate. I would have been dead on arrival at the hospital.

The doctor worked carefully, restoring the damaged and dislocated bones to their proper and natural positions, then closed up the exposed area, layer on layer of muscle and skin.

Finally he looked up, sweating and worn, and said to an assistant: "Okay. That's it. Close it up."

An assistant stitched the outer skin and I was wheeled back to my room.

Ruthe was at my bedside when the anesthetic wore off and I woke up after the operation. She and David, fourteen, the oldest of my three boys, had driven back to the hospital after being called. She had spent five miserable hours sitting by the phone. She couldn't sleep. When the phone rang, she was ready to bolt right out of the house and come to the hospital.

When she got there, I was lying on a high bed with three mattresses under me. I must have looked strange because my head was below the rest of my body. I was a sight. I looked like one of those monsters you see in the horror pictures on the late show. My head was shaved. There were tubes attached to my skull to anchor the two ten-pound sandbags that kept my head in traction.

Ruthe tells me that I greeted her with "Hi, honey."

I don't remember that. She says I talked with her for a while. "Be careful driving home," I cautioned her.

"Don't worry, I'll be careful. You get some sleep. I'll be back in a little while."

"I'll be here. I ain't goin' nowhere."

I did go places though. I went to lots of places — in my mind. I went way back, back to Philadelphia where I was born. Back to the time when I was just a little kid in the streets.

They say that there comes a time in each man's life when he takes stock of himself and tries to add up the score. Maybe it's just before he dies . . . or thinks that he's about to die. They say that it's then that an awful lot of his life comes back to him in sort of a review.

I guess this was my time to take stock. Because as I lay there in that hospital bed with tubes and things sticking in and out of me and all broke up, I thought of the things that had happened to me. Some were wonderful and some not so wonderful. My life didn't scoot by in a flash like they say it does when a man's about to drown. This was nothing like that. I must have spent a lot of those early days under dope and sedatives but there were hours — and days — and long nights, when my mind was crystal-clear. That's when I did plenty of thinking . . . and remembering.

FOUR

PHILADELPHIA IS A BIG, OLD TOWN. THE PART I was raised in, though, wasn't so very big. It was more a group of streets that made it one of maybe fifty neighborhoods — all with names — that make up the city. These streets in the Nicetown section are composed of "row houses," and are between 3700 and 4000 North on Broad Street. It's been called Nicetown for more than a hundred years, I guess. Why Nicetown? I honestly don't know. Any more than I know why there are neighborhoods on the Philadelphia municipal map called Tioga, Logan, Fern Rock, East Falls, Olney, and so many other sections with long-time names.

I was seven when we moved to Nicetown. That must have been in 1928. We used to live in Germantown, on Colorado Street. Like everything else, Nicetown has sure changed a lot since I lived there. When we moved there, it was mostly Italian and Polish. There were very few Negroes. Now it's almost all Negro. Our family lived at 1538 Kerbaugh Street. It is a corner house and that's where my Mom and Daddy still live. My sister Doris and her husband Clifton Coursey and their daughter Judy live with them. My niece Judy is going on fifteen and is quite a grownup young lady. When she thinks about it, she can be an A and B student.

Many of my earliest memories are wrapped up in that old corner house on Kerbaugh Street. It has a living room with a high ceiling and with stairs on one side going to the second floor. In the old days, I had a room to myself across from the head of the stairs. By rights it was my brother Lawrence's room, and I shared it with him. But he was much older than me and so from the earliest days he wasn't around too much. My two older sisters, Doris and Gladys, had a room of their own, with Mom's and Daddy's room down at the end of the hall in the front of the house. I was the baby of the family, so my room was the smallest. But it was a wonderful "cave." I kept the walls covered with cutouts from newspapers and magazines. Mostly they were of great baseball stars — players like Mickey Cochrane and Bill Dickey, catchers for the Philadelphia Athletics and New York Yankees. I had room for Babe Ruth and Lou Gehrig too. I even had a picture of

26

Buzz Arlett, the Phillies outfielder. Maybe he wasn't too good a fielder, but that fat old boy could sure hit! Naturally I had cutouts of the great colored stars of that era, too — Satchel Paige and Josh Gibson, battery for the Pittsburgh Crawfords, Biz Mackey, catcher for the Baltimore Elite Giants, and so many others.

Off our living room was a good-sized kitchen, and kitchen steps leading to the cellar, which ran the depth of our house. Today that cellar is more of a laundry room and play-room — with curtains and all. But when I was growing up, it was in some ways the most important place in our home. You see, my Daddy sold vegetables for a living, and each night what he didn't sell we stored in that cool, moist cellar, where those greens would keep nice and fresh.

Daddy used to get up at five in the morning. That was late compared to when I got up. I had to get out of bed at two o'clock. I had a milk route. When I'd come back from my route, I'd load my Daddy's truck while he was having breakfast. We had an old model T truck. I remember that truck very well. It had those three pedals and the spark and gas lever and it had a rack on each side for all the vegetables.

Dad didn't canvass or sell in our neighborhood, but over in Logan, in the 5300 section. Daddy was out of the house by six o'clock. Cabbages, potatoes, lettuce, chard, tomatoes, string beans, watermelon and corn on the cob, whatever the season, he had vegetables and fruit to fit it. He also sold fish on Fridays. He had a special freezer box, all metal-lined, built into the truck. It cost him $25, which in the late 1920s was a fortune. He was proud of that icebox on wheels with its cracked ice and all, and he loaded it at dawn each Friday way downtown at the fish market on Dock Street. Porgies, haddock, sea bass, perch, eels, steak cod — there wasn't noth-ing that swims hardly that he didn't carry on Fridays. Many's

27

the time I went from door to door in our neighborhood selling those fish at cut rates on Saturdays!

My father's name is John Campanella. He is white. My mother's maiden name was Ida Mercer. She is Negro. My father is Italian. His mother and father both came from Sicily. In Italian, *campanella* means "little bell."

My mother is pure American. She was born near Chesapeake City, Maryland. Daddy was born in Homestead, a small town on the Ohio River, eight miles south of Pittsburgh. His family came to Philadelphia when he was only six months old. Daddy always wanted to go back to see Pittsburgh, but he has never made it.

When I was with the Dodgers, we naturally played in Pittsburgh. My first time there, I dropped him a postcard. "Daddy, don't worry," I wrote. "You don't miss nothing by missing Pittsburgh. It's all hills, holes and cobblestones."

I don't remember it, of course, but my Daddy, who is a small but strong man with a big voice, drove a team of horses in the days right at the end of World War I. That's when the city of Philadelphia was really building and booming, with new roads, excavations for buildings and all. It must have been soon after I was born, on November 19, 1921, that Pop went into business for himself with the vegetable truck.

There were six in our family. Lawrence was the oldest. He was ten years older than me. He died in 1959. He lived in Germantown with his own family. Then there's Gladys, four years older than me. Gladys was the best girl athlete I ever saw. Basketball, track, baseball, fighting — you name it. There was practically nothing she couldn't do as good or better than most boys. Quite good-looking, too. She went to Tuskegee Institute and was "Miss Tuskegee." Gladys married a Wilberforce University boy, Eddie Johnson. Today he's Lieutenant Colonel Edward C. Johnson. He came back from Germany in 1958 and now he's in charge of the ROTC program at Morgan State College in Baltimore. Doris is two years older than I am, and she was my playing partner. She was a real good athlete too. She played basketball and starred in track. She's married and runs a ladies' sportswear and specialty shop in Philadelphia, called Mi Lords. Doris has a good husband, and like I say, they have a fine daughter, who is in high school. They live with Mom and Dad, and I guess keep the old place bouncing. Dad retired himself around 1956. He was seventy last August 29, and Mom was sixty-nine last April 28. So, like I say, he has a right to retire and enjoy life. Thank the good Lord, both my parents are in good shape and as spry as crickets. Funny thing, I look back and always think of my Mom as a big, strong woman with sturdy arms good at wielding a mop. That's because she ran our home and was always working around the house. Actually, she's about five feet four and weighs maybe a hundred and thirty pounds. Dad now says he's married to two girls, Mom and Doris. "They take turns telling me when and where to head in," he complains. Actually, he enjoys it.

The Campanella kids toed a pretty strict line, although I don't truly remember Lawrence ever being a kid, being ten years older than me. In those days, parents didn't let their children run, or run them, like today! Why, I can recall when I was still half a baby and my big sister and brother couldn't go out. We had dancing classes at school, but I hardly ever went to a dance. In fact, after supper I didn't get to go out too much.

The school I remember best, was Gillespie Junior High that took you through the ninth grade. And then you walked across an alley to Senior High, which was, and still is, Simon Gratz High. It was a big school. Just to give you some idea, in those 1930s Simon Gratz could handle better than four thousand kids at one time. By the time I was ready for high school, I truly was thinking more of playing professional ball than sitting in any classroom. Both Gillespie and Gratz High were big, gray stone buildings and sat on the same street, only two blocks from our house. So you can see, it was sort of difficult getting "lost" between home and school, but I managed lots of times. By the time I was supposed to reach Gratz, I was AWOL over in Hunting Park, scuffling and playing ball with any other truants I could dig up.

Maybe the pace was a lot slower, or something, but in those days we didn't have any gang fights. In fact we didn't have any gangs. What we did have were leagues of kids from different streets and we were always going at it in stick-ball, baseball or basketball. But mostly stickball. I don't mean just the colored boys, because for a fact there weren't but a few of us. Quentin Lee, Babe Russell and maybe a half dozen others. Italian, Poles, Irish, Negroes — it didn't matter. We were all mixed up on those teams. The most fun was those stickball games. Today stickball is played with a ball that's sawed in half. That is supposed to make it more difficult to hit and field. We played with a whole ball made of red rubber and a little smaller than a tennis ball, with small dots sprouting out all over. We called 'em pimple balls. Our bats were sawed-off broomsticks that we taped at the handle. Man, could you take a cut with those sticks — and beat that ball a mile when you caught it just right! Sydenham Street, where Quentin Lee lived, was our favorite battleground. Naturally, with traffic and all, stickball wasn't allowed in the streets, which I guess was why we got such a kick out of it. The Philadelphia police used to have red prowl cars. That was the yell. "Here comes red car!" and everybody would haul it.

Looking back, it's funny about playgrounds. The school had a fine baseball diamond across the street, but there was

30

just something about stickball in the street that beat all. In any crowded neighborhood I guess it still does.

But, all in all, the pace in Nicetown must have been a lot slower than it is today, and the kids more even-natured. Because while the police used to get on us for stickball, maybe, we seldom or almost never had any real run-ins with the cops. You hear tell about off-beat kids carrying knives and razors today? Man, we never knew what it was to carry a knife, or anything!

I have some good friends from those days. Boys like Quentin Lee, now a member of the Philadelphia Fire Department. The first time I ever was away from home, really, was with the Bacharach Giants in 1935. Quentin was along and played third base. His daddy was the first Negro policeman in Philadelphia to ride a motorcycle, not one of those three-wheel buckboard jobs, but a solo job. I remember it was black with cream spokes. I can't tell you how proud we were of Officer Lee.

When they were all much older, Lee and Herb Evans and some more boys chipped in and bought an old private house in Nicetown at 3634 North 17th and fixed it up real nice. You know, drapes, red and black color scheme, and a handsome bar. It's our social club, Club 25. For a number of years Quentin was its president, and I'm proud to be an honorary member.

I had some real good friends when we were kids. There was Jimmy Walker. We grew up together, and in 1953, when I opened my liquor store in Harlem, Jimmy was my manager. He's no longer with me, but we're good friends. Not everybody's cut out to run a store.

Then there was a boy named Philip Sampson. He was a fair athlete. He died back in '38 or '39. Nobody knew from what. He just dried up till he was nothing more than a stick! They did not speak about cancer, then. Another top boy

31

was Babe Russell. He's still in Philadelphia. He used to be in charge of our basketball team for the Nicetown Colored Athletic Club. I used to see a lot of Babe's sister Evelyn. A real nice girl and she's still mighty attractive, with a family and all. I didn't bother much with girls. There were only a few in our neighborhood. Besides, I was too busy working and playing ball when I was able to.

Of course those days were right in the middle of the depression. But do you know, none of us Campanella kids honestly knew there was a depression on! Daddy saw to that. You can be poor, but if your daddy's business happens to be food, you sure aren't going to go hungry. And we didn't.

But this for certain — any time any of us neighborhood kids had as much as two bits, that boy was really living! That reminds me of the day I was richer than Rockefeller — at least a nine or ten year old Rockefeller. I remember the boy I was playing with out in the street this day, Buddy Boyd. Buddy and me was scufflin' around when I spied some bills on the pavement. They were dirty and rumpled, but by gosh, this wasn't play money! Four one-dollar bills! Out there on the sidewalk, in front of a house on the corner of 16th and Pike! Man, when I smoothed out that paper my heart was in my mouth. Nobody was around 'ceptin' Buddy. He started yelling "Halfies!" as soon as he seen me pick up the bills. That meant he wanted to split the wad with me.

"Oh no," I shook my head. "It's all mine, man, I found it." We had a quarrel. I finally told him, to settle the argument, "Tell you what I'll do. I'll buy us ice cream cones till the money runs out!"

We had maybe three cones each and then I decided we'd better save the rest for another day. What a mistake! When I was in bed and asleep that night, Mother went through my pockets and found the money. The next thing I knew, she was standing over me and whopping me. "Where did you steal the money?" She kept yelling and hitting at the same time. "Never could earn that much money!" I took quite a pummeling before I could finally convince her I had actually found all that money. When I told Buddy the next day that my mother had found the loot, he didn't believe me.

In those days there were plenty of horses and wagons in our neighborhood. We used to hitch rides by swinging on back. This day little Eddie, one of the boys running with us, got his leg caught in a wheel, and it was crushed all to pieces. It had to be amputated. When Mom heard about that accident, she really preached to me. I didn't hitch many more rides after that. I got caught once and I still remember the whopping I got.

Besides helping my Dad with his truck loading, I worked my milk route for the Supplee Dairy, one of the biggest and oldest milk companies anywheres. I was twelve. The job started around three in the morning. My route covered maybe four miles of blocks in our general neighborhood, from 20th and Erie down past our street. That horse was the smartest I ever saw. He was so smart that when I'd start delivering he knew where each stop was! I'd drop off those bottles and pick up the empties in my wire basket and when I reached the end of the block, there he was waiting on me. He was brown with dots and, like I say, real smart. That was a pretty good area to cover and get back home by five A.M. to help Dad, get cleaned up, eat breakfast and move off to school with the other kids. That's why I went to bed right after supper. I had to get up at two. I got twenty-five cents a day. I thought it was a lot of money. I gave my mother the money each morning and she saved it up for me. When I had enough, she took me downtown and bought me a suit. After about a year, I went to work with my brother. He had a big milk route, called the Wah-Wah Dairy. He paid me

33

fifty cents a day. Lawrence worked by truck. That's how I learned to drive. I was thirteen then.

In those days I really knew how to hustle. I sold newspapers, I also had a shoeshine box that I toted around and picked up some coin. I got to admit, I was always out trying to earn some money.

I stole my first mitt. I was walking through Hunting Park one day, and the kids were playing baseball. There was the mitt lying on the ground with nobody near it. I had never owned one, and I wanted one more than anything else in the world. I looked around. Nobody was watching. I just picked it up, slid it inside my shirt and kept right on going. I didn't stop until I reached my house. I knew Mama wouldn't let me keep it, so I hid it on top of the china closet where I didn't think she'd find it. But she did, two days later.

"Where did you get it, Roy?" she demanded to know. "I found it," I said. She knew I was lying. "Where?" she asked. "In Hunting Park," I replied. "It was lying on the ground." "Go bring it back, this minute!" Mom stormed. I knew there was no use discussing it any further, so I went back to the park and left the mitt exactly where I had picked it up.

That's the onliest glove I ever remember having — for just two days — and I never even caught a single ball with it. I had to borrow a mitt from the other boys when I caught behind the plate. I never could wear a mask. I had trouble seeing through it. Once I had my nose broken as a kid, because I didn't want to wear a mask.

My Daddy is a Catholic. However, Mom and all us kids were raised in the Baptist religion. I've heard it said that God's house has many windows, each window being some faith or religion. I believe that's so. God's house does have many windows, but Dad stopped going to Mass when we were still pretty little. Mom attended the Nazarene Baptist

34

church a few blocks away, and Dad used to go with us. But he finally had to stop. It became just too embarrassing. It seemed every time the Campanellas would enter the church, the whole congregation would stop praying and turn around to stare at us. Dad was the only white man in that church. Finally he couldn't stand it any longer.

"Mama, from now on, you and the kids will go to church by yourselves," he said one day. "I'll do my Sunday praying at home. I'll try to be a good Christian without going to church."

I recall those Sundays very well. Mother sang with a group, not a choir, but a group of ladies. She had a fine strong voice. After regular church, Doris and I went to Sunday School. Mom and Dad saw to that. Yes, and following Sunday School it was straight home, where we spent the rest of the day. We couldn't play ball, go to the movies, or anything. 'Course, in those days the blue laws were really strict in Philadelphia, so there was no major league baseball or anything. And that seven o'clock curfew they still have on ball games goes all the way back to those blue laws us kids were raised under.

The kids called me "halfbreed." At first I had no idea what "halfbreed" meant. Then I found out it was because of my Mom and Dad being of different colored skin. Most of my fights came from that. Fortunately, I was a pretty good scrapper.

Doris and I would be coming home from Sunday School, and on the way the kids would sing out, teasing, "Roy, is your father really a white man?" This may seem stupid, but I honestly didn't know. It was never discussed around the house. All I knew was that my father was a wonderful man. My mother never had to do a day's work in her life.

Doris and I faced a lot that ordinary kids wouldn't go through. Many's the time we had to punch our way home.

She was a pretty good scrapper too. It wasn't only the white kids who called us "halfbreed." We caught it from both sides, white and colored. So, like I say, I learned fast to be pretty good with my fists. I had to. By twelve or thirteen, Doris and I learned to live with it. Of course by then we could analyze things better.

But I remember one afternoon in particular, when the kids were extra rough on me. It really got under my skin and I kept thinking about it all the way home. I just couldn't get it out of my mind. What *about* having a white father and a Negro mother? Was it good or bad? Was it a crime? Was it something to be ashamed of? I didn't feel ashamed. Then why did the other kids make fun of me? Why was I different? I had to find out.

Mom was in the kitchen. We were alone, just the two of us. I fidgeted a little. Finally I managed to blurt out: "Mom, is it true that Daddy is a white man?"

She had her back turned to me. She was working over the ironing board, pressing one of Daddy's shirts. She didn't stop ironing, but I could see her back stiffening. It must have been only a few seconds, but it seemed such a long time before she turned around. She looked at me for what seemed forever. Then she spoke very softly.

"Yes, Roy, your daddy is white. It makes no difference. There's nothing wrong with that. He lives in this house with us. He's a good man. He's a fine father. He's my husband. I love your father. He has given us all a good home . . . food . . . clothes. And above all, he gives us what many folks, white or colored, can't buy with all the money in the world. He gives us love, Roy. What more can anyone want?"

Mama didn't have to be told what I had gone through. It was something she must have waited for for a long time. She pulled me toward her and kissed me. "Pay no mind to what anyone says," she said. "Remember, your daddy has made

36

me very happy." Then she picked up her iron and went back to her work.

Dad never spoke about it — and I never asked him. It just didn't feel right to ask. Dad never had too much to say, anyway. He's a good, solid, dependable fella and he's proud of his family. And I'm proud of him and Mom. It was on June 17, 1959, that they celebrated their fifty-second wedding anniversary.

FIVE

AS A KID, I WAS BIG FOR MY AGE. NOT SO TALL but hefty. Maybe it was because of the diet in our family. Do you know what the main meal was? Spaghetti. When I was growing up I must have eaten a ton of it, and I still like it today. Almost always on the kitchen stove at 1538 Kerbaugh Street, there was a big pot of water heating up. Most of the time, spaghetti would go into it. I sure could twirl a fork and come up with a ball of it. I'd give a lot to be able to do that today.

But there were special days — like Thanksgiving and Christmas. What a table Mom and the girls would set. Turkey, tomatoes, rice, sweet potatoes, stuffed olives, ice cream — we had it all. The Fourth of July? It was nothing special in our house — or even in our neighborhood. And thinking back on the Fourth, the grownups carried on a bit, but not the kids. Those firecrackers and sparklers and the rest — us kids just didn't have money to burn up and blow up on stuff like that.

Christmas time was really wonderful. The girls and Mom would pretty up our home with decorations and wreaths. Yes, and our tree was always the most elegant one on the block. There were only two things I never got that I always seemed to ask for. A bicycle and roller skates. Daddy was dead set against those two things. He once told me he had enough on his mind with me getting banged up in baseball without me getting *really* messed up under the wheels of some car or truck.

Maybe that's why we never had a dog. Cats yes. We always seemed to have some old cat hangin' round the house. One in particular. He was a big old alley job, and striped like a tiger.

Next to that bike and skates, the presents I always asked for, and got, were books and magazines about baseball. That's how I learned to read, really — grabbing anything that dealt with baseball. The old *Baseball Magazine* with the Clifford Bloodgood covers — that was my favorite. I bet I got the first copy in our neighborhood each month from the corner store. And then it was run home, shut my door, and curl up on my bed with that magazine. Man, I really dug those stories, and inside-dope pieces on the stars. Babe Ruth, Lou Gehrig, Mickey Cochrane, Bill Dickey, Lefty Grove. Especially those two catchers, Dickey and Cochrane.

By the time I was twelve I thought I was ready to tackle 'most anything — just so long as it was baseball. Rainy weather, cold weather, fall and winter — any time that wasn't baseball time was a washout in my book.

But the most total washout I remember was the summer I went to church camp. I was eleven, maybe twelve. The Nazarene Baptist church, where Mom and us kids went, had its own farm out in Bucks County, way north of Philadelphia. This summer they herded a batch of us colored kids from Nicetown, Germantown, and other neighborhoods, put us in trucks and took us all out to the camp. We pitched tents, dug ditches and everything. The big deal was supposed to be swimming in the lake and hiking. Well, it started raining the day we went and it never let up. It came down until that camp looked like Noah's Ark! By the middle of the fourth

38

day it was *still* raining. Everybody was wet, homesick, and ready to pack in. Most of all, me. They rounded us up and trucked us back to Nicetown and stickball in the street! That was my first and last trip to summer camp — in fact any camp.

Camp was a bust, but the movies weren't. I got to see two of them with my sister Doris. The movie house was in Germantown and on Saturday afternoons the price was a dime. One of them was *Peter Pan* and the other was *King Kong*. I saw that Kong picture not long ago on TV. That big ape still looked and acted mean in spots, but he was nothing compared to how he looked to me when I was eight or nine.

In those days I went to Asa Parker grade school. I wasn't what you'd call a student. All I thought about, mainly, was getting out after school and playing ball. I saw my first big league game from the top of a house across the street from Shibe Park, now called Connie Mack Stadium. The A's were playing the Yankees. Nobody thought much about the poor, woebegone Phillies in those days. It was all the Athletics. The reason I saw that game and so many others from *outside* the park was because a bleacher seat cost maybe fifty cents. But for twenty-five cents you could go up on top of this big row house and still see it all. There was long benches that seated maybe five hundred or more. Like I say, for twenty-five cents you could sit up there and look straight in towards home plate.

I was on that roof the day in 1932 that Lou Gehrig hit four home runs in one game! He powered the ball over that wall in right. Yes, and I was back on that roof the day in 1934 that Bing Miller beat Detroit's Schoolboy Rowe with a bases loaded triple. That was the day Schoolboy was going for his seventeenth straight! I was only thirteen but I remember it all. The first time I had fifty cents and paid my way into the park I sat in the left field bleachers, right over the Babe. He

39

was a right fielder in most parks, but down there the sunfield was in right so they put Babe in left.

Then there was the Saturday that the Philadelphia Knot Hole Gang took all the kids from Nicetown to the game. Years later, when I was with Brooklyn, I got a kick out of Happy Felton's Knot Holers. Happy had a regular pre-game show on TV built around those kids, with Pee Wee Reese, Duke Snider, Gil Hodges, Carl Furillo and us other Dodgers giving the kids instructions before the cameras. But back in Philadelphia when I was a kid, we were still a long ways from TV, much less getting down on the field! I made it *during* a game, though, and here's how it happened. This was at old Baker Bowl. The Phillies were playing Cincinnati. I'm positive those were the teams because I remember the Phillies' Dick Bartell and the Reds' Sparky Adams got into a fight at second base. It was along about the sixth inning when somebody hit a homer that landed among us kids in those left field bleachers. The wall out there is only about twelve or fifteen feet high. In the scuffle for the ball, I simply fell out of the stands and landed on my left arm, mostly. I thought I'd broken my wrist. Naturally I tried to shake it off and get off the field and back with my buddies. The crowd thought it was real funny. I can still hear 'em laughing and hooting at "that dumb kid who fell out of the stands!"

That night by supper time my wrist hurt real fierce. I didn't want to let on that anything was wrong. I knew Dad would raise the roof. Any injury that I picked up playing ball was bad enough. But getting banged up without even getting hit by the ball — that would really have tied it. We were all at the table at supper that night — Mom, Dad, Larry, and my two sisters. I must have been awful quiet, because it didn't take Dad long to smell something fishy.

I was trying to do everything with my right hand — cut my meat, butter my bread, everything.

40

"What's it *this* time?" he asked.

"Nothing, Dad."

"Then why aren't you using your 'bread hand'? What happened?"

I finally told them what had happened at the ball park.

"All that and you didn't even get the ball?" he said. But he almost had to laugh.

"No ball, Dad. Just a toothache in my wrist."

Mom took me upstairs and painted the wrist with iodine and then fixed me a sling. I never wanted her to paint or tape me because it would look bad for baseball and me.

In those days we had a radio built into a big cabinet. To me it was the best piece of furniture in our house. I remember hearing the 1933 World Series on it. It was Washington against the Giants. I wanted New York to win. Carl Hubbell won twenty-three games that year. In the series he stood those Senators on their ears. I'd lie under the radio so I could hear the ball smack into the catcher's mitt. In my mind I was catching Hubbell. He five-hit the Senators and beat them 4 to 2.

Yes, the Giants won it all, four games to one — with Hubbell winning two.

My favorite radio program as a kid was *Heigh Ho Silver*. I used to listen to it lying on the living room floor with my head stuck under the cabinet. That way, I suppose I could hear Silver's hoofs pounding harder and louder.

The boys I ran with played ball at Hunting Park, not ten minutes from Kerbaugh Street. Kerbaugh, Sydenham, Smedley — each street had its team or at least part of a team. Most of us didn't have gloves, but what we could beg or borrow was enough. And the ball was usually beat up and taped up. And our bats were old cracked jobs that we wired and taped. It didn't matter. It was baseball.

My Dad was opposed to my playing in those games. As a

41

boy he was a good ice skater, but baseball he didn't trust. He was always afraid I'd break a leg or an arm or my nose. I'll never forget the day I did break my nose. I thought my Daddy was going to blow a fuse. I was eleven years old. We had a game in the park and I was in there with bigger boys — fourteen and fifteen. I was catching of course, and the mask was too big for me. I couldn't see good with it on, so I chucked it aside.

Sure enough, in the very first inning a boy foul tipped a pitch and the ball smacked into my face. I fell over and squirmed with pain. Then I saw the blood. It was streaming from my nose and down my shirt. I tried to stop the bleeding but couldn't. My nose hurt so bad I couldn't touch it. That was all for me.

That night I stayed up in my room until it was supper time. When I came downstairs I tried to turn my face away from Dad, but he ordered, "Turn around and let me look at you."

I turned my head slowly and tried to smile but it hurt too much. The bridge of my nose was sure swollen and cut and one eye was nearly closed.

"What happened?" he asked.

"I got hit with the ball," I said. "But it's all right, Daddy. It doesn't hurt much."

"He was catching again, Dad," said Gladys, my oldest sister. "And without a mask. Can you imagine anyone so stupid?"

"What does your sister mean?" Dad wanted to know.

"I tried the mask on, but it didn't fit right. I couldn't see through it good enough, so I took it off, and Tommy fouled one, and it got me on the nose."

"You should have seen the blood on his shirt when he got home," Gladys went on. I could have killed her.

"Aw, it wasn't much," I protested.

"Look at you!" Dad's voice was going high now. "You break your nose and you call that nothing?"

"I'll wear a mask tomorrow, Dad, honest! It won't happen again. I promise."

"Tomorrow! What do you mean, tomorrow?" he shouted. "Do you think you're going to play that crazy game again? I told you I didn't want you playing that game — and so did your mother. Why can't you play with the rubber ball like I see other kids in the street doing?"

I think he knew I wouldn't stop playing hard-ball but he didn't send me off to bed until I promised not to play hard-ball again. I broke my promise the next day, but I did wear a mask. I think that in those days I must have promised Dad a dozen times that baseball and me were through with each other. But I forgot the promise the moment I'd step out of doors.

I'm afraid I wasn't any too good a student. But I wasn't so bad either. Arithmetic didn't bother me, but English did. At least English like they taught it. History, science, geography — they weren't so tough. But the subject I liked best was mechanical arts. A ruler, a sharp pencil and clean paper — that I liked. I think that if I hadn't been so heart and soul in baseball, I would probly have become a draftsman.

Just before summer vacation the year I was twelve, the rumor got going that the Philadelphia *Independent,* a weekly Negro paper, was going to sponsor a baseball team. It was to be made up of newsboys who sold it. That sure included me. I'd been selling the *Independent* for several years. Why not? For each ten-cent paper sold, I got two cents.

Well, that rumor proved correct. I remember the afternoon they had tryouts and then handed out uniforms at the Nice-town Colored Athletic Club. They were white and beautiful, with N C A C on the front and PHILADELPHIA INDEPENDENT on the back. That's a lot of letters. But the way I looked at it, the more letters, the more official-looking they were.

Our coach was Roy Wilder. He kept sounding out names, "Quentin Lee . . . Herb Evans . . . Joe Hall . . . Jimmy Wilder . . ." I stood there with my eyes shut and a wish in my heart. He kept calling off those names and peeling those uniforms out of the box. Finally, he looked at me and told me I could have the last one. "You're pretty little, Campy," he added. "But I guess it'll fit. But don't pester me about you catching. That position ain't for you. Maybe in right field." I might have been a bit miffed, but I tried not to show it. Besides, as long as I could wear that uniform and take a cut at the ball with fellows so much older than me — well, I was really flyin'.

My sister Doris came to our first game. Walking home with me that evening, she wondered out loud why I wasn't the catcher. I told her that when I wore the mask, I'd see spots before my eyes. Doris just laughed.

"You see spots all right — the green-with-envy kind," she said. "The coach is Roy Wilder, right? And who's the catcher? His boy?"

Doris patted me on the head. "Don't fret, Roy. You'll have his job — in time."

I didn't get to catch except maybe an inning or two that season. The next spring, when they issued uniforms again, we had a new sponsor. "STEIN TAILORS 15TH AND SOUTH" was on the back. I was thirteen, practically a man I thought, but Coach Wilder didn't have a uniform for me!

I was so heartbroken, I busted right out bawling and ran home and told Mom the terrible news. She listened as I poured it all out.

"You finished?" she asked when I finally ran out of breath.

I said I guess I had. Mom told me to go out and play. That was all. Doris told me later, though, that Mom called up Mr.

44

Wilder and told him he was breaking the spirit of a boy to whom a uniform meant just about the whole world. "You wouldn't want to do that to a child, would you?" she finished. The next day I was given a new uniform. That summer I played the outfield, pitched a little, and caught some too. Also, I began to fill out.

It was during that next winter that I had my first and last go-round with the Golden Gloves. In those days the Nicetown Boys Club didn't allow colored boys for membership (I understand that's all changed today) and so I joined the Wissahickon Boys Club over in Germantown. It was just a good walk — or better yet a run. I'd go up there and play basketball with their team. A fellow named Russell Allen coached us and he noticed I was getting pretty nifty with my hands and elbows.

"You might do pretty good in the Gloves," he said. "How about giving it a try? I'll put you down for the one-forty-five-pound class."

This was maybe a month before the bouts. Daddy always felt that my brother Larry and me should know how to use our fists.

"Never pick a fight," he used to tell me. "But once you're in one you should be able to give a good account of yourself."

Dad didn't just talk. He backed it up by getting us one of those heavy punching bags and hanging it in the cellar. I got so that I could really bang that bag.

I joined the Wissahickon Boys Club boxing team and we did pretty good. We boxed Germantown Boys Club, Nicetown, Roxbury, and Christian Street "Y." I won my share in the 145-pound class. Came the Golden Gloves and I was ready. Doris, who always seemed to know what I was doing, knew about me being entered, but she wouldn't tell Mom. Of course Dad knew it too. We used to fight three 2-minute rounds, and I guess that still holds in the pure amateurs. The

45

Gloves were held in the Philadelphia Arena in West Philly. It was the first time I'd fought in a place that big, or before a crowd that large. Doris was there, but Dad stayed home. She was proud that I got past my first two men. I had a good right, along with a short jab; and at my weight, I was taller than most of the kids.

The boy I found in the semi-final, a white boy, like to broke my nose in the second round with a clean right. Man, did I see stars! My beezer started bleeding and never did stop the rest of the fight and for an hour later. I could hardly breathe. He beat me fair and square on a decision. But I still think that until he landed that right, I was doing pretty good on points. That bout marked my first and last Golden Gloves. I dunno. Maybe if I'd entered them the next year I would have done better. But by that time I was so much with baseball and so little with anything else that nothing much mattered. Including school. But this for the Golden Gloves. They may be just a newspaper promotion but can you tell me a better way for getting a boy squared away with himself? If he wants to test his courage and his skill, the Gloves are the place for it. So-called "gang fights" or "rumbles" with fists, knives or belt buckles never proved anything good.

At Gillespie, the teacher who meant the most to me was our gym instructor and coach, David Patchell. He also taught hygiene.

The school baseball diamond was across the street from Gillespie and Simon Gratz High. It was late spring, 1935, and I was going on fourteen and in the eighth grade. We played everything over on that playground, but all intramural. Indoor baseball, touch football, basketball, and volley ball. Whatever the sport, I seemed to feel that I *had* to be on top. Maybe it was because in sports I felt that I could gain the recognition and standing any kid wants.

One day I boffed that softball clean over the fence into the street. Walking back to Gillespie after the game, Mr. Patchell said he wanted to talk to me in his office.

"Anything wrong, Mr. Patchell?" I said.

"Nothing wrong," he said. "I just want to talk to you."

He was working at his desk when I reached his office. He turned around, smiled and asked me to close the door and sit down.

"Roy," he began, "about that ball you hit this afternoon. You're fourteen and I'm a grown man. But I can't hit a ball that far. I've been thinking about you. If you were to go through high school, I think you might earn a scholarship at some college. I see you as an outstanding football end — and almost as good at basketball. But baseball . . . that's your favorite, isn't it?"

"It sure is, Coach," I said. "As far as I'm concerned, it's the onliest sport there is."

"That's fine," he said. "Then be sure to use baseball in the right way. In time you may get the chance to play ball — to catch — in the Negro big league. I want you to be sure to try to live and to conduct yourself right, so that if the chance comes there will be nothing against you."

"But Coach," I protested, my voice going high and excited. "The way you talk, I been flirtin' with trouble. Honest. I'm not in *no* trouble with the cops!"

Coach Patchell waved his hand like he was brushing a fly off his nose.

"Of course you're not," he said.

Then he told me that while maybe I didn't realize it, I was so physically mature, I tended to brush through and over the other boys in our games. He didn't say anything for a while, letting his words take hold. I could tell that he was trying to lay it out for me as good as possible.

"Gillespie has less than twenty per cent colored — maybe closer to ten per cent," he said. "But whatever the sport or the game, the other boys always make you captain. Not because you're bigger than they are. They respect you for yourself and your leadership qualities. That's a nice thing, Roy. You're aggressive out there . . . real aggressive. Keep it that way. But keep it in its place. Right, Roy?"

I never forgot what Coach Patchell told me from that day to this.

SIX

By THE SUMMER OF 1936, WHEN I WAS PUSHING fifteen, I was playing sandlot ball with boys and men in their early twenties. No longer was I considered just another kid and a nuisance. I played ball like a man and that's all that mattered. Being colored didn't seem to matter either because the Nicetown Giants (the senior team of the Nicetown Colored Athletic Club) were the onliest colored team in that six-team Philadelphia sandlot league. I was still playing for the Giants, late that summer, when I was invited to join the American Legion team for Loudensluger Post No. 366. I caught up a storm there . . . and I was the only Negro on the club. I was beginning to attract attention. People in Nicetown were talking about "that Campanella boy."

It was when I was playing Legion ball the next spring that I met the man who was the most responsible for my moving ahead. That was Tom Dixon, catcher for the Bacharach Giants, a prominent Negro semi-pro team around Philly.

I didn't know he was there in the crowd that particular day, but I had quite an afternoon. We won the game and I drove in five runs with two home runs and a double. I must have handled myself pretty good behind the plate too. After the game, Tom Dixon came onto the field and stopped me.

48

He introduced himself. He didn't have to do that because I'd seen him catch for the Bacharachs. He was one of my heroes.

"Would you like to play with the Bacharach Giants?" he asked.

For a moment I was too stunned to answer.

"I know you have to go to school," he followed up, "but how about weekends?"

"You travel, don't you?"

"We sure do, boy!"

"Well," I said, "I'd sure like to, but I've never traveled any place. My folks would never leave me travel out of the city — sleep away from home and all that. I'd sure like to play with your team, but I'm afraid my mother wouldn't let me."

"Suppose I had a talk with her?"

"It's okay with me," I said, "but I think you'd be wasting your time."

When I got home that evening I mentioned to Mom that Mr. Dixon had talked to me and that he might come around and talk to her too. I let it go at that, but I was thinking plenty the next day at school. When I came home, Mom sat me down and told me what had happened.

That afternoon, two sleek Cadillac sedans with whitewall tires had pulled up in front of our house. Tom Dixon got out of one and Jack McGowan, owner of the Bacharachs, out of the other. Apparently they gave Mom both barrels, starting out by telling her that both the cars were used by the club in its travels . . . and picking it up from there. Mom listened to first one, then the other as they praised me to the skies. I would "go places," they predicted. "Never mind that," she said. "What I'm more interested in is what place are you going to take my Roy to right now?"

"Beach Haven, New Jersey, for a game Friday night, and

49

from there to Hartford, Connecticut, for a game on Sunday," said Dixon.

"He can't play on Sunday!" snapped Mom. "He goes to church on Sundays."

Then McGowan stepped in. "I promise you he'll go to church. I'm a church-going man myself, Mrs. Campanella. So I'll take him with me, personally, before the game. He'll eat good food and stop at good hotels. We have an honest, God-fearing bunch of boys and we play an honest game of ball. No cussin', no swearin', no gamblin' . . ."

Mom still wasn't convinced. Then he came up with the convincer.

"We'll pay your boy thirty-five dollars for the two games," he said.

That did it. Although Mom tried not to let on. She made out as if she was trying to make up her mind, but it was made up all right — snapped up and closed. Thirty-five whole dollars just for playing baseball! That jarred Mom. It was big money to her. After all, the depression was on real bad. There were some weeks that Dad didn't make that much money in six whole days with the vegetable truck.

"All right. Roy can go."

"Good," said Mr. McGowan. "You're a very wise woman, Mrs. Campanella. You don't have to worry about Roy one bit. We'll watch out for him."

As they got up to leave, Mom looked Mr. McGowan in the eye and said, "Mr. McGowan, the money . . ."

He started to tell her that nobody, including big leaguers in the white leagues, got paid in advance. But something in Mom's eyes, together with a sharp nudge from Tom Dixon, stopped him. He reached into his pocket and fished out three tens and a five and handed it all to her.

By the time Mom finished telling me all this I was up out of my chair and standing before her. I kissed and hugged her

50

and told her she'd never be sorry. I'd make a lot of money some day.

"I'm letting you go just this one time," she said. "And I expect you to behave yourself! You understand, Roy?"

I sure did.

I felt like a man as I sat between two of my teammates in the back seat of one of the two black Cadillacs speeding to Beach Haven . . . wherever that was. I was going to play my first professional game of baseball. I looked at the other five fellows in that car. They were grown men . . . real grown. And so were the players in the other machine. You see, we carried nine regulars, two extras, and of course Mr. McGowan, the big boss.

In the back seat, the others were dozing. So I closed my eyes too. But I couldn't sleep. My mind was too full of things. I pictured how it would be the first time I came to bat. In my mind, I saw myself stepping into the first pitch and knocking it a mile. I imagined myself cutting down base runners with bullet-like pegs to all bases . . . and finally, to put the icing on the cake, I'd end the game with a tie-breaking homer and be carried off the field on my teammates' shoulders.

Talk about the Hot Mikado.

I was in a dream world then, but what a different feeling I had when I walked out on the field that night. My teammates almost had to carry me onto the field, not off it. I was never more scared in my life. All of a sudden I began to realize this wasn't Nicetown any more. This was professional ball. This wasn't a bunch of high school kids. These were men. These weren't the home-town folks and friends watching; these were strangers who didn't know whether Roy Campanella was a ball player or a violinist. This wasn't the Loudensluger Post team; this was the Bacharach Giants!

For the first and onliest time I wished I was back home, sleeping in my warm bed instead of sitting on the bench, cold and scared, wondering what it would be like to play under lights for the first time. All my life I had wanted to play baseball every minute of every day. But now I was ready to sit on the bench and let Tom Dixon do all the catching.

I didn't sit there too long. Tom Dixon came over with shin guards, chest protector and flung them at my feet.

"Put 'em on, kid, and catch batting practice — might as well get the feel of things before the game starts."

"You mean I'm gonna start catching right away . . . tonight?" I asked.

Dixon looked down at me. "That's what you're here for, ain't it?"

I nodded. I was so nervous Dixon had to help me strap on the tools. Once I squatted behind the plate and caught the first pitch, I was all right. The nervousness left me. When the game began I was sort of sorry it was Dixon who was doing the catching.

But again I didn't sit on the bench too long. In the fifth inning, Dixon stuck a finger in the ball and tore a fingernail loose. He looked at his bloody finger. Shaking it dejectedly, he walked toward the bench and called to me. "Okay, kid, it's all yours."

McGowan turned to me and ordered. "Go in, kid."

All of a sudden, I got nervous again. This time another player helped me with the shin guards and chest protector. I wasn't thinking no more of hitting home runs and throwing out the runners. I was worrying now about dropping a pop up and making a wild throw and striking out. But that feeling, too, lasted just one pitch.

The Bacharach's star pitcher was a veteran named Swimmy White. Today he's a bartender in a high class place in Philly. (When I was so sick, Swimmy, Quentin Lee and so many of those old boys sent me a giant "Get Well" card with their signatures all over it.)

Among Swimmy's other pitches — in fact it was his pet pitch — was his "dipsy do." Driving toward Beach Haven that first day, he had described it as an "up and down" pitch. I wondered what kind of ball can jump both up and down. In curve or out curve, sure — but not up and down. Swimmy just told me to rest easy, he'd show me. Warming him up that evening, sure enough, he had the craziest acting pitch I'd ever seen!

"Just signal with your hand if you want it to jump or fall down," he had said. "And be sure you block that ball if there's a man on and my pitch happens to go in the dirt."

Actually, that pitch is illegal. To throw it, Swimmy scuffed up the hide of the ball with a small piece of emery paper that was glued into the palm of his glove. So actually, it was an emery pitch.

We won the game, 3 to 1. I didn't do anything outstanding. But for a kid that was running scared when he took over the mask and the mitt in that fifth inning, I didn't do anything bad either. I didn't get a hit, but at least I didn't make an error. Even if I had to box a few of Swimmy's up and down pitches, Tom Dixon said, "You did fine, Campy. There's no need to be nervous no more. You're gonna be all right." He especially liked the way I threw out the only runner that tried to steal on me.

The plans called for the team to stop off at New York on the way to Hartford for Sunday's game. We spent the night at the Woodside Hotel in Harlem. That was headquarters for all visiting Negro teams who played in New York or in the area around New York. I was no longer frightened as we zipped through the flatlands of New Jersey toward the big city. My heart was lighter, and I even bantered a bit with the other fellows. Also, I noticed that they looked at me a bit dif-

53

ferently. It was as if I was being accepted. They had seen me do a man's job, and to them I was no longer a wet-eared kid. To tell the truth, I didn't feel like a babe in the woods any more. For the first time I began to feel the excitement of a new adventure. I didn't know where it would lead me, but I was eager to go. Quentin Lee, who played third base for the Bacharachs and was my oldest friend, was my roomy on that trip. He'd been to New York a few times with the team. But for me, it was the first time — except for camp — I'd ever been away from home, let alone out of Philadelphia. I just couldn't wait to see Times Square, Broadway, the tall buildings, the bright lights, Coney Island, the Polo Grounds, and Yankee Stadium. I also looked forward to staying at a hotel for the first time.

Mr. McGowan rode in the same car I did, and he was full of ribs. He warned me about not losing the key to the pitcher's box . . . about making sure I'd get a can of striped paint for the batter's box, and things like that.

As we neared the Holland Tunnel, under the Hudson River, he suddenly turned to Tom Dixon and said excitedly, "Oh-oh — we forgot to get a gas mask for Junior, here."

"Gas mask?" I blurted. "What gas mask?"

"Why sure, didn't you know?" Mr. McGowan said. "You need a gas mask to get through the Holland Tunnel or else you'll suffocate!"

I half-believed him. Then I saw one of the fellows smile. I grinned, too. I was happy. They were pleased with me. I had been accepted.

It was close to midnight when we rolled into lower New York and on uptown. We went by way of Broadway. I'd never seen so many lights and people and excitement in all my life. It looked like the whole world was having a party.

Dixon, sitting next to me, must have sensed what was going on in my mind.

54

"I know just how you feel, kid," he whispered. "That's the way I felt the first time I rode through here. I wasn't much older than you are now. Exciting, isn't it? It still gets me a little bit even now when I come through here."

We were past Columbus Circle now. I felt a little bit embarrassed, Dixon speaking to me so confidentially. I wanted to tell him how I felt, what was in my heart, but I couldn't express myself with the right words. So I said nothing.

"This is the big time, kid," he continued. "Broadway, New York. When you make it there, you make it big. Bojangles Robinson . . . Henry Armstrong . . . Duke Ellington and so many others of our race. Even that kid Joe Louis. He'll make it big — real big. But until you make it here, in the big town, you ain't nothin', kid. You just ain't nothin'."

"What do you mean?" I asked. "I don't understand. What has dancers and fighters and band leaders and New York got to do with playing ball?"

Dixon started to answer and then he stopped.

"Never mind, kid," he said. "You're too young to understand. Some day you will, though."

I understand now what Tom Dixon meant. It wasn't Broadway or New York, it was the things they stood for: the big time, the top cabin, first class, the big leagues . . . success. But big time baseball back in those days was closed to members of my race.

Tom Dixon, my first tutor and counselor, told me something else that night that stuck with me.

"I'm not one for talking," he said. "But I want to give you one piece of advice. Let this stick in the bones of your head if nothing else I tell you does. Don't see yourself small. If you start off aiming small, you'll always be small. Aim for the bright lights back there. Aim for that big time and that big money. *Reaching* never hurt a man no matter what his color is. Remember, success ain't gonna chase you. You got to go after it. You're still a kid, but you got a good head on your shoulders and you got a way with you behind that plate. You got it, kid. You're gonna be a better catcher than I ever hoped to be. You can make it, kid, if you keep your nose clean, a sharp eye out and your tongue in your mouth."

"Hey, Tom," one of the other Giants remarked good-naturedly. "You missed your target. You'd have made a fine preacher."

The cars finally came to a stop. We were in front of the Woodside Hotel, at 141st Street and Broadway. The streets were all lit up there, too, although not nearly as much as on lower Broadway. This, I was told, was Harlem, *the* place in New York for Negroes.

I don't know about the rest of the team but Quentin and me headed straight for bed. I was awfully tired but I couldn't fall asleep. My head was bursting with things. There was the new and strange surroundings, the first time in a hotel bed; the noise and bright lights outside, my first game, the trip to Hartford tomorrow; there were my folks back in Philadelphia, the school and the kids in Nicetown. There was Tom Dixon talking so earnestly and so strange. He liked me. I could see that. And he was trying to tell me something. What did he mean — really? I was still trying to figure it out when I finally fell asleep.

The next morning I was up bright and early with Quentin. We dressed quickly and went downstairs. We bumped into Mr. McGowan in the lobby. He was all smiles.

"Make your bed, Campy?" he asked.

"Why no, I didn't," I said. "I thought —"

"Son," he broke in, "be sure to always make your bed. An unmade bed is the baddest possible reputation for the team."

"Yes, sir," I said and hurried back to my room and made up my bed and Quentin's too. When I came down again, Mr. McGowan gave me a pail.

"Get this filled with steam, boy," he said. "And bring it up to my room . . ."

"How can I fill it with steam?" I asked him.

Then I saw the other fellows were laughing and I realized he was still working the rib. "Why sure," I said, "and wouldn't you like a can of that striped paint while I'm about it?"

Mr. McGowan laughed fit to bust. "You catch on real quick, kid . . . real quick."

That was the last time Mr. McGowan pulled a gag on me.

Quentin and me had a fast breakfast. I couldn't wait to get out on the street and see something of New York.

"How far is it to where we saw all those bright lights?" I said.

"A good hike in the subway," he said. "We don't have time to go down there. There's plenty to see right here. Besides, until it's night, Broadway is pretty much like Market Street in Philly — only with more noises and people."

As we walked through the lobby of the Woodside and out into Seventh Avenue, a sight met my eyes that stopped me in my tracks. It was a great big blue and white bus with BALTIMORE ELITE GIANTS painted along its sides. To me, and I guess to any Negro kid, the Elite Giants were like the New York Yankees. If a colored boy had dreams of making it in the big leagues it was the Baltimore Elites — or the Pittsburgh Crawfords, the Newark Eagles. Teams like that. The Negro big league consisted of the Negro American League, made up of cities in the West, and the Negro National League, with the same number of teams in the East. The Babe Ruth of the whole shebang was Josh Gibson, the big catcher for the Pittsburgh Crawfords. He was almost as big as the Babe — but all muscle. He could hit a ball a mile.

But in those days, Baltimore's Elite Giants were really big and really colorful. They packed 'em in wherever they played.

Out in the street that morning, I just sort of drank in the sight of that big, bright-painted bus. Finally I said to Quentin, "That's class with a capital K, ain't it!"

Tom Dixon wandered over. I was asking him how his finger felt when another fellow joined us.

"Tom," he said, "I need a catcher — a good young kid I can break in to give me a rest. I'm beginnin' to get beat. You know anyone?"

"Biz," said Dixon with a big grin. "You're standin' right next to him. Biz Mackey, meet Roy Campanella."

That introduction by Tom Dixon was in some ways the most important introduction of my life . . . at least up till then. Mackey, a strong-looking man with a wonderful smile, looked me up and down.

"I've heard reports on you, Campy," he said. "Big for your age, ain't you?"

"A little, maybe," I replied. "But I'm learnin'."

That's about all that was said. But later that day Biz Mackey came up to my room. He didn't waste much time.

"How'd you like to take a ride with us today?" he said. "To where?"

"To Philly, to play the Philadelphia Stars."

I almost swallowed my gum. "I'd sure like to, Mr. Mackey," I said. "But I'm going to Hartford with the Bacharachs."

"That's okay," he said. And then he reached into his pocket, pulled out a card and wrote an address and phone number on the back of it.

"Here," he said. "Give me a call in the next few days. You live in Philly, don't you? Well then, just don't forget. And good luck in Hartford."

But I did forget.

We played the Hartford Gems on Sunday and it was a real close game. They had a pitcher named Johnny Taylor.

What a pitcher he was. He had great stuff. We won, though. I got two singles and caught the whole game. The ride back to Philadelphia that night was wonderful. I was really beginning to take hold and felt strong as a bull. Late that night as they turned me loose in front of my home, Tom Dixon said the Bacharachs were going to play Tuesday night in Woodhaven, New Jersey. There would be fifteen dollars in it for me.

As I ran up our front steps, the light was on in the living room. It was after midnight, but Mom was waiting for me. I started to tell her about the whole weekend. Mom just listened . . . and listened, with a smile on her face. She finally broke in. "It's late, Roy. Real late. The rest of this can wait until tomorrow. Meanwhile it's a school day. Now scat!"

"Just one more thing, Mom," I said on my way up the stairs. "On Tuesday night they're playing in Woodhaven, over in Jersey. It's another fifteen dollars. And it all goes to you! Fifty dollars for three games. Not bad, right, Mom?"

"Not bad, son. Not bad at all," she said. "Now —" and she clapped her hands — "to bed, Roy! Quick!"

That Tuesday afternoon I could hardly wait to pick up my uniform and get started for Woodhaven.

"A man named Mackey phoned," said Mom. "He wants you to call him downtown at the Attucks Hotel."

I reached him on the phone. "Hello, Mr. Mackey. This is Roy Campanella."

"Oh yes, Roy. You didn't call, so I guessed you might have forgotten. I'd like to see you. Can you drop over to the hotel?"

"Well sir, it's this way," I stammered. "I'm just now on my way to Woodhaven with the Bacharachs."

"Well, just stop by on your way," Mackey replied. "I won't keep you long."

59

Less than half an hour later I was in Biz Mackey's room at the Attucks Hotel. He was the same nice man with that big smile. He sat me down and began telling me what it was like to play with the Baltimore Elites. He painted it real big and I was plenty impressed. It sounded like I dreamed it would be.

"I can get you sixty a month, and expenses," he finished enthusiastically.

"But I'm getting much more than that now," I said with a good deal of regret. "You see, Mr. Mackey, I'm getting fifteen dollars a game . . . sometimes twenty."

Biz Mackey's brow wrinkled. "But that isn't the big leagues, son. This is only a start. There's no telling how much you can be making in just a few years."

Before I could think of an answer to that, he was out of his chair and digging into a large suitcase. He took out a brand-new uniform and tossing it to me said, "Here, try this for size."

He didn't have to whip me. Just feeling the material in that uniform was enough. I slipped it on and then he tossed me a cap. I walked over to the dresser mirror and took a long look at myself. And then I passed my fingers lightly across the chest letters. I tried to keep my mouth shut, but I know my lips moved as I repeated the magic words "Baltimore Elite Giants."

SEVEN

I JUMPED THE BACHARACH GIANTS. I COULDN'T
even wait to finish out the day and the game with the Bacharachs. I went downstairs with Biz Mackey and climbed
aboard that big blue bus that meant big league.

"Don't see yourself small or you'll always be small. Aim
for the bright lights and that big money . . . success ain't
gonna chase you. You got to go after it . . ."

Those were the words Tom Dixon had said to me that
Friday night driving into Harlem. I didn't think then that
it would all happen so quick. I hadn't even thought when
Mr. Tom had introduced me to Biz Mackey the next morning, and he had told me to look him up, that it could happen
— at least, not so soon. But here it was only a few days
later. And here I was, riding that big Baltimore Elite Giants
bus to an exhibition game over in Norristown, Pennsylvania.
Then, that night, we were to play a regular league game
against the Philadelphia Stars at the old Penn Railroad
Field at 44th and Parkside. Biz Mackey was both manager and
catcher. Before I climbed aboard the bus, he told me he'd
use me in both games!

Hog dog! The Baltimore Elite Giants, with Roy Campanella, "The Boy Wonder," working behind the plate. If Tom
Dixon could see me now. Not only was I *reachin'* high, I
was *grabbin'* high.

The Elites won both games. True to his promise, Biz
Mackey let me catch a few innings in each one. I only got
one hit. But it was my catching more than my hitting that
the crowd seemed to like. I hustled those hitters almost as
hard as I chattered to my own pitcher. Down at the Parkside Field that night, many of those Philly fans recognized

61

me. They really let Biz have it — and me too, but all of it good-natured.

"Hey, Biz! Wotta you doin', robbin' the cradle? . . . You better get that kid home and in bed by ten . . . What *is* this — the Negro National League or the Playground League?"

It didn't bother me none. In fact I loved it. I knew I had a lot of friends in those stands, some maybe from Kerbaugh Street. They were pulling for me. So I was nearly fifteen. I felt a lot older and bigger and stronger and wiser than fifteen.

There was no curfew in colored night ball. You played till you finished the game. It was almost two in the morning when I reached home. The light was shining through the living room window. Mom was up and waiting for me, and I expected the worst. I'd told her I'd be home before midnight, and here it was close to two in the morning. I also had told her I'd bring home that fifteen dollars from the Bacharach game. I had thirty-two cents in my pocket.

Mom's voice was cold when I walked in that door.

"Where have you been?"

My eyes traveled from her angry face to the leather strap dangling from her right hand — the same strap Dad used on me more than once! I tried to soft talk her. "Mom, I'll bet you can't guess what happened tonight — I played in the big league tonight!"

"Big league, you say. I don't care where you played. Coming home at this hour. You're getting to be a bum, just like the rest of those baseball bums!"

"But Mom —"

I stepped back as she came at me with the strap and hit me across the hip with it.

"Don't, Mom!" I shouted.

She hit me again and again, screaming "Bum . . . bum

62

". . . bum!" with each whack. But she couldn't keep it up. She burst out crying and then she grabbed my head and brought my face down on her bosom.

There was nothing that broke me up worse than hearing Mom cry.

"Don't cry, Mom," I pleaded. "Please don't cry. You didn't hurt . . . don't, Mom, please don't."

She drew away from me, the tears streaming down her cheeks.

"Roy . . . Roy. Don't you realize how you worry me when you stay out this late? Don't you know what it does to your father?"

"I'm sorry, Mom. Honest I am." She started dabbing at her eyes with her handkerchief. I knew she was calming down a little.

"Mom," I said. "Something wonderful happened to me today. Look!" I pointed to the lettering on my baseball shirt that I'd worn home. "This is the big league of colored baseball. They want me to play for them. Regular!"

That brought Mom around fast. "How much did they pay you?" she asked.

"They didn't give me anything tonight, but —"

"No money?" she screeched. "You're not in any big league!"

I tried to explain that I'd be paid by the month now, not the game, but Mom wouldn't hear me out.

"Who is this man and what's his name?" she demanded.

"Biz Mackey," I said proudly. "Next to Josh Gibson, he's the onliest catcher there is! He's tops."

"Biz . . . Buz!" she hollered. "What kind of name is that? Where is he?"

I mentioned the Attucks Hotel, how it was the same man that called in the afternoon. "You don't want to call him now. It's awful late."

"Late?" she snapped. "It wasn't too late for him to keep a fifteen-year-old boy out."

I stood there, fidgeting on one foot and then the other as she called the Attucks Hotel. I could imagine her getting Biz Mackey out of bed to bawl him out — and having him wind up by telling her to keep me home if that's how she felt. That conversation was mostly one-way.

"I thought you were going to give my boy some money . . . Who? . . . Tom Wilson? . . . That's not very much . . . Very well, then . . . Tomorrow morning? All right . . . good night."

Mom put down the phone. "The owner of the team, a Mr. Wilson, will be here in the morning. Now go to bed."

The next morning I tried to convince Mom that I should stay home from school so that I could be there when Mr. Wilson called, but she cut me short.

"Young man, you just get to school, and on time, or I won't even consider letting you play ball for the Giants or anybody else!"

When I got home from school, Mom told me what had happened. Biz Mackey and Mr. Wilson had come by our home. She had agreed to let me play, but only with the understanding that I couldn't make any long trips until summer vacation. My pay would be $60 a month. The money would be sent home to Mom, but I could keep the expense money.

I finished out the spring term in a daze. On June 23, I met the Baltimore team in Philadelphia and took off with them on a tour of Pennsylvania, West Virginia and Ohio. In some ways, that was the most valuable summer I ever spent.

As a catcher, Biz Mackey was one of the best I ever saw. A big fella, about six-one and around 225 or 230. Biz was a switch hitter. But it wasn't his hitting that made me whistle; it was his catching that really impressed me. And how he impressed me. He wasn't really so fast on his feet as he was quick. At blocking low balls, he was a master. But even more than that, Biz was a thrower like you seldom see today.

I had a strong arm and a fast one, even in those days, but it was a scatter-arm. I'd get the ball away so hard on my peg to second base that it was fifty-fifty whether it would be on the bag or out into center field.

"How do you think you'll ever make a catcher?" Biz would say. Man, in those days I was *his* boy, but he rode me unmercifully. Most of that riding was because of my throwing.

In his earlier days Biz had been a shortstop too, and he knew all about getting the ball away quick. "You don't have to throw the ball that hard," he'd preach. "Learn how to get it away quick, and you can throw easy."

That's what he hammered into my head, fast hands and a soft throw. He didn't let up on me. The sternest, hard-ridingest coach I ever knew.

Biz wasn't satisfied for me to do just one or two things good. He wanted me to do everything good! And the onliest way I was going to improve myself was by working at the game, working . . . working . . . working. Not just *playing* at catching, but *working* the position!

There were times when Biz Mackey made me cry with his constant dogging. But nobody ever had a better teacher.

The pattern of my life in the Negro National League began for me the summer of 1937. We were away from home for nearly two months. The schedule was a rugged one. Rarely were we ever in the same city two days in a row. Mostly we played by day and traveled by night; sometimes we played both day and night and usually in two different cities. We traveled in a big bus and many's the time we never even bothered to take off our uniforms going from one place to another. We'd pile into the bus after the game, break open boxes of sandwiches and finish the meal with some hot coffee as we headed for the next town and the next game.

The bus was our home, dressing room, dining room, and hotel.

I always carried an extra pair of shoes, socks, underwear, shirts, pants, a couple of ties, handkerchiefs and a sports jacket. What else could I need?

I loved the life despite the killing schedule. Looking back now, it's difficult for me to understand how I stood up to it. Besides the constant go, there was the handling of the pitchers.

Anything went in the Negro National League. Spitballs, shine balls, emery balls: pitchers used any and all of them. They nicked and moistened and treated the ball to make it flutter and spin, dip and break. Not only were there no rules against it, there weren't enough spare baseballs around to substitute clean unmarked ones for the damaged ones, like they do in the big leagues. I was never sure what a ball would do once it left the pitcher's hand, even when he threw what I had called for. A man could get hurt catching in the colored league.

We had a pitcher named Bill Boyd, a spitballer who chewed slippery elm, a soft, greenish-colored bark that gave off enough juice not only to make the ball do tricks when he threw it, but also when the infielders or outfielders threw it after the batter hit it. That's if they ever hit it. Why, Boyd would mush up the ball so bad, there were times when I hoped the batter would connect. Hitting Boyd was an art; catching him was a nightmare.

One day Boyd complained about me to Mackey.

"I like the kid," Boyd told the manager. "He gives me a good target, but he don't know nothin' about catchin' spitballs, and he's going to get hurt back there."

66

Biz Mackey shrugged. "Well, he ain't goin' to learn, either, if he don't get back there and catch."

When Mackey told me Boyd's complaint, I sought him out.

"Mr. Bill," I said, "don't you worry none about me. You just throw whatever you please. I'll stop 'em! Nothin's gonna get past me."

Mackey really took me in hand then. There wasn't a time when we were together that he wasn't explaining something new about catching.

"There's so much to learn about catching, kid," he'd say. "There isn't a game in which you can't learn something, if you look for it. You gotta figure to yourself, now what's the hitter looking for up there, what's he think I'm telling the pitcher to throw? You gotta try to fool 'em, keep 'em off balance, learn what bad pitches they'll go for and what good ones they'll let by. There ain't a player who ain't got a weak spot. You gotta find it.

"A good catcher is worth his weight in gold to a pitcher as well as to the team," continued Mackey. "He can make a fair pitcher look good by calling the right pitches. Or he can ruin him by calling for the wrong ones. You gotta learn to handle pitchers like they were babies sometimes, each one different. You gotta scold some, you gotta flatter some, you gotta bribe some, you gotta think for some, and you gotta mother them all! If you can do all those things, son, you'll be the biggest man in the league."

I took that advice to heart. I began to take charge; and as the season wore on, I found myself working as many games as Mackey. I improved steadily. I broadened out, became stronger, and my hitting was sharper.

The Elites were playing through the Midwest — a long tour which took about a month. At the beginning I didn't mingle much with the others on the team. I was the youngest and only a spare on the team. Also, I didn't have the kind of

67

money to spend in jazz dives and such — not when I was making $60 a month and all of it going home except for seven dollars spending money. Finally, I just wasn't interested in going to those places.

But a fellow can't be a hermit. He's got to go out once in a while with the boys. He's got to pick up a tab now and then.

One day I approached Vernon Green, the club secretary, and talked him into letting me draw against the next payday. I'd repay him in plenty of time to send a check home. By the time the team hit Philadelphia, I was broke.

That first night home, I was treated like the prodigal son. Mom really spread a table: Pork chops, spaghetti Caruso, the works. My brother Lawrence and his wife were there. So were Gladys, on vacation from college, and Doris, and of course Mom and Dad. Things were pretty lively, with me the center of attraction. I told them everything that happened to me, about the places I'd been, the things I'd seen, the games I'd played. Finally, when I began to run dry, Dad spoke up.

"Son," he said, "where is your check?"

"They didn't pay anybody yet," I lied.

"Why not? It's almost the end of the month, and it was due on the fifteenth. You always send it home to your mother by the twentieth."

I had got myself in deep enough. I tried to shrug it off by saying "Don't worry, Pop. It'll come."

"Never mind," he said. "I'll get it. I'll go down there tomorrow."

I didn't know what to say. Kids seldom do. It takes a while for them to learn that telling the truth beats a lie four ways from Sunday. Tell the truth and you don't have to remember what you say; tell a lie and you got to remember everything you say.

I didn't have the nerve to go to Vernon Green and ask him

to cover for me, and there was no way I could detour Pop from going down to demand that sixty bucks I'd already spent.

It was late the next day when I walked into Mr. Green's cubbyhole at the park.

"Your father was down here earlier, raising cane," he said.

"I know," I replied. "What did you tell him?"

"I told him we had a bad trip, and that I wasn't able to meet the payroll until we got back East." Then Mr. Green's grin would have split a watermelon. "And I gave him the sixty dollars."

I thanked that man from the bottom of my heart.

"Don't worry," he said. "Pay me when you get the money. There's no big rush. But remember this: What you did was wrong. Never tell a lie like that to your daddy. Not only do you put yourself in a hole, you pull us all in there with you."

The next day we played the Philadelphia Stars at the old 44th and Parkside field. It was in a late inning that I caught hold of a pitch real good and rode the ball clear over into a tennis court in left center. As I trotted around the bases, I could see that two fellas playing tennis had stopped and were watching me. One of them had the ball.

After the game, the fellow with the ball showed in our dressing room. It was my old gym instructor from Gillespie, Mr. Patchell.

"Campy," he said. "I see you're still hitting the ball. Now that you're a professional, how do you like the life?"

"It's great, Coach," I said. "What with a fellow like Biz Mackey here, giving me pointers, and with the fine gang we've got — well, I'd be crazy *not* to like it. Yessir, I like it fine!"

Our second baseman, Sammy T. Hughes, was dressing nearby, and I introduced him to Mr. Patchell.

"Mr. Hughes," he said, "Roy, here, was one of my boys. I'm proud of him. If he lives right and continues to behave, there's no telling how far he can go. Isn't that so?"

Sammy was quite a bit older than me. "Mr. Patchell," he grinned. "Don't worry about Campy none. He's doing fine . . . yessir, just fine."

I never did see Mr. Patchell again.

When I returned home early in September, I was convinced more than ever of one thing. For better or worse, my future and my life was going to be baseball. If the colored big league was as far as I could go, I would be the best in my own league. Another thing — quite a few Negro league players were drifting south with the season. I mean really south. To Puerto Rico, Cuba and even to South America. I had traveled as far west as Chicago and Kansas City. Right from that first day, I liked travel. That, along with my love of baseball, made the game a combination of the two things I wanted most to do. Play ball and travel.

That fall, in school, I just couldn't work up any steam for the books. Try as I might to concentrate on my schoolwork, my mind wandered off. I'd look at the teacher writing on the blackboard, and I wouldn't even see him. The teacher would be Satchel Paige and the blackboard would be the baseball diamond. The chalk lines the teacher would be writing were the baselines and there'd be old Satch, grinning down at me, getting ready to give me that old dipsy doo.

Yeah, here I was sitting right in this classroom, batting against the great Satch Paige. I had batted against him, too, just a few weeks ago. Couldn't even get a loud foul off him. Man, you ever try to hit Satch's hesitation pitch?

I was nearing sixteen. Part of growing up was that when a boy was sixteen he could get his working papers. I argued with my folks about continuing school. They were dead set

70

against me quitting, but they knew too that my marks were dropping like stones off a roof.

One day Mr. Wilson visited our home again and told my parents that he'd like to have me play regularly with the Baltimore Elite Giants. He wanted me to start training with the team the next spring, but it meant that I'd have to quit school.

"I'll give Roy ninety dollars a month, instead of sixty," Wilson said. "And that's only the beginning of what he can make in baseball."

Mom decided it was useless to buck the tide much longer. One night in early November she and Dad had it out in the living room for about an hour.

"I don't like the idea of Roy quitting school," Dad said.

"You can lead a mule to water, but you can't make him drink," she said. "Baseball has ruined Roy for school. But I do think that there's a future for him in baseball. Not only Mr. Wilson tells me, but a lot of others too. Playing ball, professional ball, he's doing something his whole heart is set on."

"Well, I've tried to stop him," finished Dad. "But like you say, Ida, he's baseball crazy. And our friends and the papers too say he's pretty good. If you think it's the thing to do, I won't try to force him with the books."

I was supposed to be up in my room studying during that talk between Mom and Dad, with my door shut. It was cracked open enough to hear every word. Dad got up, threw down his paper and started to climb the stairs. Then, turning, he said, "Ida, it's a queer thing, isn't it, that we should have a son who'd be so different."

"Different?" Mom said the word softly.

"Yes," said Dad. "This business of white and black. For you and for me, honey, I wouldn't change it one bit. We've been able to raise four fine kids. God willing, they're going to work out fine . . . and be happy. But the baby up there. He's too nerved up about this baseball business. I hate to think that with him it could lead to disappointment. To be good enough to rate the big league — the white league — may be one thing. But not to be able to get his chance to make it because of the color of his skin — that could be very difficult for him."

It was quiet downstairs.

"Roy is a smart old boy," Mom said finally. "Maybe that Negro league isn't the best there is. But it sure isn't the worst there is, either. They pay our boy good, real good. And in time he can earn more money than he could in any other line. And to love what you're doing, John, that's important, too." She paused. "Would he be better off as a porter — a shipping clerk, or perhaps work in a fruit and vegetable store?"

"To be happy with what he's got and who he is — that's more important," said Dad. "The Lord only knows how much I want Roy to be happy. Lately, I notice Roy don't laugh much. This striving to prove he belongs with older men playing a boy's game — if that's his way of proving he belongs, then I hope he'll come out the other side — on top. But I hope by then he can still laugh. A boy needs to laugh."

I lay in bed with the light out thinking about what Dad had said. It was true, there wasn't much to laugh about. Not for me there wasn't. Now that I think about it, there wasn't much time for me to be good-natured Campy until ten or eleven years later — when I was with Brooklyn.

Two weeks later, on November 20, 1937, the day after my sixteenth birthday, I left school. To do that, a boy should at least be grownup enough to go into the world and earn his way. That's exactly what I aimed to do with a mitt and a mask and a bat and a ball. For me, the baseball diamonds around the East and the Midwest and in Puerto Rico,

72

Mexico, Cuba, and Venezuela were about to become my place of business.

EIGHT

.THE DAY I QUIT SCHOOL I WROTE A LETTER to Tom Wilson, owner of the Baltimore Elite Giants. I told him that I had my working papers and that I was ready to begin work. Baseball work. It was maybe a week later that I got a reply.

"Keep yourself fit and report to Nashville, on March 20," he wrote. "We'll play an exhibition game before paying customers on the second or third day in camp. So be ready. You've got a future in Negro Baseball, boy. Don't forget that."

It was March 17th, Saint Patrick's Day, and I was getting ready to leave for my first spring training trip. Mom came to my room. She sat on the bed, watching me finish dressing. I had a green tie, bright green, and I put it on.

"Quite an Irishman, arcn't you?" chuckled Mom.

"Colored, Italian, Irishman — it's all the same. They're all people, ain't they, Mom?"

"They sure are, 'ceptin' some are spoiled a little worse than others. But you're right, son. As long as people are clean and honest in their hearts, they figure to be decent in their heads."

My little suitcase was all packed including the extra socks and the handkerchiefs that Mom had ironed that day, and three white shirts instead of two. Man, I was really beginning to arrive.

"Roy," she said, "last year you got along pretty good without having this book as your own personal private property.

73

But this year, you're a year older. Things could become one year more complicated. Not on the ball field — off it. Whenever your mind is confused about something and your heart is troubled . . . turn to any page and start reading. Pretty quick you'll feel much better, and stronger."

Mom handed me the Holy Bible, brand-new and just bought. Inside the cover she had written in ink: *For Roy from his Mother, March 17, 1938.*

The train left Philly station around four in the afternoon. I was aboard, in the last coach, with my suitcase, a magazine, and a neat brown paper bag. In the bag were four sandwiches, a couple with chicken and a couple with veal cutlets. The ticket, one way, cost $14.90. And on top of my ticket that Mom had bought, I had food enough to last me till the train was 'most to Nashville.

By the time we got to Washington, it was dark. I watched the people going into the diner to eat supper. That didn't bother me one bit. I had Mom's sandwiches. Two for dinner, and one each for breakfast and lunch, and I'd be in Nashville. That wasn't tough. In fact that was pretty good! I'd traveled on trains enough to know my way around — the quiet and polite way with a smile for folks and sticking to my own business.

By ten o'clock I was ready to turn in. I had the whole seat to myself, so I loosened my tie and my shoes and spread out. I hadn't been asleep long when I felt a nudge on my shoulder. I looked up through the smoke. The lights were dim, but the old man's face looking down at me beamed.

"That's you, ain't it, Campy?"

"It sure is — what's wrong?"

"Nothin' wrong, boy. I thought maybe you could use a bit of food — follow me."

I followed that white coat and that ring of snowy hair. The train must have been rolling through North or maybe

South Carolina. It was rockin' and pitchin' from side to side, but that steward walked as smooth and easy as if he was walking down Market Street at home.

Maybe six cars back, we crossed over into the diner. At one end, just off the narrow hallway, he opened the door to a kitchen. The chef was in there, along with a couple of waiters. Chef threw me a big smile.

"Hello, Campy," he said, grabbing my hand. "I seen you play. You tag that ball real good, son. Real good! Sit down and maybe I can hustle you a li'l old steak and ice cream or something."

That night, with the train rolling toward the Deep South, I sat in that diner with a white tablecloth and polished silverware and tied into the biggest sirloin I'd ever seen. With those waiters sitting around playing cards, some of them still in their white jackets, and with baseball questions flying this way and that, we had quite a bull session.

Finally the questions came around to colored baseball and what players like Satchel Paige, Josh Gibson and so many others might do if the color line was dropped.

That was a little over my head. "I'm sixteen," I said. "I hope I've got years and years of baseball ahead of me. If I'm lucky I should. Maybe, well maybe one day, we'll be able to play on an even basis with the whites. It sure would be a wonderful thing. From what I've seen, my league right now has players in it who are better than some I've studied upstairs. But to try and guess when will that day come — I just don't know. All I know is that my job right now is to get my hits and to make myself the best catcher I possibly can."

Training in Nashville, or any place else with the Elites, was nothing like my Dodger years at Vero Beach. In the big leagues the first week and more is spent pretty much just loosening the winter kinks and getting your arms and legs in shape. But that's not how it was — ever — in the Negro league. No sooner did you pull on your uniform and crack a sweat than you were in a game, playing before paying customers.

Play yourself into shape! That was the only way the Negro leagues got on the ball. Man, we didn't just sop up sun and orange juice and run laps and play "pepper" and listen to theory on the "pickoff play" those first few days after reaching camp. No sir — regular exhibition games with the hat being passed. And often as not, those old boys were hard as iron and limber as a rubber tube right from the gun. The reason for that was because they'd never stopped playing ball, really, from the season before! I didn't know much then about baseball in Cuba and Puerto Rico and Venezuela and Mexico, but it didn't take me long to find out.

I'll never forget the barbecue that our club owner, Tom Wilson, threw at his farm about twenty miles outside Nashville. It was a wonderful spread, with racks of spare ribs, mountains of Southern fried chicken and hot biscuits, dunked in syrup and honey. Yes, and black-eyed peas and gravy. When we bussed back into town late that night, I thought my stomach would burst. But next day I still had my appetite. That's another thing. Just like in the big leagues, us players didn't get paid one red cent until the regular season started. So I depended on my mother for spending money. She'd send me six or seven dollars a week, along with strips of postage stamps and a reminder to write home!

I'd write home about all the good things I could think of. And in those days the fact that I was wearing the mask and swinging a bat made everything seem pretty good. But I neglected to write about the day I opened a letter from Mom while two of my teammates, Andy Porter and Robert Griffin, were in the room. When I opened the envelope, out fluttered a five and two ones, along with that strip of stamps.

76

Griffin and Porter saw those greenbacks. "Say, Porter," said Griffin nice and easy, "can you shoot craps?"

"Sure," said Porter. "How about you, Roy?"

"Not me," I said. "I don't know nothing about it — and I don't care to."

"Aw, c'mon up to my room, and I'll show you," said Griffin. "There's nothin' to it."

Wanting to be one of the boys, I went with them to Griffin's room and listened as Andy Porter explained the fundamentals of that old man of indoor games: craps. As he talked, Andy rolled the dice a few times for demonstration purposes.

"You see how it goes?" he said.

"Yeah, I think so," I said.

Andy bounced the cubes to me. "Okay, man — shoot!"

"For how much?"

"Two bucks," said Griffin, tossing a wrinkled dollar bill onto the floor. Porter dropped another beside it. We were on our knees in a little circle. As I pushed out my two bucks, I rattled those dice and turned 'em loose.

"Eleven! That wins, don't it?"

"Yeah," said Porter real quiet, and looked at Griffin with sort of a strange look. "Shoot again."

"Two more?" I said, asking more than declaring.

Again they covered my two bucks. Again I shook those bones a real long rattle and let 'em spin.

"Eleven again!" I cried, sweeping in the bills. "How much this time?"

"I'm tapped out," declared Griffin.

"Me too," said Porter. "I only had two bucks. Lend me something for a few days, will you, Roy?"

"Sure," I said, and handed each man a dollar, along with the dice.

As I walked down the hall, I heard what sounded like

77

Porter's voice complain, ". . . and I thought you gave him the *other* dice, you dumb cluck!"

That spring we played a series of exhibition games in New Orleans. We practiced on the Xavier University diamond. The New Orleans baseball club of the Southern Association worked out at Pelican Stadium. I'd go there every chance I got, mostly in the mornings, and sit in the stands by myself and study the form of the big leaguers, especially the catchers. The Chicago Cubs came through town and I enjoyed watching their regular catcher, Ken O'Dea, work with the pitchers. He taught me something. I noticed the way he moved his body on every pitch to make sure he got directly behind the ball. I made a mental note of that.

Dizzy Dean, the great pitcher, had been sold by the Cardinals to the Cubs that winter. He worked out in the bullpen, near where I sat. I watched Dean very carefully, and I couldn't help but wish that I'd caught him in his prime.

It was in New Orleans that I learned that an oyster loaf (the kind New Orleans is famous for) and a bottle of pop could last me all day. Know what's an oyster loaf? It's a giant guinea hero sandwich — a loaf of Italian bread sliced down the middle with oysters instead of salami, pickles and goat cheese. For thirty-five cents a day I lived on oyster loafs, and that made my spending money stretch a fair distance of ground.

Playing with the Elites that summer was the greatest. The long bus rides were still fun. The new towns and the big cities were always something new. To a kid of sixteen, playing in Louisville one night and up in Philadelphia the next, that was about as big league as there was! Some of the others, specially the older players, would complain plenty about long and tiresome bus rides to nowhere, about fleabag hotels, greasy spoon restaurants — yes, and sleeping in the

78

bus as we rolled cross country. To me, it was exciting. Not only exciting, I was advancing at my position. As that season wore on I began to share the catching with Biz Mackey fifty-fifty. Instead of growing distant as I grew better, Biz gave me everything he could. I was becoming a good instinctive catcher, doing the right thing without thinking about it. But my hitting was something else again. Biz tried to get me to cut down on my swing and meet the ball better. "With your power you don't need to kill it. Don't kill the ball. Just meet it. It'll go plenty far!" Even then I had a big hitch in my swing that I never got rid of entirely. But Biz helped me to smooth it out some.

The next spring Tom Wilson decided I was ready to take over the catching job completely. He traded Biz Mackey to the Newark Eagles, a team that a few years later had a big kid named Don Newcombe as its star pitcher.

With my promotion to the first-string job in 1939, I got another $30 a month raise. I was now earning $120 a month — in season.

Around the league, my capacity for work began building me a name. Twice that summer I caught two double-headers in one day. One of these was a double-header in Cincinnati on a Sunday afternoon, a bus ride to Middletown, Ohio, for another twin-bill that night. Three hot dogs and a few bottles of pop was all I needed for fuel on the ride to Middletown.

That year Baltimore won the pennant, and I hit the ball real good in the playoffs against the Homestead Grays — with my idol Josh Gibson catching for the Homesteads. One game I got five hits including a homer, and in the series I drove in seven runs. The Elites won three games out of four.

It was quite a team. I'll always remember that bunch. Jim West was the first baseman. Sammy Hughes was at second,

Pee Wee Butts at short, and Felton Snow, who later was to manage the team, was at third. The outfield had Bill Wright in right field, Henry Kimbrough in center and Zolley Wright in left. Eggie Clark shared the catching with me. Besides Byrd we had Andrew Porter, Jonas Gaines, Bob Griffin and Bill Glover for pitchers. After Mackey was traded, George Scales, an infielder, was made manager.

Then came snow. There was quite a call for most of the Elites, the champs, to play ball in the tropics that winter.

I got an offer to play ball with the Caguas club in the Puerto Rico winter league. I was interested. Not only would I be working at my trade, I'd be paid a lot more than for anything I might be doing around home. I went down there with a couple of teammates, Lennie Pearson and Billy Byrd. It was my first trip across water, and I sure enjoyed it. Down there with the fences way off, nobody was hitting those home runs so easy. I hit eight that winter to beat out Buck Leonard, a veteran Negro league first baseman built like a wrestler. Before that, the most homers hit in one season was six, by Josh Gibson.

I learned to speak some Spanish in Puerto. Not so much for social as for baseball purposes. Few of those Latin American pitchers spoke English. So I had to learn their lingo to understand how they thought.

That winter set the blueprint of my life for the next seven years. Baseball in the United States each summer, baseball in the tropics each winter. I was playing the game fifty out of fifty-two weeks. With the Elites my pay rose to $150 per month.

It was along about then that I started thinking about girls. I never was much of a ladies' man. I was always kind of speechless whenever I was around with girls. Besides, I didn't have time for romancing, what with being on the go all the time. But I did meet a nice girl back home in Philadelphia. She lived in my neighborhood and we had gone to school together. I got to seeing her more and more. Her name was Bernice Ray.

Even though we were both young, Bernice and I decided to get married. That was in 1939. I had a job and I was making some money and we both felt that we could swing it. We agreed that when the time came for me to go on the road, she would remain with her folks. In fact, we never did have our own home.

Joyce was born the following year. Then came Beverly a year later. I was away most of the time. When I wasn't playing in the Negro league, I was down in the Caribbean. It wasn't any kind of a setup for a good marriage. What can anyone say about a marriage that doesn't work out? We just agreed to call it quits. The divorce came in several years later.

NINE

I WAS ALMOST EIGHTEEN YEARS OLD WHEN Hitler marched into Poland. It was September 1939. I can still hear those Baltimore newsboys shouting "Extra! Extra! Hitler invades Poland!" It didn't mean too much to me then. But some of the older fellows began to roll their eyes.

"What's next?" asked Felton Snow. "I sure hope we don't get mixed up in this thing."

It was about eighteen months later, in April 1941, that I received my Greetings from the draft board.

At the time I was in Hot Springs, Arkansas, training with the Elites. The United States wasn't at war yet, but the boys were being called up from everywhere. I rode the train back to Philly, thinking about what branch of service I'd land in.

Being a married man with two children, I was not subject to an early draft. But if Uncle Sam wanted me, I was ready, for whatever job he had in mind for me.

My draft board was up in my old neighborhood, above the firehouse at 22nd and Hunting Park Avenue. I had no trouble passing the physical, and they told me to expect a call in from sixty to ninety days.

"Can I keep on playing ball until I'm called?" I asked.

"Yes," they said. "But let us know where you are at all times."

I went back to the Elites. A month later, the draft board called me back and told me baseball was out. I would have to take a job at a defense plant.

"But I don't have any trade," I said. "I'm a ballplayer."

That made no difference. I was given a job at the Bendix Aviation plant in Philadelphia as a porter, with a mop and broom. The salary was $40 a week: take-home pay, $32.50. Two weeks of it was all I could stand. Then I went to the draft board.

"You said I'd get a defense job," I complained. "Do you call that a defense job — sweeping out the plant?"

"But we don't have anything else for you right now," said the head man.

"Then let me go back to playing ball," I said.

Those men put their heads together and finally told me to go back to the ball club but be sure to keep in constant touch.

So, it was back to the ball club. This second time, I didn't worry about the call or anything else . . . just baseball. My draft board knew where I was without me sending postcards from each town. I wasn't going to take any powder.

I was catching regular and I was hitting a ton. I was named to the Eastern All-Stars for the annual game against the West. The game was played at Comiskey Park in Chicago.

82

Leaving Chicago after the game, I picked up a paper and saw my name in big black type. The headline read, CAMPANELLA VOTED MOST VALUABLE.

This was the story:

Roy Campanella, youthful catcher of the Baltimore Elite Giants, was awarded the handsome gold trophy as the most valuable player in the East-West game, which the East won 8-3, here today. Campanella, playing his first year in the Classic, stole the show from his more experienced teammates with a brilliant display of heads-up baseball.

At bat, where he is a terror against National League flinging, he wasn't his usual successful self. He collected only one hit in five trips against the quintet of Western pitchers, but his four failures were more than compensated for in the ninth when he beat out a roller off the great Satchel Paige for the only hit off Paige in the two innings the famed Kansas City Monarch ace worked.

The big part of Roy's glory, however, was his grand fielding, which stamped him as the favorite among the fans, and among the newspapermen who voted him the trophy over Buck Leonard, Hilton Smith, Manual Martinez and Billy Horn, who also figured high in the balloting.

Campanella nailed Tommy Sampson on an attempted steal of second in the second inning; rifled a peg to Martinez in the fifth to make the game's only double play, catching Cleveland at second after Horn fanned; went to the stands for Ted Strong's foul fly; and twice nipped fleet Western base runners with speedy fielding of intended sacrifice bunts. In three of the four cases mentioned, Roy's brilliant work halted impending West rallies.

I still have that write-up at home, along with the trophy, which I keep along with my other trophies and awards in my den.

That fall I drifted with the season back to the Caribbean, to Puerto Rico and the team at Caguas, an interior town twenty miles from San Juan. Back then in 1941, Caguas was a town of around 20,000, not much more. Today it's closer to 35,000.

A Negro ballplayer, playing Negro ball in the States, might not have lived like a king, but he didn't live bad, either. Actually, with the Elites, we were never in any one town long enough to think about the poor side of cities. Sure, we knew it was there . . . as a matter of fact we had a lot of players in both leagues who had come from slum neighborhoods of big towns. Playing ball was a way to beat that, to move on to something better. After all, we were entertainers. We were out there to give the paying customers a show. I don't mean the sort of clowning that the Harlem Globetrotters put on with their basketball, we just played as good as we knew how. And we were always wanted for exhibition games when we were on the road — games against both white and colored teams. We had some great players, and those white semi-pro clubs used to really bear down against us. Phil Rizzuto, the great Yankee shortstop, played for the Bushwicks as a youngster. He once told me that when the Bushwicks played Josh Gibson's Homestead Grays, they would store the baseballs in the icebox. Freezing the balls was supposed to deaden them and help to keep those heavy-hitting Homestead Grays down to size. It never stopped Josh.

Puerto Rico is a long way from Brooklyn, the home of the Bushwicks, but the fans there were just as wild about baseball. Long before those early 1940s, the American sugar interests in Puerto had brought baseball to the island. In 1941, the Puerto Rico winter league was made up of eight teams from as many cities. In San Juan, the biggest city, Sunday double-headers always drew crowds of more than 15,000.

There were teams from San Juan and Santurce, a suburb of San Juan. Then, swinging west from San Juan and circling the coastline of the island, there were teams in Aguadilla, Mayagüez, Ponce, Guayama, and Humacao. And finally, directly south of San Juan, between it and Guayama, is Caguas, the city my team represented.

Puerto Ricans know their baseball. They've played the game many years, and during the winters they've seen plenty of pretty fast professional ball. In order to keep the league more or less in balance, it used to be that three American players were signed by each of the eight clubs. We all signed regular contracts and were subject to being traded, just like in the States, which tended to keep the pot boiling. During the week there were no games, just practice; but on Sundays there was always a morning and afternoon game in four of the eight league towns. With a season about four and a half months long that made a schedule of around forty games for each team.

In Caguas, I shared a nice apartment with two other boys, Lenny Pearson from the Newark Eagles and Bill Byrd from the Baltimore Elites. Our team was the Sugar Kings, and we were owned by the Eastern Sugar concern. Santurce was a Shell Oil team. The Don Q rum company financed the San Juan club. Satchel Paige was the big show in Puerto during those years. He pitched for Guayama, and it was always full house each Sunday in whatever town Guayama played, because the fans could count on Satch pitching.

Caguas is a sugar cane town. That winter of '41, we covered that island real good. We traveled by automobile. The sixteen of us would pile into four cars and off we'd go. We returned to Caguas every night. That wasn't bad. After all, the entire island is only a bit over a hundred miles long, and forty miles wide. Humacao, on the east coast, is just a skip from Playa de Humacao where they load the sugar boats.

There's wharves there and a nice beach too. Humacao is only fifteen miles from Caguas with the beach just beyond. I enjoyed being a beach boy. There's no prettier blue and green water anywhere than the Caribbean. I heard that there were sharks not far off shore but didn't put much stock in it. Matter of fact, I never swam that far out to investigate. But one day, when I was splashing in the shallows, glad to be alive and a ballplayer in Puerto, something scraped against my leg. Sharks! I made a beeline for shore. Man, I didn't know if I was swimming or running on those waves! Actually, the "shark" was a big jelly fish — the red and purple kind with stingers a yard long. Lucky for me, he barely stung me. He might have been just saying "Hi, Campy," but I sure wasn't staying to shake his hand. That monster cured me of going down to the sea, at least to swim.

Puerto Rico has many handsome yacht clubs and boat basins. To sit on the wharf and watch those pretty yachts come into dock — well, I used to spend quite a bit of time admiring those boats, never dreaming that one day I would have a yacht of my own.

Another thing we used to do a lot in Puerto was fish. Not only off a pier for pan fish, but deep-sea fishing, too. Many's the time I caught dolphin that weighed better than forty pounds and sharks too. But I never did tie into a tuna or a sail.

It was in Puerto that I got to know green bananas as a diet. When I first saw them in the market I thought they weren't ripe. But after eating *platanos fritos,* practically by the bunch, I know how good those green fried bananas are. Papaya was another good new fruit taste — but I can take or leave avacados, which really isn't a fruit but a vegetable.

On Sunday, December 7th, I was in bed reading a Spanish newspaper and thinking about the day's double-header. We were to play Santurce. A radio in my room was playing music when, suddenly, it cut out. The announcer rattled off a bulletin in Spanish.

The Japs had bombed Pearl Harbor.

"Pearl Harbor," I said out loud. "Where in heck is Pearl Harbor?"

Later, I mentioned it to some of the other boys. They had heard it too, and of course by then we all knew that Pearl Harbor was our big Hawaiian navy base. Fifteen years later, I was to mutter a silent prayer for all those boys on the *Arizona*. This was when the Dodgers stopped off at Pearl following the '56 World Series. We were headed for Japan on a good-will baseball junket. But that morning, Pearl Harbor sure seemed a long way off. I was worried, of course, because it seemed that the war everyone had been talking about was really started now. But we were paid to play ball, and on Sunday, December 7, 1941, we beat Santurce two games.

All visiting Americans in Puerto Rico had to register at the United States office in San Juan. I was classified 1A. They stamped NAVY across my papers and asked me my business.

"Business?" I piped. "I don't have no business."

Business or no business, they would give me a month to close it, sell it, or burn it.

We had a tough time getting back to the States. There were no planes flying to New York in those days. Just boats, and it took time to get passage. Lenny Pearson and me finally were able to buy tickets. We boarded the *Coamo* at San Juan. She was part of a convoy heading over to the East Coast. Everything was blacked out. German subs were supposed to be in those waters. We hit a terrible storm and it took us seven days. It wasn't no pleasure cruise. One day we were off the Virginia coast when suddenly the *Coamo* pulled out of the convoy and headed straight for shore. I was on deck when the commodore of the port at Hampton Roads yelled through the bullhorn.

"You have to have some kind of signal to come busting in here!"

Our captain bullhorned him right back. "A submarine just surfaced out there. We couldn't stick with the convoy."

Pretty quick, a destroyer took out from the Roads at full speed and dropped depth charges all over the area. I don't know if they hit anything, but those cans of TNT sure must have given that sub an earache. Four torpedo boats escorted us to New York where the *Coamo* put in at the Bull Lines pier. I was never so happy to see the East River.

My draft board called me two weeks after I got back. They sent me for another physical and again I passed, but they wouldn't take me into any branch of service. I asked why, and they said, "Haven't you got a wife and two kids?" I said, "Sure," and they said, "That's why." I was reclassified from 1A to 3A.

They wouldn't let me play baseball either. They didn't want me to travel, but stay right at home and take a job in a defense plant. They promised me a legitimate defense job this time.

The Disston Steel Mill in North Philly had been converted to an armor plate plant — armor plating for tanks. I was given the job of operating a huge hammer-press which pounded slabs of red-hot steel ingots into long, thin strips. Not only was it hard work; it was dangerous. One day, the fellow on the machine next to mine had his arm smashed to a pulp by the hammer. That scared the wits out of me. The next morning I asked the foreman to have me transferred.

"I ain't aiming to get my arms mashed," I told him. "I got a family to worry about and a baseball career."

The foreman switched me to another department where they assembled tank parts. That's what I was doing just before the spring of '42, when my draft board told me I could go back to baseball. I rejoined the Elites in New Orleans.

That summer I got a wire from the Cleveland Amateur Baseball Federation inviting me to play for a pick-up Negro All-Star team in a benefit game at Cleveland. I'd be paid $200 — more than a month's pay with the Elites. It was for a good cause, too: the profits were to go for promotion of sandlot baseball in Cleveland.

I went to Tom Wilson to ask permission. He nearly blew his roof.

"See here, Campy!" he stormed. "What do you think I'm runnin'? An employment agency or a baseball team? Here we got a game with the Grays Sunday, and this gink back in Cleveland not only wants you but Sammy Hughes too. You expect me to hold up the pennant race while you two go traipsin' around playing outside ball for extra dough?"

I pointed out that the New York Cubans had let off Imp Barnhill for the Cleveland game. "Two hundred dollars," I added. "That's a lot of money to turn down."

"Yeah, it sure is!" snapped Wilson. "And I'll fine you more if you jump the club to play that game!"

That night, Hughes and I compared notes. We decided that just this one time we'd risk it. The day before the Cleveland game, Sammy and I just got up and left by train. What can Wilson do to us? Dock us maybe a couple of days pay? That's only about twenty bucks. It didn't turn out that way. When we returned to the club two days later, Wilson, who was also president of the Negro National League, said: "You boys took an expensive trip. I'm fining each of you $250."

We gaped. I wasn't a scared fifteen-year-old any longer. I had a wife and kids. I wasn't about to take that.

"You didn't fine me a nickel," I said. "You just think you did."

The Negro All-Star game that year was played the following week in Chicago. Although I'd been picked, I rode the bench. Josh Gibson, getting old, but still the best catcher around, was behind the plate for the East. In the fifth inning, with the East behind, the fans began to yell for me. Tom Wilson had to let me play, but he took a last dig at me by sticking me — of all places — at third base. Things sure seemed strange out there; but, fortunately, I had only one chance in the field.

When I returned to Baltimore, I thought perhaps Tom Wilson and his $250 plaster might have cooled off. But it still stuck. And I wasn't about to pay it. I didn't play any ball that next week, and it was while I was cooling my heels that a wire arrived from a man named George Pasquel in Mexico City.

I HAVE HEARD ABOUT YOUR DIFFICULTIES WITH YOUR CLUB OWNER, TOM WILSON. WOULD YOU CONSIDER FINISHING OUT THE SEASON IN THE MEXICAN LEAGUE STOP YOUR PAY WILL BE ONE HUNDRED (100) DOLLARS A WEEK PLUS EXPENSES STOP PLEASE ANSWER PRONTO STOP JORGE PASQUEL

Would I? I caught the first train to Philadelphia, and bright and early next morning I paid my draft board another visit. I was getting to be a familiar face around that place, but I couldn't help that. My 3A status hadn't changed, and so I explained the situation. I was told, "Keep in touch with this office after you arrive at your destination in Mexico — and good luck."

TEN

I WENT TO NEW YORK AND CAUGHT A PLANE to San Antonio. There a man was waiting for me as I came down the gangplank with a small zipper duffel bag in my hand. I was traveling light.

If things didn't work out in Mexico, I didn't want to spend time packing. If this Pasquel fellow was as good as his word, I could buy whatever I needed for that country.

This man's name was Guillermo Ferrara. He came right up to me, shook my hand and told me he was a representative of the Mexican League. Another fellow was with him, but I never quite got his name.

"How was the trip?" asked Ferrara.

"I'm here. That's what counts, ain't it?" I smiled.

Ferrara couldn't understand why I didn't have any real baggage.

"I've got my spikes and my mitt," I said. "Yes, and a toothbrush, a clean change and the clothes on my back. I'm down here to play ball, not to strut in no fashion show."

The two Mexicans shrugged at each other and led me to their car. It was an old model but it ran. I climbed into the back seat, with them up front and we were off to Monterrey.

"That's where you're playing," said Ferrara. "They need help . . . bad, *si?*"

"Where is this place at?" I said.

"Maybe three hundred miles from here." He patted the steering wheel. "She's a good car — fine engine, sturdy tire. We get there fine."

Well, we just bumped along that road south. I was tired from the plane ride. There seemed to be dust everywhere.

91

I was feeling hot, dirty, dusty. Punko, period. Right at that moment, if a turkey buzzard had flown in and dropped a message from Tom Wilson saying "All is forgiven, come home," I think I would have headed straight back to Baltimore. But really, I wasn't about to do nothing like that. Pasquel had wired me the money, plus twenty-five extra, for the trip down . . . things were all fouled up at the Baltimore end, and, for a fact, not much better than that in Philadelphia, where Bernice and me had separated. The few times I'd been back to Philly I'd stayed with my folks on Kerbaugh Street instead of with Bernice and her folks.

No, I wasn't about to change my mind. Mexican ball and me just had to get along real good. I'd heard about that thin air at high altitude and how a batted ball rode a mile. Monterrey . . . Pasquel . . . sombreros and hot tamales — and that hundred bucks a week most of all. Campy was fixin' to do all right!

We stopped to eat outside the small Texas town of Cotulla, not far from the border. It was a little old roadside restaurant with gas pumps out front. Ferrara and his buddy said the food was "ho-kay," they'd eaten there on the trip up that same morning. And I was hungry. We sat in a booth. When the waitress came over, I noticed she looked at me sort of funny. But she didn't say anything. I knew what she was thinking, though. I'd lived long enough in places like Nashville and New Orleans to know her mind. But she couldn't decide whether I was colored or not.

After we'd eaten, the waitress handed Ferrara the check. She put her hands on her hips, faced me square, and came out with it.

"What is this guy? Mexican, American or what?"

"He's no Mexican," said Ferrara, nice and easy like.

"Hearing him talk and all, I thought not," she snapped. "But if he's an American, he sure ain't no white man. Don't

92

you know we've got laws against niggers eating in a place reserved for whites?"

"I'm real sorry," said Ferrara, cool and polite. "But we're finished now. Here's your bill, tip and all. Good night!"

And out we went, into the Texas night, with Laredo on the border and the customshouse our next stop. I had a hundred dollars in American money in my pocket. At customs, when I changed it into pesos, they handed me a bag of hard money, heavy enough to sink a body in their Rio Grande. The rate of exchange those days was a little better than five-and-something to one.

Later, as we drove deep into Mexico, a cow wandered onto the road and right into our headlights. Ferrara, a good driver, swerved sharply and we caught that old cow only a glancing blow. After that there wasn't any incident, not even a flat. "Sturdy tires!" he crowed. I thought about that and laughed to myself. There in the back seat, with my money bag loaded with silver, I almost felt like some pirate chief. I have to laugh now that I think back on what a strange passenger list that old car carried that night back in '42. Bumping along through that Mexican back country, I finally dozed off. But as I went to sleep, I couldn't forget, quite, that little incident in that roadside dump of a Texas eating shack.

We reached Monterrey early next morning. The manager of our team, Lazaro Salazar, a Cuban, was having his troubles getting the hitters to back up his pitchers and vice versa. The League consisted of such towns as Chihuahua, Mexico City, Puebla, Vera Cruz, Monterrey and others.

I plunged right into things. Those Mexican pitchers aren't big for the most part, but they're tricky. In air that thin the ball doesn't take off, break and dance like it does in the heavier air of the States. And when a batter with a home run swing connects, the ball *really* rides! Monterrey was in fifth place when I arrived. The fact that I had picked up so much Spanish in Puerto Rico — well, it really helped. Those pitchers knew what I was talkin' about. And after I first got there, and they briefed me on different hitters in the league, I knew what *they* were talkin' about.

It was early in October and I'd almost forgotten that there was a World Series going on in the States. This particular day we were playing Puebla. It's a little town high in the mountains and down there it's called "the City of Churches." It's a real pretty little town and God must like what they've built for Him. For a fact, in some of those towns I got to going to church again — not my old Baptist church because they just don't exist in those Latin countries, but just going to Mass and sort of letting that beautiful ceremony seep into me. It sure didn't hurt.

Anyhow, like I said, we were playing Puebla and we'd beaten 'em. I'd dressed quick and was fiddlin' around with a battered old portable radio in the little outer office when suddenly I tuned into a play-by-play of the World Series: it was the Cardinals and the Yankees. I remember that moment so well because right after I tuned in, Mort Cooper, the Cardinals catcher, picked Joe Gordon off second! That must have been a throw. That was the series where Johnny Beazley won two games for the Cards. After losing the first game, St. Louis simply ran the Yankees out of the park, winning the next four. It was the first time the Yanks had been beaten in a series since 1926, also by the Cards.

Monterrey finished second that year. The people down there liked my work and they paid me every dollar of my contract. Before I left for home, our manager, Salazar, said I'd be hearing from him. That winter he was to manage the Marianao team in Cuba and he wanted me as his catcher. I told him I'd be interested "at the right figure." As a token of his appreciation Mr. Pasquel, the owner of the whole

94

Mexican League really, paid my way back to Philadelphia on a flight from Mexico City straight through. I sure liked the way that man operated.

I wound up playing the winter of '42-'43 for Salazar in Cuba and enjoyed every day of it. What's more, when spring rolled around I'd about forgotten about the Baltimore Elites. That $250 fine still held, I guessed. Well, let it. I was now averaging $400 a month, practically the year round, and had reached the point where my Spanish was almost as good as my English. I began to think I could make myself into a real native in Cuba in the winter and in Mexico in the summer. That's where I returned to — Monterrey. That '43 season was a good one. Monterrey became a real good road team — drawing both fans and money. Not only that, we won our first Mexican League pennant that year. Off his '43 record Salazar might have got himself proclaimed a president or a senator or something pretty important in the government. But instead, true to his Cuban blood, he returned to Cuba while I got a good offer to go back to Puerto Rico — this time with Santurce. That's where I spent that winter of '43-'44, in Santurce, playing with Luis Olmo's Shell Oil team. Olmo played for a time in the Dodger outfield, under Leo Durocher.

When I returned to Philadelphia in the spring of '44 to spend a few days with my folks and my two babies, I intended to spend the summer in Mexico again. But one day I got a call from Baltimore. It was Tom Wilson. He told me he was willing to forgive and forget. That is, if I'd forgive, Tom would forget about that old fine of $250. He needed a catcher so bad that he was willing to pay me $3000 for the six months season, plus a bonus of $300 if the club did well.

We both did well that year . . . the club and me. In fact I took down that $3000 and the added $300 after both the '44 and '45 seasons.

ELEVEN

IT WAS IN THE SPRING OF 1942 THAT I FIRST started hearing rumblings about the possibility of Negroes being allowed to play in organized baseball. What with the war going on and a shortage of players, there was some agitation for the admission of colored players into the major leagues. I paid no mind to all that idle gossip. Maybe there was a shortage of players, but the Negroes were dying in the war as well as the whites. There were no bars there, but there were bars in organized baseball.

I had little faith that these bars would ever come down, at least in my playing lifetime. During my six years in professional baseball, I had played against nearly all of the white stars in post-season exhibition games and I did well in those games. But the color line in the big leagues did not take a man's talent into account. Never once did it occur to me that I would some day be playing in the majors. I was a ballplayer, and I played ball; and I made as much money as I could doing it. But all my ballplaying was confined to the Negro leagues. As far as I was concerned the big leagues were as far away as Siberia.

So I was kind of surprised when there was a knock on my hotel door one day, and a fellow came in. Before he even introduced himself, he said: "How'd you like a tryout with the Pittsburgh Pirates?"

I stared at him blankly for a moment, and he had to repeat the question. Finally I said: "Sure, who wouldn't?"

The Baltimore Elites were playing in New York that day; and, as usual, we were staying at the Woodside Hotel. The fellow went on to explain that he already had arranged with the Pittsburgh club for a three-man tryout. He chose, besides myself, Dave Barnhill, a pitcher with the New York Cubans, and Sammy Hughes, who played second base with the Elites.

"You'll receive a letter shortly from William Benswanger, president of the Pirates," the fellow said. "He'll tell you when to report."

And the man left.

I don't mind saying I was impressed. The fellow sounded so sincere, and he seemed legitimate enough. He said he was a newspaperman, and the trials were being arranged by his newspaper, the *Daily Worker*. I had no idea at the time that it was a Communist paper. Deep down I think I knew that nothing would come of it, yet I kept waiting and hoping for a letter. But weeks passed and no letter. So I dismissed the thought from my mind and went about my work as if nothing had happened.

Then, one morning, there was a letter. It was from the Pittsburgh club. It began with the attempts made by the *Daily Worker* to get me a tryout. It went on to say that the Pittsburgh club would be only too happy to arrange such a tryout, but it contained so many buts that I was discouraged even before I had finished reading the letter:

"You must understand that you would have to start at the very bottom . . . you must come up through our minor league farm system in the conventional manner . . . it might take you years to reach the major leagues . . . the pay would be small . . . there is no guarantee that you would ever make it . . . your years of hard work might be for nothing . . ."

The letter was signed by William Benswanger, president of the club.

I didn't let my feelings stop me from replying to the letter. The prospect of playing in the big leagues, no matter how remote, was too wonderful to let slip by without making a try for it. I answered promptly. I wrote that I'd be only too glad to start in the minors and work my way up. All I wanted was a chance, I said.

Then I waited for an answer. I waited . . . and waited . . . and waited . . . and finally I decided I had been a fool to have built my hopes so high against my better judgment. I knew I should have forgotten all about it but I suppose I became stubborn.

One day in Philly, my sister Doris and I went to Shibe Park. The year was 1945, the last summer of the war. Doris was carrying Judith and was far enough along to be a bit uncomfortable. We made our way into the park and into the upper balcony. It was real early — at least an hour before the game — and the Phillies were on the field having batting practice. Sitting up there, I spotted Hans Lobert, the Phillies manager. Lobert I knew. He had seen me play several exhibition games in Shibe Park. Suddenly I was hit by an impulse. I bought Doris a scorecard and a bag of peanuts.

"You comfortable?" I asked.

"Why sure I am, Roy," she said. "Why? You got business on your mind?"

"Maybe. I want to leave you for a few minutes. I want to go down there and talk to Hans Lobert about something."

Doris just smiled. "Tell him for me you're ten times the catcher anybody he's got is! Yes . . ." and she chuckled, "tell him that for me."

I made my way down to the field right beside the Phillies dugout. Lobert was talking to somebody nearby. When he saw me, I waved.

"Can I speak to you a minute, Mr. Lobert?"

Soon he came over to me. He was one of the bowleggest gentlemen I ever saw — and one of the nicest, too.

"Hello, Campy — what are you doing away from the Elites?"

98

"An off day," I said. Then I let him have it, both barrels. I told him that there had been talk around that the major leagues might be about to break open old Jim Crow. "You can use a catcher," I said. "And I'm a good catcher. I can help this club!"

Mr. Lobert put his hand on my arm. "Campy," he said. "When I tell you there's nothing I could use more and better than *you* right now, I'm not kidding you. But I haven't heard talk about any bars being lowered. Tell you what you do. There's a pay phone out there in the lobby. Why don't you go out there and call Mr. Gerry Nugent, the president of our club? You can tell him I suggested you give him a ring. He's in his office."

Hans Lobert must have understood the wild sort of gleam in my eye. He extended his hand and shook mine. "You're a good catcher, boy — a real 'class' catcher. Good luck."

I found a vacant phone booth right quick, and the Phillies number. As I slipped the nickel into the box I half whispered a prayer, and crossed my fingers for luck.

I told the secretary my name, that I wanted to speak to Mr. Nugent. On business.

Finally, a voice on the other end came through nice and clear.

"Hello."

"Is this you, Mr. Nugent?"

"Yes . . ."

"Mr. Nugent, this is Roy Campanella. I was wondering if maybe you could give me a tryout. I been keeping tabs on the Phillies, and it strikes me that you could use not only some catchin', but hittin' too. After nine years with the Baltimore Elite Giants — I'm ready."

He didn't reply for a moment or two. Then, Mr. Nugent told me that he knew about my record with the Elites.

I managed to get in the information that I'd just been

99

down to the field and had talked with Mr. Lobert. "He suggested I call you, sir," I finished.

Mr. Nugent was a fine gentleman . . . but I could sense that now he was giving me the sweet talk. He told me that I knew as well as he did that there was the unwritten rule about Negroes in organized ball and that he was powerless to do anything about it.

"But I want you to know I appreciate you taking the interest to call me," he said.

As I hung up the receiver, I felt real bad for a minute. I knew I had no right to. After all, what did I expect? Did I expect Hans Lobert and owner Gerry Nugent to go busting the bars down for me — right there and then? I hadn't lost anything by that call. And maybe one day . . . well, maybe one day . . .

I swallowed hard, bought a hot dog and a bottle of pop and started upstairs again. Doris was there waiting. There couldn't have been a thousand people in the stands yet.

She read my face like a book. "Don't worry, brother. Now you just sit down here and let's enjoy this old ball game."

I never did call Mr. Nugent again. I figured I had been a fool even to hope that I would be given a chance to play major league baseball. Organized baseball was in another land. The frontiers were well guarded. No one of my race could sneak in.

I didn't worry about it long. I was too busy catching and playing ball every day. By now I was the best catcher in the Negro leagues, with the exception of Josh Gibson, who was not only the greatest catcher but the greatest ball player I ever saw. I don't know how much the modern fans know about Josh Gibson — he died prematurely in 1947 — but when I broke in with the Baltimore Elites in 1937 there were already a thousand legends about him. And once you saw him play, you knew they were all true. He hit the ball so

100

far, so often, that you just didn't have to go making up stories about him.

Let me give you an idea. Josh hit home runs in every major league park he ever played in, and in almost all of them he hit balls up into places other hitters never even knew were there. He was the right-handed Babe Ruth over a period of fifteen years, without ever having a bad season. In 1931, when he was nineteen years old, Josh hit seventy-five home runs. Ten years later, playing for the Homestead Grays, he hit more home runs in one season in huge Griffith Stadium in Washington than the whole American League put together. Walter Johnson said then that Josh was worth $200,-000 to any big league ball club. In today's market that would be more than tripled.

The greatest hitting show I ever saw was an exhibition Josh put on during a barnstorming stop in one of those small West Virginia towns set in between the mountains. The park had this small plank fence around the outfield, and then, about ten yards behind it, the hills started rising. Well, the first time up, Josh just did clear the fence; the second time, he reached the base of the hill. By this time he was getting the range, so the third time he came up he hit one pretty well up on the slope. Then he came up for the fourth time, and he hit the ball . . . well, it must have gone halfway up the hill. I always figured that if he had come up one more time he just might have hit the ball clear over the hill.

That was the kind of hitter Josh Gibson was.

Like Babe Ruth, when Josh hit a ball right it didn't matter much where the fences were. They once measured a ball he hit in Monessen, Pennsylvania, at 513 feet; but I wouldn't want to say it was any longer than the fourth home run he hit that day in West Virginia.

Now after all I've said about his hitting, I'm going to say something that might sound a little crazy. I always looked to

101

his catching more than his hitting. Nobody but a catcher would say that, I know, but I was a catcher.

Josh was a big, powerful man. He was six feet two inches tall and he weighed about 230 pounds. Most of the weight was above his waist. He had a huge chest, tremendous shoulders, and the biggest arms I've ever seen. With all that weight, he moved around behind the plate with such effortless grace that everything he did looked easy. There never was a better receiver. His arm was strong and always accurate.

I had a very erratic arm when I broke in. It was strong enough, all right; but I never was too sure where the ball was going. I'll always be grateful to him for the help he gave me when I was a skinny little catcher away from home for the first time, and he was the great man of baseball. He tried to show me how to set myself to improve my speed and accuracy, and when I'd have a bad day against the Grays he'd come over to me in the locker room and try to give me a little confidence. "It's just a matter of practice," he'd tell me. "You got the arm, that's the important thing. The rest of it is just practice, practice, practice."

Nobody ever had a smoother, more rhythmic swing than Josh. That was the thing that used to impress people more than anything else, the distance he could get with the easiest sort of a swing. I used to take a real hefty cut myself, and he'd always tell me, as Biz Mackey had, "Roy, you don't have to swing that hard to give the ball a ride. If you hit it right, it'll go."

And I'd tell him, "Mr. Gibson, I'm not a big fellow like you. I got to swing hard." I tried to cut down on my swing, but in a way I was right. The natural ease with which Josh could do anything on a ballfield was something you had to be born with. Josh, for instance, was the only power hitter I ever heard of who hit the ball where it was pitched. When you get

102

a young ballplayer who can hit the long ball, you try to get him to pull, so that he can get the full sweep of his power, and also so that he can take advantage of the shorter fences near the foul lines. But Josh's power was to all fields.

He did just that, as a matter of fact, the first time I ever saw him play. I was a young kid then, paying my way into the bleachers at Baker Bowl, Philadelphia, and Josh was catching for the Pittsburgh Crawfords, the greatest Negro team ever put together. Satchel Paige was the Crawfords' star pitcher; Coop Papa Bell, the fastest man in the league, was in center; and Judy Johnson was at second base. The Crawfords were so good, and so cocky, that when they barnstormed against local teams after the season they used to advertise that Satchel Paige would strike out the first nine men and Josh would hit two home runs.

Unfortunately, the Crawfords were wrecked in 1937, the year I came into the league. President Trujillo of Santo Domingo decided he wanted to win the Latin American championship that year so he put up some real money to bring Gibson, Paige, Bell and some of the others down there. Trujillo got his championship, but the Crawfords had to go out and hustle themselves up a bunch of kids to play out their schedule. Gibson, Paige and the rest of the boys came back the next year, but the Crawfords sold Josh to the Homestead Grays. Paige went to the Kansas City Monarchs, and that was the end of what must have been the greatest battery of all time. Satchel will be the first to say that the best catcher he ever had was Josh Gibson of the Pittsburgh Crawfords and the toughest batter he ever faced was Josh Gibson of the Homestead Grays. And Satch barnstormed with all the big league greats. People have asked me many times how I think Josh would have done in the majors. I don't see how there could be any question about that. The players who were great in the Negro leagues would have

103

been great in the majors. It's a matter of ability, as I see it, not of league. Josh had it, that's all. He had more of it than anyone I've seen before or since.

It was three years after the Pittsburgh Pirates episode in 1945 that I started hearing rumors of Negro players actually being scouted by the major leagues. This time I paid no attention to it at all. I had been fooled once. That was enough. We were playing in Ruppert Stadium, at Newark. I was unstrapping my shin guards for my turn at bat when somebody nudged me.

"Look over there in the stands," the fellow whispered. "That man in the aisle seat is a scout from the big leagues."

"Well, what of it?" I replied. "My job is to play ball, not worry about who's watching."

I didn't believe him, of course. As I found out later, he was right. I was being scouted and the man in that aisle seat was Clyde Sukeforth, then coach of the Brooklyn Dodgers. I didn't know it then, of course. If I had thought it was true, maybe I'd have tightened up. Anyway, I wouldn't let myself believe it. I only wanted one thing in my mind at a time.

I was twenty-three years old, had a family to support, was veteran of nine years in professional Negro baseball, and I figured my future was still before me. I was one of the best catchers in the league now and I could not expect to progress any further in baseball; there was no place to go from where I was. Between the Elites and winter baseball in Latin America, I was making a decent living, $3000 a year in the summer and another $2000 in the winter. I caught almost 150 games a year and that was hard work, I suppose. But not to me. It's just a question of getting used to it. I caught winter and summer over eight years in a row. In the colored leagues a player who didn't play didn't get paid. There were no averages to go by. What paid off was being in the lineup. A fellow who was around all the time got the notice.

104

I was sitting on top of the world in October of 1945. I had just finished another successful season. Once in a while I wondered how much longer I could go on. I couldn't imagine life without baseball. But I'd shrug off those thoughts. Heck, a good man could go on playing until he was forty, I told myself. That means I could still play for another sixteen years. What was the sense in worrying that far ahead now?

I was getting ready for another season of winter ball in Venezuela when I got a telephone call from Mrs. Effa Manley, owner of the Newark Eagles, a good Negro team with a fireballing young pitcher named Don Newcombe.

"Roy," Mrs. Manley said, "we're getting together a Negro All-Star team to play an exhibition series against a team of major leaguers. Five games. I want you to catch. You interested?"

"Sure," I said. I wasn't due in Venezuela until the following month, and I could use the money. Besides, it was always a challenge to play against major leaguers. "Who's running the other outfit?" I asked.

"Dressen," Mrs. Manley said. "Charlie Dressen."

Dressen had a pretty good team. He had men like Eddie Stanky, Buddy Kerr, Whitey Kurowski, Tommy Holmes, Jim Russell, Frank McCormick, Ralph Branca, Virgil Trucks, Hal Gregg, Red Barrett and Vic Lombardi. We played five games, four in Brooklyn and one in Newark, and we didn't win one. We opened with a double-header at Ebbets Field. Hal Gregg beat us in the first game, 4-3, and the second game, with Trucks pitching against us, was called because of darkness and rain, with the score tied at 1-1.

Now we were in Newark. It was on a Friday night. Our team was getting its brains belted out, 11-0. Ralph Branca was blazing the fast ball past us and the lights at Ruppert Stadium weren't helping us either. I had just finished buckling on my knee guards and was walking toward the plate to take Bill Byrd's warm-up pitches to start the eighth inning when I heard a voice say:

"I'd like to see you after the game, Campanella."

I turned around, just in time to see Dressen's back as he trotted toward the coaching box behind third base. I yelled to him, "Sure, where?"

"In front of the ball park."

I nodded . . . and spent the rest of the inning wondering what it was all about. But as I said, I think of only one thing at a time, and by the time I had dressed, stuffed my things into the zipper handbag and half-groped my way out of the park, I had forgotten about Dressen. I was waiting on the corner under the street lamp for the bus when I heard a shrill whistle. "Hey, Campanella!"

Dressen was coming toward me. I didn't know much about the man — only what I read in the papers. He was supposed to be one of the smartest coaches in baseball, and he was Leo Durocher's right-hand man on the Dodgers. Durocher was the manager and Dressen was his coach. That's all I knew about him.

"Where are you staying?" Dressen asked me.

"Up in Harlem. At the Woodside Hotel."

"Mr. Rickey wants to see you. Do you know how to get to the Dodger office?"

"No. I've been to Ebbets Field, but only in the team bus. I wouldn't even know how to get there by myself."

Dressen took an envelope from his pocket and talked as he wrote.

"Take the A train. That's the Independent subway line. Get off at Jay Street, Borough Hall. Ask anybody where Montague Street is. It's only a couple of blocks from the station. The number is 215."

Dressen turned to go. "Be there at ten o'clock sharp to-
106

morrow," he said. "I'll make an appointment with Mr. Rickey for you."

All the way to Brooklyn, I tried to figure it out. I had heard something about a new Negro league being formed. It was to be called the United States League, or something like that. Branch Rickey was supposed to operate one of the franchises in Ebbets Field. His team was to be called the Brown Dodgers. There was talk about signed contracts, a uniform schedule, first-class hotels and travel accommodations. Yeah. I had heard that before.

I was on the A train. For the third or fourth time I took the envelope out of my pocket. "Get off at Jay Street," I read again.

I looked at my watch as I waited for the elevator inside the building of 215 Montague Street. I had had no trouble finding the address. It was just as Dressen said, only a few blocks from the subway. It was five of ten. Good, I was prompt. I liked being prompt. People liked you for it, and I wanted people to like me.

I liked Charlie Dressen the first time I talked with him. He seemed sincere. He didn't beat about the bush. He came right out and said what he thought. That's the kind of a guy who would stick by you. I didn't know Branch Rickey, of course, but I had heard he was a devout man. And he was all baseball. We had the same things in common. That's what I was thinking as I was being led into the office of the president of the Brooklyn Dodgers.

The first thing I noticed about Branch Rickey was his eyebrows. They were thick and wild-growing. They came over his horn-rimmed glasses. He was chewing an unlit cigar. He was older than I had imagined. Maybe sixty-five or sixty-seven. But his eyes were alert and probing and his grip, when we shook hands across the big mahogany desk, was firm and powerful.

We must have sat there for four or five minutes without saying a word.

His eyes, which had been looking almost through me, looked down and rested on my body. I pulled in my stomach self-consciously.

"What do you weigh, Campanella?" he asked suddenly.

"Two-fifteen, maybe two-twenty."

"Judas priest!" he growled out of one side of his mouth while chewing his stogie in the other. "You can't weigh that much and play ball."

"All I know is I've been doing it every day for years," I told him.

Mr. Rickey took the soggy cigar out of his mouth and said, "How old are you?"

"I'll be twenty-four next month."

"Are you sure that's your right age? I've been hearing about you for a long time, Campanella."

"Mr. Rickey," I said, "I don't know what I can tell you except that I was born on November 19, 1921. Today is October 17, 1945. That makes me twenty-four next month, and that's the truth. The God's honest truth."

Mr. Rickey didn't give me a chance to do much more talking after that. He told me all he knew about me, and it was plenty. He explained how he had investigated into my background. He told of assigning Oscar Robertson, an old-time first baseman of the Negro league, to follow me around. Robertson, being a Negro, could get into the clubhouses and find out facts on the colored league.

"The boy's not too old, Mr. Rickey," Robertson had said. "He started early."

Mr. Rickey kept reading out of a little black book. It astonished me to find out how much he knew about me. Finally, he finished reading. He looked at me hard.

"I've investigated dozens of players in the Negro leagues,"

108

Mr. Rickey said. "I've tried to learn as much as I could about their personal habits, their family life, their early childhood, their education, their social activities, practically everything there is to know about them. I've rejected a number of possibilities who I'm sure have the ability. They're lacking in other requisites. It's either character, habits or what have you. You're different. Your record is good — no arrests, no trouble, good family, a hard worker who loves baseball, a man who gets along well with people."

He went on talking and I found myself just half listening. Finally, he barked out:

"You like to play with me?"

Here it is, I thought to myself. Here's what he's been leading up to. He wants me to play for his Brown Dodgers. I didn't want any part of them.

"Mr. Rickey," I said, "I'm one of the highest paid players in the colored league. I earn around three thousand a year, and I make around two thousand playing winter ball in Puerto Rico, Venezuela and Cuba. I've worked for the same man for nine years. I like the man. I'm doing all right."

"Make me one promise," he said. "Promise me you won't sign a contract with anyone unless you've talked to me."

"I don't sign no contracts," I said. "I just play ball."

"I'll get in touch with you," he said, and he got up from his chair. I knew the interview was over so I took my hat, shook hands with him and said goodbye.

It was almost two o'clock when I got into the subway at Borough Hall. My head was swimming from that four-hour grilling. Whew! Mr. Rickey was certainly a man with the words. I wasn't sure I had understood everything he said.

I was still trying to make out what Mr. Rickey had been talking about when I rode the train back to Baltimore where I was now living with my new bride. Yes, I had gotten married again. I had known the girl a long time. We had met

109

when I made my first trip to New York way back in the Bacharach Giants days.

It was in Harlem on that first Saturday morning in New York. I felt lonely, sort of, as any boy of fourteen might on his first day in the big city. After all, I didn't have too much in common with my teammates, who were much older than me. I made friends with the bat boy of the Pittsburgh Crawfords who was also stopping at the Woodside Hotel. We took a walk. A few blocks from the YMCA, where we were headed to play a game of ping-pong, this boy recognized two girls coming our way. He introduced me to them. One was Ruthe Willis.

She told me she was a basketball player . . . and a pretty good one too. I thought at the time she was kidding. It wasn't long after that that I found she was some athlete. In fact, she can play a good game of basketball today and she throws a baseball as good as most boys. Until recently she coached a girls' basketball team over in Glen Cove.

For a time, I dated Ruthe whenever the team came through New York. Between us, we spent plenty of change on movies and sodas for two. Ruthe of course was just coming along in high school then, and so a year later, when I began batting all over the country with the Elites — well, we gradually stopped seeing each other.

We met again in 1944. It was while the Elites were playing in New York. I remembered where she lived, up around 152nd Street, and called her up. Luckily for me, she was home. Yes, she'd be glad to see me. We went out that night and had dinner together. She took me bowling. I thought I was pretty fair myself, but I was no match for her. She was a 200 bowler!

We began seeing a lot of each other again. She had been married and divorced. During the war she worked as a secretary, then as a nurse's aide. We found time to do a lot of

110

things and go a lot of places together — Coney Island, Jones Beach, Rockaway, Playland. One thing we didn't do. We didn't go bowling any more.

Ruthe and I were married early in 1945. We took an apartment in Baltimore. Ruthe attended most of our home games but remained behind with David, who was then a year old, when the club went on the road.

Ruthe sensed right away that something was troubling me when I got home after my talk with Mr. Rickey.

"There's something on your mind," she said later that evening. "Do you want to tell me about it?"

"Oh, nothin', honey," I said. "It's just that Mr. Branch Rickey, the owner of the Brooklyn Dodgers, had me down to his office today. He wanted me to join up with a new team he's starting — the Brown Dodgers. At least, I think that's what he wanted. Honey, that man sure can talk. He talked so much that he gave me a headache."

A week had passed since my interview with Mr. Rickey. I was in the lobby of the Woodside Hotel. The place was buzzing with activity. There were players from nearly every team in the Negro leagues. We were all gathered there for a short vacation in New York before heading to different places for the winter league season. There were players from Baltimore, Newark, Philadelphia, Chicago, Cleveland, Kansas City, St. Louis, Memphis. I had forgotten all about my visit to the Dodger office. I had more important things on my mind. I was busy getting ready for a trip to Caracas, Venezuela, to play with a picked team called the American All-Stars. We were going to play as a unit for several weeks, then split up. Some of us, including me, would remain to play with the various teams in the Venezuelan league for the rest of the winter. The others would return to the United States.

Among those who planned the brief stay in Caracas was a good-looking, well-built young fellow from the Kansas City

Monarchs. He was new to the league, just one year. His name was Jackie Robinson. I didn't know him well. I remembered him as a good, hustling ballplayer who could hit the ball sharply and run like a deer.

Robinson was in the other league — the American — but I had played against him in two games, in the All-Star game in Chicago during the summer, and in Baltimore later in the season. I remember that game in Baltimore very well. The fellows were telling of this boy Robinson before the game. A couple of them had seen him in a game against Josh Gibson's Homestead Grays the night before in Washington and he had gone 4 for 4. "He runs like Ty Cobb," they were saying, "and he murders those inside pitches."

I made a mental note to pitch Robinson outside. The game developed into a wild, free-hitting contest. We'd get three or four runs in an inning and then they would. Robinson was getting his hits, even on outside pitches. Late in the game, we were trailing by four runs, but our club exploded for seven in the eighth inning and regained the lead. Suddenly, Jackie and a couple of the other Monarchs noticed the scoreboard didn't correspond with their tally. The two team scorebooks were checked, each against the other, and they didn't correspond. The Monarchs insisted the scoreboard owed them a run.

Finally someone suggested the official scorer be consulted. The managers went up into the press box, but there was no scorer. Sam Lacey of the *Baltimore Afro-American* newspaper had left the long-drawn-out game. The argument continued with both sides refusing to budge. The Monarchs finally walked off the field in a huff, and the game was declared forfeited.

I was reminded of that incident when I spotted Robinson in the lobby of the Woodside Hotel.

"Hey, Jackie!" I shouted out. "Where's the official scorer?"

I was grinning when I said it and he grinned back. "Yeah," he smiled, "you guys cheated us out of a run."

We shook hands and talked for a while.

"How about a game of cards, Campy?" Jackie asked me, "Gin rummy — half a cent a point?"

"Okay."

Up in my room, Jackie was dealing the cards. We finished the first hand. I pulled out a cigar and lit it. Jackie said he didn't smoke.

"I hear you went over to see Mr. Rickey last week," he said casually.

The surprise showed on my face. "Yeah, that's right," I said after a while. "How did you know?"

"I was over there myself," he said. "What happened with you?"

"Nothing much. We talked, or rather Mr. Rickey did. Man, he's the talkingest man I ever did see."

"Did you sign?"

"You mean did I sign to play for him?"

"Yeah."

"No. I didn't. I did agree that I wouldn't sign with any other team before next season, but I let him know right quick that I didn't want to play for no Brown Dodgers. Heck, Jackie, I'm an established star in our league. I've put in a lot of years, and I'm not going to give it up to take a chance on something that's just getting started and might not last. No sir, not me."

"Did Mr. Rickey tell you that he wanted you for the Brown Dodgers?" Jackie asked.

"No, come to think of it," I said. "He didn't even mention them. He didn't mention signing with anybody in particular. But I told him I wasn't interested in signing. I told him I was making three thousand for six months with Baltimore and two thousand more playing winter league ball. I told

113

him I got a bonus of two or three hundred at the end of each season, too. And Mr. Rickey said, 'that's good money,' and I told him, 'darned right it is.' And then he started talking about something else. I don't know what. He talked about everything. How about you?"

"I signed," Jackie said quietly. "But it's a secret. Mr. Rickey told me to keep it quiet, so you got to promise me not to tell anybody."

"Sure, okay, I won't say anything. It's okay for you, I guess. You've only been in the league one year. I'm a little younger than you, but I've been at it longer, and I'm established. And I've got kids to think about. You can take a chance with a new league, and it don't make much difference. But it's like I told Mr. Rickey, I can't afford to."

Jackie waited until I was finished. Then he picked up the cards from the table and shuffled them idly.

"I didn't sign with the Brown Dodgers," he said quickly. "I'm going to play for Montreal."

Jackie wasn't calm now. His voice was loud with excitement. He knew he was revealing something important, something eventful. He watched me carefully, waiting for my reaction.

"What do you mean, Montreal?" I asked.

"I'm going to be the first Negro in organized baseball," Jackie said. "I'm flying up to Montreal tomorrow for the official signing ceremony. It's going to be a big thing — cameras and everything. Mr. Rickey says that in a year or two I can make the big leagues. Do you realize what this means, Campy? It's the end of Jim Crow in baseball. I'm all excited. I'm proud, and I'm scared, too."

I sat dumfounded. My cigar went out, but I didn't realize it and kept puffing away. For the longest while I didn't say a word. I just sat and stared at Jackie. He didn't seem to notice how I felt. His face was all lit up. His eyes were looking past

114

me. He was a picture of happiness. Then he grinned at me. I grinned back, and broke into a laugh.

"I'm really happy for you, Jackie," I said. "I know you'll make it, and I wish you all the luck in the world. Now take a good look at yours truly. You're looking at a dumb boy. Man, you're looking at the all-time prize. So that's what it was all about. Well, I'll be darned."

"Sure," Jackie said. "Now remember, not a word about this. I guess I shouldn't even have told you."

"Don't worry, I won't tell a soul."

"It's only for a day. I'll sign at Montreal tomorrow, and then it'll all be in the papers. It'll be okay then to talk about it. I can't wait until tomorrow. It's been hanging on my neck like a yoke."

Jackie got up to leave. I put my hand on his shoulder.

"I'm glad for you, Jackie, real glad. Don't you be afraid of nothing. You're a good ballplayer, you'll make it. It won't be as rough as you think. I've played with white teams, lots of them — with them and against them. They're men, just like us. There's nothing to worry about."

"I hope so," he said. "I sure hope so."

TWELVE

I COULD HAVE GIVEN MYSELF A SWIFT KICK. Here Mr. Rickey had been trying to sign me for the big leagues, maybe; and I had thought he just wanted me for another colored team. I really felt bad. What should I do? My first impulse was to pick up the telephone and call Mr. Rickey. But I knew I couldn't do that. I had promised Jackie I wouldn't say anything about it. Then I remembered that

115

Mr. Rickey had said he'd get in touch with me. I wasn't too hopeful, but the only thing I could do now was to go to Venezuela and wait.

We weren't to leave for Venezuela until two days later. The day before we left, I was in the lobby at the Woodside Hotel when the radio that had been playing music cut out and a voice broke in with a news bulletin.

"The Brooklyn Dodgers baseball club announced today that Jackie Robinson, star infielder for the Kansas City Monarchs of the Negro National League, has signed a contract to play next season with the Dodgers-owned Montreal farm team of the International League. Robinson, a former student at UCLA, will be the first Negro to play in organized baseball."

A deep silence followed the announcement. Then the lobby of the Woodside went wild. Everybody started yelling for Robinson all at once. It was not until then that they recalled they hadn't seen him all day. He had gone up to Montreal with Mr. Rickey for the historic announcement.

The news broke big. Streamer headlines spread Jackie Robinson's name across all the newspapers. Some even played the story front page. The editorial pages gave it a big play. Almost immediately sides were taken. Some said it was a good move; others said it was bad. Branch Rickey was regarded as a patron saint of the Negroes in some quarters; in others he was accused of exploiting the Negro without regard for the trouble he might be starting for them. The politicians joined in the act. Some were sincere; others saw it as an opportunity to get Negro votes.

The whites weren't the only ones who argued it pro and con that day of October 23, 1945. A sharp difference of opinion existed among the Negroes, too. Even the ballplayers, those who stood to gain the most from it, didn't know for sure how to accept the news of Robinson's signing. They were divided just like the whites, but for different reasons.

A bunch of fellows were discussing Jackie's signing on the plane ride down to Venezuela. Jackie, not due to report to the Montreal club until February, was with us, but he was sitting at the other end of the plane.

"I don't know. I just don't know how it's gonna work," said Felton Snow, manager of the All-Stars and a veteran infielder of the Negro leagues. "How's he gonna travel with them, and who's he gonna room with? And how about when they play exhibition games in the South or during regular season in Baltimore?"

"Yeah," said Buck Leonard, the big first baseman. "I'm afraid you're right, Felt. I'm afraid Jackie's in for a lot of trouble."

I didn't like that kind of talk.

"Yeah, and you may be wrong, too," I said. "You guys are imagining all kinds of things. I say if Robinson handles himself right, it'll work out fine. And I'm sure he's smart enough to do it. I've played with and against white guys most of my life, and I never got into any trouble."

"But you didn't play against those Southern boys," said Marv Williams. "Jackie's gonna run up against a lot of them in organized ball. Did you read some of those stories? I read where a Southern ballplayer said he'll quit before he plays on a team with a colored man."

"Huh," snorted Quincy Troup, a catcher and outfielder, and an older fellow the guys respected for his sound judgment. "Did you read what Mr. Rickey said about that? He said that even if they do quit, they'll get tired of working in some cotton mill or lumber camp and be glad to come back into baseball after one year."

We all laughed at that. Sam Jethroe, the skinny outfielder of the Cleveland Buckeyes, who was considered the fastest man in the colored leagues, said:

"Well, I hope Jackie makes it, because if he does, then I know I can."

I felt the same way, but I didn't say anything. I knew I could play in the big leagues, but I wondered if I'd ever get the chance again. I had had it once — and I muffed it.

When the KLM airliner landed at Miami, I went to the back of the four-motor job to sit with Robinson. We resumed the card game that had ended so abruptly in my hotel room at the Woodside, and by the time we had passed over the Caribbean and the plane set down in La Guaira, I owed Jackie around ten bucks. That night at the hotel I addressed an envelope to Brooklyn. In the letter, I informed Mr. Rickey of my address in Venezuela and wrote that I would be only too happy to see him again when I returned to the States.

We had a real strong All-Star team. We played an international series involving Venezuela, Cuba, and the United States. We won eighteen of the twenty games. Robinson played shortstop and I caught and played the outfield. After the exhibitions were over, a good many of the fellows, including Robinson, returned to the States. I stayed down there to play with the local Vargas team. One of the rival clubs was managed by Lefty Gomez, who was a great pitcher with the New York Yankees. He was very kind to me.

We won the pennant but I played with half a mind on the game, the other half back in the States. I kept waiting to hear from Mr. Rickey. The big league spring training season started, and still no word came. Finally, on March 1, I got a cablegram.

PLEASE REPORT BROOKLYN OFFICE BY MARCH 10. VERY IMPORTANT. BRANCH RICKEY.

I wasn't going to wait for the 10th. Man, I was ready to leave right then! I wasn't going to blow this chance. I ran into a little difficulty, though. The owner of the Vargas team didn't want me to go, although we had a big lead. I was the only catcher on the team. This little problem was solved, however, when Sam Jethroe, our center fielder, volunteered to catch. I caught a plane that day and flew back to New York.

Once more I got on the A train, this time without written directions. Also, this time I knew exactly why I was making the trip. But this time Branch Rickey was not there when I arrived at his office on Montague Street. I was told he was in Sanford, Florida, taking charge of the operation of the Dodgers training base for minor leaguers in the Brooklyn farm system. I was told Mr. Bob Finch, Branch Rickey's assistant, would take care of me.

Mr. Finch resembled Mr. Rickey somewhat, but he was easier to understand.

"Mr. Rickey is interested in signing you to a contract with the Dodger organization," he said. "He's sorry he couldn't be here to sign you personally. But he felt he should be on hand to take care of any emergency that might arise in Florida."

I knew what Mr. Finch meant. Mr. Rickey wanted to be on the scene of Jackie's training debut to make sure there would be no trouble.

"However," Finch continued, "Mr. Rickey told me to call him the minute you got here, and we'd see to your transportation."

While Finch was calling Sanford I couldn't help but think that soon I would be in Florida and, after all these years, finally getting a chance to play in organized baseball. They'll probably room me with Jackie, I thought to myself. And they'll probably start me at Montreal, the Dodgers' top minor league club.

Finch was talking to Mr. Rickey. Or rather, he was listen-

119

ing mostly. Occasionally, he would say, "Yes, I see . . . uh-huh . . . all right" and "Mmmmmm." When he finally hung up, I knew that something was wrong.

"Uh, Mr. Rickey says you can't go to Sanford right now," he said. "There's been . . . uh . . . some unpleasantness regarding Robinson. Something about local civic authorities. Also, some teams have refused to go through with their exhibition commitments because of the Negro situation on the Dodgers. Mr. Rickey feels it would not be wise to have you join the Montreal club at this time. He suggested I try to place you with our Danville club."

"Where is Danville?" I asked.

"Illinois. Class B. In the Three-I League. You know, the league is composed of cities in Illinois, Indiana, and Iowa."

"Oh," I said, nodding my head as if I knew what he meant. Actually, I had little idea of what classifications in organized baseball were all about. There was one real Negro league and that was it. But whatever this Three-I League was, it would be all right with me.

The call to Danville came through in a few minutes. Again I waited to hear what was going to happen to me. I knew the answer before he hung up.

"They don't want me?" I asked, although it was more of a statement than a question.

"Nope," he said. "They don't want you."

I was beginning to sweat a little under the collar. They were tossing me from team to team with nobody wanting anything to do with me. They were playing catch with my career and all I could do was listen, and hear one side of it at that. First I was bitter, then I became angry. Nuts to them, I thought. I don't need them. I can live without them. I was really ready to chuck the whole thing. But I felt awful too. I decided I should have known better than even to hope this white man's league would want any part of fellows like me.

120

They were already beginning to get on Jackie. Maybe I was better off to have never even gotten started.

Finch was talking and trying to calm me down. He kept assuring me they'd find a spot for me in the Dodger organization.

"We have to expect these things," he said. "We all realized from the start it wouldn't be easy. You have to have patience . . . and courage."

Mr. Finch was right. After all these years, I should have known they wouldn't welcome me with open arms. But this was all a new experience for me. I'd always gotten along well with white folks. Not since I was a kid had I experienced any racial trouble.

"Mr. Rickey told me to try Nashua," Finch was saying. "He thinks Bavasi will take you."

"Nashville?" I was surprised that a Southern city would take me.

"No, Nashua. It's in New Hampshire. Also Class B. They've got a new general manager up there, fellow named Buzzie Bavasi. Buzzie is one of the finest young fellows in the organization. He's smart and progressive. You'll like him."

While Finch was talking with Bavasi, I saw his face light up. I didn't know whether I should feel happy or not. After he hung up, Finch turned to me and grinned. "It's all set," he said. "Bavasi will take you. I'll arrange for your railroad ticket to Nashua, and some expense money for you. I'll have someone pick you up at the railroad station. When you get to the park, report to the manager. His name is Walter Alston. Let's see, this is Tuesday. You come back here Thursday morning ready to go."

I was about to leave when Finch suddenly remembered something. "Oh, by the way, Campanella," he said, "you're going to have company on your train ride to Nashua. A young Negro pitcher named Don Newcombe."

121

I was going to be the first Negro catcher in organized baseball. Thinking about it, there was only one thing that made me sad. Tom Wilson, my old Baltimore boss, had died a month earlier and so he had not lived to see me make good. Thinking back, he was a tough man at times, but a real fair man too. The nicest and truest thing that I can say about him is that he was a sportsman all the way.

THIRTEEN

MY SALARY AT NASHUA WOULD BE A BIG $185 a month. For five and a half months of play that would make my first year's salary in organized ball exactly $1017.50. That was about $4000 less than I'd earned the year before when I earned $3000 in the Negro league and another $2000 in winter ball. My friends told me I was crazy to leave the tops in one league for the bottom in the next. They just didn't understand.

"Campy, you're making the biggest mistake of your life," I was told. "Look how far you're going down. You're getting on, and you're too old to start way down there. You're never going to make the majors."

They just didn't understand. But Ruthe did. Lord how she understood. When I took the Dodger's proposition to her and laid it out for her as best I could, she said, "Campy" — she's always called me that — "for how long has it been . . . for how many years is it that you've been trying to make the major leagues? Whether you admit it or not, it's been practically your life's dream. Even way back there that first day we met, you had no time for anything but baseball — really. If others starting out in the minor leagues live on what we'll be making, then we can live on it too. No, money

122

is not the important thing, now. This is the big opening — the big opportunity you've dreamed and worked for, always. Don't pass it up, and don't worry. We'll make out just fine!"

Nashua is a nice little friendly town in New Hampshire. In 1946, it was a Class B team in the New England League. The people don't have much racial prejudice. Ruthe and little David went up there with me and we lived at the hotel. The townspeople were friendly and the players leveled with Newcombe and me one hundred per cent.

Both Bavasi and Alston were friendly and very cooperative and the opposing players didn't bother us, either. Sure, the bench jockeys gave us a pretty hard time but it didn't bother me, and Newcombe took it good. I wasn't in Nashua long before I got a letter from Mr. Rickey. It cautioned me to stay out of disputes on the field, play ball all the way and turn a deaf ear to any taunt or sarcasm from opposing players.

All in all, it was pretty good at Nashua. A poultry farmer, a fellow named Jack Fallgren, offered a hundred baby chicks for every home run hit by a Nashua player. I hit thirteen home runs during the regular season and one in the playoffs so at the end of the season I shipped fourteen hundred baby chicks home to Philadelphia, and Pop started a little poultry farm just outside of town. The first home run I hit was on opening day against the Lynn club of Massachusetts. The pitcher was a big sidearm right-hander by the name of Walter Cress.

The outfield fences at the Nashua ball park were a long way from home plate. It was practically impossible to hit one over the fence because the outfield stretched nearly to the horizon. I think that's why this poultry farmer offered those prizes. All my homers were inside-the-park jobs. I had to run them all out. Walter Alston, the manager, was also our first baseman, and he batted third, right ahead of

123

me. Well, I ran him so hard he got tired. Finally, one day he changed the lineup.

"From now on, Roy," he said, "you bat third and I'll bat fourth. I just can't run those bases like I used to."

There was just one unpleasant incident. It happened early in the season, when we were playing the Manchester Giants, a farm team of the New York Giants. The rivalry between us was as heated as that between the parent teams in the National League. I had crouched behind the plate to flash the sign to the pitcher, Dick Mlady. It was in the second inning. Sal Yvars, the Manchester catcher, was at bat. He bent over and scooped up a handful of dirt, then flung it back into my face.

I flung the mask aside and charged him. "Try that again," I said through my teeth, "and I'll beat you to a pulp." Man, I was burning.

That's all there was to it, though. Yvars didn't say a word. He didn't even claim it was an accident. But he gave me no more trouble after that. Neither did anybody else. Oh, I was called names. All players are called names, both colored and white. Baseball is a game where tension sometimes is at fever pitch, and many times the opponents will call each other vicious names.

Oftentimes I've had balls thrown at my head and three times in my big league career I was seriously injured by head pitches. That's all part of the game.

It was a few days after the Yvars incident that Alston approached me in the locker room.

"Roy," he began, "you're a little bit older than the other fellows on the club, and a great deal more experienced. They respect you. If I'm ever thrown out of a game, I want you to run things."

I stared at him.

"Me, Skipper?"

124

"Yes, you. What's the matter? Don't you think you can?"

"Sure I can, but —"

"No buts," Alston interrupted. "I know what you're thinking. Well, forget it. These boys are for you all the way. You're one of them. They liked the way you stood up to Yvars. They're behind you a hundred per cent. Besides, I want it that way."

"Okay, Skip," I said. I had a lump in my throat this big. I was so proud I nearly burst.

The next day I walked into Buzzie Bavasi's office and threw a piece of paper on his desk.

"I guess I don't want this any more," I told him.

It was a telegram I had carried around in my pocket for almost a month. It was from George Pasquel, president of the now outlawed Mexican League, offering me quite a bit more money than I was making at Nashua to come down and play for him. I had kept the telegram because I wasn't certain how I would be received in organized ball. Now my mind was made up. Pasquel would have to keep his pesos.

The next day, the front page headline in the *Nashua Telegraph* read: NASHUA STAR GETS MEXICAN LEAGUE OFFER. Underneath, there was the story.

Mexican League baseball, which is raising havoc with major league magnates by luring their star ball players south of the border with fantastic bonuses and salaries, reached up into the newly formed New England League today. Roy Campanella, Negro youth who is now rated as the outstanding catcher in the league, revealed today that he had been offered $5,000 a year for three years to play baseball in Mexico by George Pasquel, fabulously rich president of the Mexican Baseball League. Campanella stated he will ignore the offer.

Campanella, one of the four Negro players in organized baseball, said he preferred to take his chances on making good in the Dodger System, although the salary offered him by the

125

Mexicans is more than he could hope for in Class B ball. From all reports, Campanella is considered by scouts to be one of the outstanding young catchers in baseball today.

As far as is known, Campanella is the only New England League player to receive an offer to join the Mexican League. Although Campanella refused to reply to Pasquel's invitation, his boss, Buzzy Bavasi, hot under the collar over the approach, plans a blistering letter to Pasquel, warning him to keep hands off his players.

I sort of became the assistant manager after that. This talk with Alston gave me a lot of confidence. I began to take charge out there on the diamond, and I huddled more with the pitchers. It wasn't more than a couple of weeks later that I became the acting manager when Alston was thrown out of a game in the sixth inning for beefing too much over a called strike.

In the seventh, the Lawrence team had us by two runs. We had a man on base with one out. The pitcher was due to bat next. I looked over my bench and called out, "Newk, grab a stick."

Newcombe, who was my roomie, shuffled over to where I was sitting on the bench, grinned, and said, "Any instructions, Mr. Manager?"

"Yeah," I answered. "Hit one out of here."

And that's just what he did, too. He fouled off a pitch, then sent the next one clear over the fence in right center smack into the Merrimack River. That tied the score and we went on to win, 7-5.

The fellows really put on a show for me in the clubhouse after the game. They said I was the greatest manager since John McGraw.

Alston joined in the fun. "That's the last time I'm ever going to get thrown out of a game," he chuckled. "If I don't watch myself, you'll have my job."

126

"Aw," I said, "Newk did it, not me."

"What you talking about?" Newcombe howled. "I would have bunted if you hadn't ordered me to hit one out of the park."

All in all, I had a pretty good year. I only batted .290, but I drove in ninety-six runs and I led all the catchers in the league in putouts and assists. We finished second, just a game and a half out of the pennant — and then we beat Lynn in the playoffs for the championship.

I was voted the league's Most Valuable Player. I was really up in the clouds when I flew back to New York at the end of my first year in organized baseball.

I wasn't home more than a couple of days when I got a telephone call to come to the Dodger office in Brooklyn. Mr. Rickey wanted to see me.

"I suppose you're wondering what we have in mind for you." Mr. Rickey began.

"Yes, sir."

Mr. Rickey struck a match and put it to the end of a half-burned cigar. He puffed once and said: "I want you to scout for me."

I kept looking at the half-burned cigar. I didn't know what to say. Me a scout? Scout who? I figured it was best to wait.

"I want you to scout the Negro World Series for me," Mr. Rickey said, as he lighted another match and put the flame to the burned-out end of the cigar.

"Yes, sir," I said, not even knowing what he wanted me to look for.

"I want a report on any boys you consider major league prospects," he went on. "But, besides the usual data — power, arm, speed — I want you to find out things about their background. That's important, very important. We don't want to take any risks if we can help it. I'm sure you

127

realize that. You know most of these men. You've played with most of them. You can mix with them and find out things that my regular scouts can't possibly learn."

"Yes, sir."

"Mail your reports to Harold Roettger. He's in charge of our farm operation, and has the file on many of the Negro players."

"Yes, sir."

"Oh, yes," Mr. Rickey added as if it was an afterthought, "I'll put you on the payroll for three months — at five hundred a month."

"Yes, sir!" I said, as I grabbed my hat and headed for the door.

It wasn't until I was out in the street that I did a double take. What was it that Mr. Rickey had said, "for three months, at five hundred a month." Man, that was $315 more a month than I'd gotten for playing ball for Nashua. Maybe I was in the wrong business. Maybe I should be scouting instead of catching. Or maybe this was Mr. Rickey's way of sweetening up the pot a little after the year I'd put in . . . and winning that Most Valuable Player and all. I decided that was what it was for — mostly.

A few weeks later, Harold Roettger got a large envelope with my report on half a dozen Negro players. The players I recommended most highly belonged to the Newark Eagles: Larry Doby, who played second base, and Monte Irvin, who played the outfield.

I was getting ready to leave for Venezuela for another season of winter ball when I got another call to visit the Dodger office.

"We're interested in Doby," began Mr. Rickey, "but I understand the Cleveland Club of the American League has shown a desire to sign him. And I wish they would. It is my fervent hope that every club in baseball sign a colored

128

player. Right now, the Dodgers are the only club to have Negroes. I dare say that within five years there will be at least one Negro playing in every league in the country."

Mr. Rickey was to get his wish but it wasn't until next summer that the Cleveland Indians signed Doby. The Dodgers did sign Monte Irvin but didn't keep him. Fresco Thompson, who was Mr. Rickey's chief scout then, signed Monte in Puerto Rico that winter while he was playing for the Santurce team. The Dodgers considered Irvin a free agent because the Newark Eagles had disbanded. But Mrs. Effa Manley, owner of the Eagles, insisted she still owned the players and that the Dodgers had no right to sign Irvin without paying for him. She asked for $5000. Mr. Rickey withdrew all claims to Irvin and the Giants got him for that figure and sent him to their Jersey City farm club in the International League. Monte later advanced to the Giants and helped them win pennants in 1951 and 1954.

I was promoted to Montreal in the International League, but in October of 1946 I went down to Venezuela to play winter ball. I was the catcher and manager of the Vargas team. Newcombe was one of my pitchers. Luis Aparicio, whose son now plays shortstop for the Chicago White Sox, was my shortstop. He was a heck of a ballplayer. He could field and he could hit better than his son. He used to bring little Luis down to the clubhouse. I also had Sam Jethroe and Suitcase Simpson on my team.

Lefty Gomez, the old Yankee pitcher, managed the Caracas team. He beat me out for the pennant on the last day of the season. Newcombe gave up only three hits, but he walked thirteen men and we lost the game 2-1. That was the wildest I ever saw Big Newk. It was only his third defeat. He won ten for me.

There was fun, too, in the winter leagues. I remember one time we were playing the Santurce team and Big Luke

129

Easter was playing third base for them. I was on second base and the next batter singled. I ran to third, but Big Luke got right in my way. So I just tore into him and knocked him flat and kept on going for the plate. Luke must have bounced right up, because I could hear him chugging right behind me. I didn't even bother to look back. I crossed the plate and kept right on going. When I got to the dugout I yelled to Newcombe, "Take care of him, Newk!" And I didn't stop until I reached the clubhouse.

FOURTEEN

I FELT LIKE A LOST SHEEP AS I SAT IN THE REAR of the last coach of the Atlantic Seaboard train speeding to Miami. Jackie Robinson sat next to me. Facing us were Don Newcombe and Roy Partlow, a veteran pitcher from the Negro National League. We hardly seemed part of the spring training expedition made up of the Brooklyn and Montreal clubs. It was in February of 1947, and we were all headed for Havana, where both clubs were to train.

I was excited, of course, about making my first trip with a big league club, but I was scared too. I didn't know what to expect. Playing in Havana was no new experience for me. I had played in Cuba many times before, but always on Negro or mixed teams.

Robby and the rest must have felt the same way I did, but they didn't say anything.

When we arrived in Havana, the Dodger players were put up at a swank tourist spot, the Hotel Nacional, on the edge of town overlooking the sea. They had a swimming pool, cabanas, beach chairs in the daytime, and music, dancing, and big, tender sirloin steaks flown in from the States in the evening. The Montreal team, except for Robinson, Newk, Partlow and myself, were put up at the Havana Military Academy; not as elaborate as the Hotel Nacional, but it had a country club atmosphere with large grounds, clean rooms and good meals.

The four of us stayed at a downtown hotel in the busy section of town. Each day the ball club sent a limousine to the hotel to drive us to the Gran Stadium, where we practiced with the other Montreal players, then return us to the hotel. Maybe it was the food. Maybe it was the segregation. Maybe it was a combination of both, but Robinson developed stomach trouble that bothered him during most of the spring training period at Havana. I wasn't happy either, but felt I was getting that big opportunity. Nothing else mattered.

I tried not to notice the things that bothered Jackie. Not that I didn't mind them. It's just that some men can have the same problems and yet face them differently. And I had trouble enough of my own without having to worry about where I was living and what I was eating. I got a soreness in my right shoulder after the first few days of training, and I could hardly throw a ball during the exhibition games between the Dodgers and Royals. I didn't want to mention it to my manager, Clay Hopper, because I was afraid he wouldn't let me play. I kept hoping the soreness would work itself out.

Several years later, Bob Edge, who used to do play-by-play and a post-game TV show, "Club House Quiz," at Ebbets Field, told me of the first time he saw me play.

"Mr. Rickey, Ernest Hemingway and I were sitting in a box on the first base line," said Edge. "Hemingway was interested in a prospect playing outfield for Montreal. The boy never made it, and I can't remember his name. He was also interested in seeing Jackie play." Then Edge laughed.

"The first time you came to bat, I thought you were carrying a watermelon on each hip. 'My Gosh, Mr. Rickey, with a build like that, how can that catcher, that Campanella, get off his haunches?' Mr. Rickey chuckled. Anyhow, you hit a line drive single. The way you went down to first I knew that no matter how fat you looked, you could run. Watching you catch that night . . . handle pitchers . . . and take charge . . . well, Campy, I've got to say that that night you impressed Hemingway and me."

"Bob," I said, "did you mention that to Mr. Rickey?"

"We both did," said Edge. "And again, all Mr. Rickey did was chuckle."

One day, Hopper called Clyde Sukeforth, the Dodger coach, over to the side of the batting cage and said:

"Campanella can't throw a lick. I thought you told me he had a great arm."

"He has," said Sukeforth, who had been a catcher himself and who was the biggest booster I had. "He owns one of the strongest, most accurate arms I've ever seen."

"Then where's he hiding it? I haven't seen him make a good throw yet."

When Sukey told me what Hopper said, I had to admit that my arm was sore. He went to Hopper.

"Campy has a sore arm. He's afraid of cutting loose because he might strain it. He thinks that it will come around in a few more days."

Before too long, the arm was as strong as ever. Hopper seemed happy with me, but I didn't share his feeling. Even though I was training with the Dodgers, I felt that I was further away than ever from a job with them. The team was crawling with catchers. There was Bruce Edwards, then being called the best catcher in the National League. There was the veteran Bobby Bragan, and there was a promising big youngster named Gil Hodges. It just didn't look like

132

there was any room for me. I had a nice time, but when I left I didn't know whether I'd ever be back.

That feeling lasted throughout the entire season at Montreal. I batted well over .300 most of the year but tailed off badly and wound up with a .273 average. That slump hurt the club. We blew a fourteen-game lead and lost the pennant to Jersey City on the last day of the season by two percentage points. Man, was I blue. Even the fact that I was voted the Most Valuable Player in the league failed to cheer me up.

I went down to Caracas to forget about it. Again I was playing manager of the Vargas team. I did a lot of thinking while I was playing and managing, but my mind wasn't on the game. I kept thinking about my future. I was really troubled. I felt I needed advice, so I sat down and wrote what was for me a long letter to Al Campanis. Campanis was my friend. He had been a ballplayer in the Dodger organization, but when he saw he couldn't get very far he decided to go into the teaching end of the game. He had helped me at Montreal, and I figured he'd give me sound advice. Here's what I wrote:

Dear Al,

First of all, I want to thank you again for your help and your friendship. You're one good Greek.

Things are going smoothly down here. We're playing about .500 ball and are in third place. Newk is wild, but he's really humming that pea, and I expect a lot of wins from him.

Once more, I'm coming to you for advice. You always told me I was sure pop to make the Dodgers, but the way things stand, I'm wondering. There's an awful lot of good catching on that club. From what I've heard, Edwards had a terrific season. And there's Bragan, and Hodges, and so naturally, I ask myself: "Where does Campanella fit in?"

Do you think I'd have a better chance to make the club

133

if I tried out as an outfielder? I understand the Dodgers are hurting for a right-handed hitting outfielder. I've played it a little bit in the colored league, and once in a while here for the Señors. What do you think? Would I just be kidding myself?

Best of luck, Al. Hope to hear from you soon.

Campy

Jackie Robinson was already a member of the Dodgers — in fact, he had been up there for a year — when I was ordered to spring training with them in February of 1948. This time the club trained in Ciudad Trujillo, the capital city of the Dominican Republic — the Spanish-speaking two thirds of the Caribbean island known as Hispaniola. That's where the tomb of Christopher Columbus is located.

It may seem strange that Mr. Rickey chose to train his club there. Actually it was not strange at all. He was determined more than ever to erase the color line in baseball. That was just as important to him then as the immediate success of the Dodgers, maybe even more important. He hadn't forgotten the cool reception the people in the South had given Robinson during spring training only two years before. Havana wasn't much better, and training there had cost too much money.

In Ciudad Trujillo, Mr. Rickey had been offered a $50,-000 guarantee. More important, unlike Havana or Florida, there was no segregation among the ballplayers in the Dominican Republic. Besides Robinson, the Dodgers had another colored player, Dan Bankhead, a speedball pitcher. They stayed at the Hotel Jaragua. I was still on the Montreal roster and I stayed with the team at a swanky suburban location in San Cristobal where many of the diplomatic representatives to the Dominican Republic were living.

I was in real good shape that spring, and I must have made a good impression on Leo Durocher, who had returned as manager of the Dodgers from his year's suspension by Commissioner A. B. (Happy) Chandler. After a couple of weeks of training, Durocher confided to me that he intended to move Gil Hodges to first base and move me into the catching spot. He told me he was going to talk to Mr. Rickey about it.

The next day Mr. Rickey called me to his suite at the Hotel Jaragua.

"Roy," he told me, "you're the best catcher we have, and I'm going to bring you up to the Dodgers."

I gulped.

He watched me. Then, "You will be brought up as an outfielder."

I gulped again, but I still felt good.

"You will be brought up as an outfielder," Mr. Rickey repeated, "because I don't think you can make it as an outfielder."

What was that? What did you say? What kind of a crazy statement is this? That's what I wanted to say to him, but instead I said:

"What do you mean, Mr. Rickey?"

He looked me straight in the eye, as only Mr. Rickey can, and pointed a finger at me.

"I know you can make the Dodgers as a catcher," he said, "but I want you to help me do something bigger, something very important to me, to you, and to all baseball. I want you to become the first colored ballplayer in the American Association. Do you want to do this?"

I just sat there in a daze. My head was swimming. I couldn't figure out what he was saying.

"If I weren't to bring you up to the Dodgers, people would wonder why," he was saying. "If you were brought up as a catcher, you'd make the club. But I don't want you to make the club. I want to send you to St. Paul to lower the barriers in that league. Therefore, you will work out here with Montreal as an outfielder, and shortly before we return to the United States you will join the Dodgers — as an outfielder. You will fail — but your failure will be a glorious success. You will be optioned to St. Paul, and become their catcher. If you do the job there, I will bring you back at the end of the season. But first you will pioneer the Negroes into the American Association. Do you understand?"

I let the words sink in. Then I said quietly:

"Mr. Rickey, I'm a ballplayer, not a pioneer. Sure, I'm a colored man. I can't hide that, and I don't want to. But when I'm hitting or catching, I think only of what the pitcher is throwing — I don't think of the color of my skin or his. If you want me at St. Paul, that's where I'll play. Because it's in my contract. For no other reason."

I got up to leave and the last thing I heard was something about instead of making the minimum of $5000 in Brooklyn, I would be paid $6500 in St. Paul.

April 1, 1948, will be a day that will stick in my mind forever. That was the day I walked into the clubhouse at Vero Beach in Florida and the clubhouse boy handed me a Dodger uniform. It was the happiest day of my life, even though I knew I would not be a Dodger for long. I was a big leaguer at last — with no possible chance of making the team.

Yes, that was really April Fool.

FIFTEEN

WHEN THE WAR ENDED, VERO BEACH, ON the east coast of Florida about a hundred miles north of Miami, turned into a ghost town — a naval air training station with wooden barracks, a mess hall, a recreation center, and an airfield.

The buildings with their surrounding grounds struck Mr. Rickey of the Brooklyn Dodgers as an ideal spot for a baseball training camp. Mr. Rickey took over this former air base, and today's "Dodgertown" is the result. You've got to see it to realize what it really is — a giant baseball talent factory.

At Vero, I landed with the A squad, but I got little chance to work behind the plate. Gil Hodges did most of the catching and I'd usually get in at the tail end of the game.

Nevertheless, Leo liked my style. He told me he'd open the season with me behind the plate. That's what he told Mr. Rickey too.

"I'm going to switch Hodges to first base," Durocher told Mr. Rickey. "That's where he belongs."

"Who will catch for you if Hodges plays first base?" Mr. Rickey asked.

"Campanella," Leo said unhesitatingly. "Campanella and Bruce Edwards."

Mr. Rickey frowned. "But I have something else in mind for Campanella," he said. "I want him to go to St. Paul."

"The devil with St. Paul," Leo barked. "I'm thinking about *my* club, not St. Paul!"

"Don't you think Edwards and Hodges give you enough protection?" Mr. Rickey asked.

"I'm not sure," said Leo. "All I know, Campanella is the

best catcher in camp. Besides, Hodges is a natural at first base."

As he talked, Durocher could sense he was fighting a losing battle. Finally he agreed to do without me. He was to keep me around until cutdown time on May 15, but I was only to sit on the bench, not go behind the plate except maybe to finish out a game. But Leo did get Mr. Rickey to promise, that if he needed me for the pennant race around midseason, I would be recalled from St. Paul. At the time, I didn't know any of this, but what difference would it have made if I had?

I was about to get my first big league trial — on the bench.

The sports writers picked the Dodgers to win the 1948 pennant. Why not? They had done it under Burt Shotton the year before. However, from the start it looked like a different team, losing four of the first seven games, without a single Dodger pitcher going the distance. Impatient, even when things were going good, Leo wanted to change the entire lineup. Things got worse and Durocher's temper followed suit. He bawled out Reiser and Robinson, accusing them of not being in shape. Jackie said his arm was sore, but Leo wouldn't listen. He vowed he was going to get Jackie in shape or else. The next day he had coach Clyde Sukeforth hit grounders to Jackie until he nearly dropped. That started a feud between them that lasted a long time.

With Robinson out of the lineup, things got worse. Our attack sputtered to a new low. With Bill Voiselle pitching, Boston shut us out 3-0 on a three-hitter. Durocher was frantic. He had replaced Robinson at second base with Gene Mauch. Now he wanted to switch Billy Cox from third to second and put Spider Jorgensen on third. Cox didn't want to play second so he jumped the club and went home to Harrisburg, Pennsylvania.

138

Leo was desperate. After we had lost four in a row, he said, "Campy, you're catching tomorrow."

Next day I caught Rex Barney, who only allowed four hits — three by Bob Elliott, Boston's third baseman. I got a walk in four times at bat. I remember it because that was the first complete ball game I'd caught in the majors.

We returned to Brooklyn to play the Giants the next day, with me looking forward to getting my first hit. But there was no "next day" for me. Durocher stopped me on the field as I came out for hitting practice.

"Sorry, Campy," he said, "but you'll have to go out to the bullpen. I can't play you any more. The old man really tied into me for letting you catch."

"Sure, Skip," I said. "I understand."

I understood, I guess, but I sure was hurting inside.

The team continued to slide. Edwards did most of the catching, with Hodges once in a while going behind the bat. Edwards's arm was sore and Durocher kept after Mr. Rickey to let him work me. Nothing doing. The feeling between the two men became strained. Looking back now, I think that started the rift between Durocher and Mr. Rickey that finally ended with Leo being fired in August.

May 15 finally came around. That was the deadline for cutting down to twenty-five men. We were scheduled to play a night game against the Braves in Ebbets Field. I was in the clubhouse ready to go out on the field when Jake Pitler, one of our coaches, told me that Durocher wanted to see me in his office.

"Well, Campy," Durocher said, "this is it. You're going to St. Paul. I suppose that's no surprise to you."

"No, Skip," I said.

Leo looked at me a moment. Then, "What's Rickey giving you to do this?"

"Sixty-five hundred."

"It ain't enough!" he snapped. "It's worth more to you to go out."

"But Mr. Rickey told me if I stayed with the Dodgers I'd get only the five thousand minimum, and that he was giving me the extra fifteen hundred to go to St. Paul."

"Bunk," said Leo. "You'd be earning a lot more up here. You ought to get more to go to St. Paul. I'm going to see to it that the old man gives it to you."

I walked back to the clubhouse and started to pack my things. I was getting ready to leave when Jackie Robinson came in from infield practice to change his shirt. He didn't have to be a mind reader to know I'd gotten the ax.

"Where *you* going?" he asked.

I looked at the man who had broken the color line in baseball and grinned.

"I'm going to St. Paul, man. I'm going to open up a new league."

Next morning, I stopped off at the Dodger office to pick up my plane ticket and expense money. I knew what else to expect from Mr. Rickey: a pep talk on the responsibility I carried in being the first Negro to play in the American Association. I was surprised when Mr. Rickey opened with a blast.

"What do you mean by telling Durocher you're not satisfied with the salary I'm paying you?"

"Salary? Not satisfied?"

"You know what I'm referring to, young man. What kind of an ingrate are you? You're just starting out and already you're complaining."

"I'm not complaining, sir," I said. "I never told Durocher I wasn't satisfied. He asked me what I was making and I told him. He told me it wasn't enough and that he was going to speak to you about getting me more money. That's all there was to it."

140

"It's nobody's business but yours what you're making," Mr. Rickey snapped. "If you want more money, come see me. Don't go talking to Leo Durocher or anyone else about it."

On the plane trip West, I wondered what it would be like in St. Paul. Mr. Rickey's last words had stayed with me.

"Just be Roy Campanella and everything will be all right," he said. I thought about that. I also thought about what Mr. Rickey said about bringing me back, if I did well with the Saints.

I felt better when I arrived in St. Paul. For one thing, my old boss, Walt Alston, was now manager of the Saints. I knew I'd have at least one friend. In a way I looked forward to St. Paul because it meant I'd get more work. Man, you can get mighty tired sitting around doing nothing. In the Negro league I'd caught a hundred and fifty games a year, then maybe another hundred in some Latin American country.

Those St. Paul papers didn't exactly roll out a red carpet for the first Negro to play in the American Association. An article in a St. Paul paper of May 21, 1948, said: "The acquisition of Roy Campanella, Negro catcher, sent down by the Dodgers, came as a surprise to the Saints since they already have two veteran backstops — Ferrell Anderson and Stu Hofferth."

I broke into the Saints' lineup on Saturday, May 22, in Columbus. Next day, the paper mentioned my debut.

"Roy Campanella, Negro catcher, on 24-hour recall from the Dodgers, made his bow in St. Paul livery, fanning twice and going hitless in four trips, in addition to making an error attempting to pick a runner off first base."

The story went on to criticize Alston for using me over the regular catchers, "only because the Dodgers had sent Campanella to St. Paul to break the color line." If my debut

141

was any indication of my ability, I'd be back in the Negro league real quick.

I wasn't happy about my first game in Triple A baseball, but I wasn't upset either. I'd been around too long to get the shakes because of a bad day. I just hustled and kept my mouth shut. In Minneapolis a few days later, I began to tune up my batting eye. I hit two home runs in Nicollet Park, but we lost. Then, back home at Lexington Park, I hit a home run and a triple in an 11-6 victory over Minneapolis in the first game of a Memorial Day double-header.

From then on there was no stopping me. I ran right through the league. It made no difference if the pitcher was right- or left-handed. I tagged them all. In two successive days I drove in eleven runs. Against Louisville I hit a home run, a triple, and a single, and batted in six runs. Next day I got a pair of home runs, a single, and batted in five runs.

Those base knocks stopped the other kind of knocks. The writers and fans treated me swell. After twenty-five games I was hitting .333 with eleven homers and thirty-three runs batted in. The St. Paul writers and fans were worried now that the Dodgers would recall me. On June 28, an item in the newspaper read:

"Fears that Brooklyn might recall Roy Campanella, the Saints' slugging catcher, were dispelled today when Stu Hofferth, No. 3 backstop, was dispatched to Cambridge as pilot of the Eastern Shore League club." The story ended by saying; "Campanella was presented with an appropriate Father's Day gift yesterday . . . a seven and a half pound son born right after the double-header."

The story was wrong about the first part and right about the second. On Sunday, June 27, Roy, Jr., was born. That made it four. There was Joyce; she was eight then . . . and Beverly, seven . . . and David, five.

Joyce and Beverly lived with their mother in Philadel-

142

phia. Joyce is now married and has a child but Beverly lives with her mother. David was Ruthe's son by a previous marriage, but he belonged to her, which made him ours; and now, with Roy, Jr., David had a baby brother!

Back in Brooklyn, things weren't going good for Leo Durocher and the Dodgers. The team had sagged to sixth place. Durocher was keeping tabs on what I was doing in the Association, and he kept after Mr. Rickey.

On June 30, in a night double-header at Toledo, I played right field the first game, caught the second, and collected three hits — a single, a double, and a home run. I was pulling off my uniform in the clubhouse when Manager Alston came over.

"I've got news for you, Roy," he said. "Bad for me, but good for you. The Dodgers want you back. Right away."

I guess I didn't look too happy about it because Walt asked, "What's the matter? Do you like the pitching in this league so much that you don't want to go to the big leagues?"

"It ain't that, Skip," I protested. "It's Ruthe, my wife. She just had a baby, and she's only been home from the hospital three days. I don't know if I can move her. If she can't go now, I wouldn't want to leave her to do all the packing because she's not strong yet."

"I'll call Mr. Rickey as soon as we get back to the hotel and see what he advises," Alston said.

When we finally got through, Mr. Rickey was sympathetic.

"Roy," he told me, "fly to St. Paul at once and consult your doctor about the advisability of moving your wife and baby. If it's all right, then take the plane to New York. If not, telephone me right away, and we'll make other plans."

I didn't have to call him. The doctor said there was no danger involved in Ruthe flying to New York with the baby. Ruthe was joyful over the news of my promotion. Being a

143

New York girl she was especially happy about leaving immediately.

We cleared out of the apartment in nothing flat and soon Ruthe, the baby and me were on a plane. Ruthe's mother, who had come out just before Roy, Jr., arrived, followed with David on the train.

Flying to New York I had time to think. What a difference compared to that other trip six weeks before, when I'd been flying the other way. In thirty-five games, I had batted .325 and drove in thirty-nine runs. Of my forty base hits, exactly half went for extra bases.

"Ha! Fat as ever."

That was Leo Durocher's greeting to me as I walked into the Dodger clubhouse at Ebbets Field two nights later. It was early evening, two hours before game time. The Dodgers were dressing, preparing to go out for batting practice. As I shook hands with Durocher, he yelled out: "Hey, guys, look who's back!"

Pee Wee Reese, the Dodger captain, who occupied the first locker against the wall, looked up and grinned. "Welcome back, Campy," he said, extending his right hand.

"Good to be back," I answered.

Gil Hodges came over to shake hands. "It's sure good to see you," Gil said softly. He always speaks softly, does big Gil.

"How's it going?" asked Jackie Robinson.

"Can't complain," I said, "but it's nicer up here."

Carl Furillo, who had the locker back near the shower room, walked over to my locker, in the center of the room.

"Hear you were murdering 'em in St. Paul," he said.

"I did okay."

"Hope you saved a few hits for us," called out Duke Snider. "We could use a few around here."

John Griffin, the Dodgers equipment man who must have

144

come with the franchise, pulled a uniform out of the trunk and tossed it to me. "Knew you'd be back before long," he grunted.

"You were more confident than I was," I replied, trying the suit for size. I noticed the number on the back of the shirt as I got into it: 39.

"How're you feeling?" Durocher asked.

"I'm in good shape," I said. "Been playing every day."

"And you won't stop now," he said. "Get out on the field. You're catching tonight."

I stared at Leo. I hadn't expected to break into the lineup that quickly.

"What's the matter, nervous?" he asked.

"No," I said, "just sorta bewildered."

The stands were filling with people as I stuck my head out of the Dodger dugout. Ebbets Field was a bedlam of noise. And no wonder. The Giants were the opposition and the fact that the Dodgers had lost five in a row and were just one step out of the cellar didn't mean a thing. Nothing else mattered when the Giants and Dodgers locked horns.

I could feel the excitement as I stood by the batting cage waiting my turn to hit. It was a sweet feeling, one that would be repeated many times during the next ten years of rivalry between the two New York clubs. But never quite so sweet as that night of July 2, 1948.

I remember a little later, standing behind home plate, wearing my shin guards and chest protector, with my mitt under my left arm and my hat and mask in my hand.

"Ladies and gentlemen," the public address loudspeaker echoed around the packed park, "our organist, Gladys Gooding will now sing our National Anthem."

I almost bawled standing there at attention. Then I said a little prayer. I wanted so very much to make good.

Now Whitey Lockman was coming to the plate. I squatted

145

and gave the sign to Ralph Branca. Thirty-three thousand let out a roar as Ralph's first pitch came right down the pipe.

"Strike one!" sang out plate umpire Jocko Conlan.

In the second inning I came to bat with no score. I took a ball and a strike. Then Andy Hansen threw a fast ball, I swung, and the ball sailed high and far toward right center field, hitting the wall for a double. I got three hits that night; but the Dodgers lost the game 6-4 and flopped into last place. That was the only time that I ever played with a last place club in Brooklyn.

The next day I got a triple, two singles and a walk; and the following afternoon I crashed two home runs and a single, good for four runs. We won both games and climbed out of the basement. The last game of the series, on July 4, was a killer. The Giants led by scores of 2-0, 5-3, 8-6, and 12-9 before we came up with four runs in the bottom of the ninth to win 13-12.

That series provided the spark the Dodgers had lacked. We won sixteen out of the next nineteen games, and by August instead of battling to get out of the cellar we were challenging for first place. I caught every game. Edwards, who had been the No. 1 catcher, went to third base, and Hodges, the No. 2 catcher, was converted into a first baseman. All three of the team's catchers were now playing at the same time.

The Dodgers' bid for the flag was to be made without Leo Durocher. The breach between Durocher and Mr. Rickey widened. Finally Durocher left the team to manage the Giants, and Burt Shotton was brought out of semi-retirement by Mr. Rickey to pilot the Brooklyn team again.

After Durocher left, Mr. Rickey brought up Carl Erskine from Fort Worth and Carl immediately became a winner. The Dodgers climbed into first place in early August, but then three straight losses to the Giants dropped us back

146

into second. We never recovered. We wound up third, behind the Braves and Cardinals.

SIXTEEN

NINETEEN-FORTY-NINE WAS MY FIRST FULL
year in the major leagues. In the All-Star game at Brooklyn,
I caught the entire game. (I was to catch the '50, '51, '52,
and '53, too, without relief: that remains an All-Star record
for a catcher.)

That '49 season, I hit .287, made twenty-two home runs,
and drove in eighty-two runs in one hundred thirty games.
But that year really belonged to Jackie Robinson. He led
the league in batting with .342, cracked thirty-eight doubles,
stole thirty-seven bases and was voted the Most Valuable
Player.

That '49 team started a dynasty that was to bring the
Dodgers five pennants in eight years, and their first world
championship. That club had Gil Hodges at first, Jackie
Robinson at second, Pee Wee Reese at shortstop, Billy Cox
at third, Carl Furillo in right field, Duke Snider in center,
and me behind the plate. The only position that required
shuffling was left field.

My old roomie, Don Newcombe, was brought up from
Montreal in '49 and he teamed up with Preacher Roe, Ralph
Branca, and Carl Erskine to give us strong rotation. Then
we had such pitchers as Rex Barney, who pitched a no-hit,
no-run game against the Giants, Jack Banta, Joe Hatten, and
Paul Minner to call upon.

We whipped the Giants 10-3 before a record opening day
crowd at Ebbets Field, and we were off and running. By

147

July 1, it had become a two-team race — the Cardinals and Dodgers.

I suffered my first head injury late in '49. When I first joined the Dodgers, I found they all wore protective helmets. The first time I saw Pee Wee try one on, I kidded him.

"What's the fancy millinery for, Pee Wee?"

"You'll wear it, too, after you get a ball stuck in your ear," said Reese.

"No pitcher has hit me in the head yet," I said. "None will. I duck too quick."

Reese shrugged. "Famous last words."

It was in a September night game. We were playing in Pittsburgh and Bill Werle, a left-hander, was on the mound for the Pirates. One minute I was digging in, and the next I was writhing on the ground. I hadn't ducked fast enough.

I could see the sweeping sidearm curve but I couldn't get out of the way fast enough. The ball hit me on the side of the head, dropping me like a felled steer. They carried me off on a stretcher and took me in an ambulance to a hospital where I stayed overnight for observation. X-rays showed no fracture.

"You're in luck," the doctor said. "No fracture, no concussion. You'll just have a headache for a while. A couple days rest and you'll be as good as new."

"Rest?" I cried. "With the Cardinals leading by a game and a half you want me to rest, Doc? Where's my clothes?"

The next afternoon, I walked into the Dodger clubhouse at Forbes Field, and asked John Griffin, our equipment man, to give me a helmet.

"From now on nobody ain't going to get me to take this off, batting, catching, or running the bases," I said. I fitted the helmet over my regular cap and turning to Reese, I said: "Hey, Pee Wee, how do I look?"

148

"You're a doll," Reese laughed. "A living doll."

As that '49 season went into its final week, it looked like the Cards had the flag sewed up. They led by five games. Then for no apparent reason they went into a tailspin, losing five out of six to the Pirates and Cubs. And so, on the final day, we were on top of the league by one game. That last day was really hairy. The Cardinals won theirs and the result was posted on the scoreboard in Philadelphia, where we were locked in a tie game with the Phillies. A defeat would mean that the season would end in a tie between the Dodgers and Cards — just like in 1946 when the Cards beat us in a playoff.

We scored two runs in the top of the tenth to beat the Phillies 9-7.

The Yankees won the first of five straight pennants for manager Casey Stengel that year, and the Dodgers met them for the fifth time in a World Series. It was the same old story: the Yankees beat us in five games. There was some good pitching in that series. Allie Reynolds beat Newcombe 1-0 in the first game when Tommy Henrich hit a home run in the ninth inning. Newk struck out eleven and Reynolds fanned nine. Preacher Roe got that one back for the Dodgers, beating Vic Raschi in the second game by the same 1-0 score.

The thing I remember best about Roe's pitching that day is that he struck out Joe DiMaggio with the most beautiful spitball ever. Sure Preach threw a spitter. I knew it and so did everybody else on the team. I didn't have a special sign for it. I would just make a fist for a fast ball, something Roe didn't have. In a situation like that he'd throw what he felt like, and sometimes he felt like throwing a spitter.

The Yankees beat us in the next three games, but I hit a home run off Joe Page in the third game and threw out two would-be base stealers in the fourth game. The biggest satisfaction I got was picking Phil Rizzuto off third base. As he jogged into the Yankee dugout, little Phil, one of the finest base runners I ever saw in my life, moaned:

"Nothing like that ever happened to me before, in all my years in baseball." Then he added: "And that son-of-a-gun made it look easy."

In the clubhouse after the game a reporter asked me:

"Campy, what is the best way to pick a man off third?"

"You throw at the runner's head," I told him. He looked shocked. "Don't worry, you never hit him. But the runner, seeing the ball coming at him, ducks, or falls to the ground. It's natural reaction. If he ducks, he's lost a step getting back, and you have a good chance to get him. If he hits the ground, he's dead for sure."

With the World Series over, I accepted an offer to go on a barnstorming tour with a group of Negro players headed by Jackie Robinson. We toured throughout the South and drew big crowds, but bad weather set in and the tour had to be cut short. It was during that barnstorming tour that I first saw Willie Mays. We were in Alabama, playing against the Birmingham Barons, a colored team. This kid was playing center field for the Barons. We had Larry Doby on third base and Larry was a real speed demon in those days. Somebody hit a fly ball to center field. The kid caught the ball, making that fancy breadbasket catch of his, and threw Doby out at the plate. I didn't believe it.

"Who the devil is that kid in center field?" I yelled to the first base coach.

"His name is Mays — Willie Mays," he shouted.

I can't recall what he did at the plate. All I remember is that throw and what a beauty it was. I saw the kid a few more times after that and the more I saw of him the more I liked him. I phoned the Dodgers one day, collect, and told them all about this eighteen-year-old kid.

150

"You'd better send a scout down quick to sign him up," I advised.

The Dodgers took my advice — that is, to the extent of sending a scout to look Willie over. The scout, Wid Matthews, came back with his story on Mays. You know what he included in the report?

"The kid can't hit a curve ball."

And the Dodgers lost the chance to sign Willie Mays — the greatest outfielder, maybe, to come up to the big leagues since Tris Speaker.

SEVENTEEN

NINETEEN HUNDRED AND FIFTY WAS A TOUGH year for me. It was the year I had my first real serious injury, a fractured thumb; it was the year we lost the pennant on the last day of the season; and it was the year I nearly went blind. My luck wasn't all bad that year, though. I made the All-Star team for the second straight year; and I was the only player on either squad to play from start to finish in that fourteen-inning game in Chicago, won by the National League on Red Schoendienst's home run.

Another boy, Tony, was born to Ruthe on August 18, and we bought our own home, a nice, comfortable Colonial type house in the St. Albans section of Queens, Long Island, not far from where we had been renting a house for the past two years. It's a pleasant community where a number of Negroes have settled. Jackie Robinson lived around the corner. Other neighbors were Count Basie, Lena Horne, and Ella Fitzgerald.

I got off to a real good start in 1950. Early in June, I went on a home run binge, hitting at least one out of the park six successive days. I needed only one more to equal the seven-game mark set by George Kelly in 1924 and matched by Walker Cooper in 1947. But although we knocked out three Cardinal pitchers, I couldn't get that seventh homer. But I soon began another streak that carried me into the last week in August with twenty-seven homers. With forty games still to play, I had a strong chance to break the Dodger club mark of thirty-five set by Babe Herman twenty years earlier.

But whatever chance I had of reaching Herman's record was lost when my right thumb was smashed by a foul tip. The accident happened in Philadelphia on the night of September 6. The Phillies' Whiz Kids, as they were called that year, had opened up a big lead over our club for the National League pennant, but we were catching up to them. With every game a crucial game for us, Manager Burt Shotton sent Don Newcombe, our ace, back against the Phillies in the second game of the twin bill after Newk had shut them out with three hits in the opener.

My roomie didn't do so badly either in trying the Iron Man role, but we couldn't get no runs for him and Shotton had to take him out for a pinch hitter in the top of the eighth because we were losing 2-0. Dan Bankhead came in to pitch for us in the eighth and the first batter to face him was Willie "Puddinhead" Jones. Puddinhead likes to hit the fast ball, so I flashed the curve ball sign to Bankhead, and Jones fouled it off. The bat just caught the top of the ball and deflected it into my thumb.

I yelled out in pain and took a look at my right hand. I got sick. The bone showed right through. I made a beeline for the bench and the blood made a red path from home plate to our dugout. Man, the thumb was just gushing blood.

Doc Harold Wendler, the team trainer, didn't need more

than a quick look to see that the thumb was broken. The edges of both bones stuck out through the broken skin at the joint. It was an ugly sight.

"Compound fracture," he muttered.

"Oh, no!" I cried, although I knew before he did what it was. It was the first time in all my years of catching I had suffered a broken finger of any kind.

"It looks like you're through for the season, Campy," said the Doc. "Of course, I wouldn't bet on it. Not the way I know you. For anyone else, there'd be no chance of getting back this season. But you, maybe. You have remarkable recuperative powers."

I forced a grin. "I'll be back in there in a week, Doc," I said. "See if I'm not."

"Maybe so," said Doc, "but right now I'm taking you to Temple University Hospital to have the thumb sewed up."

I was wrong. It was eleven days before I got back into action. The season still had eleven days to go and pretty soon we were breathing heavy down the necks of the Phillies. With two days of the season left, we were two games behind. Oddly enough, both games were with Philadelphia, in Ebbets Field. We won the first game, my three-run homer wrapping it up. We'd been nine games behind when we started the drive. Now all we needed was to beat them again the next day to gain a pennant tie.

Ebbets Field was really bulging at the seams for that final game. More than 35,000 crammed into every available space. I don't know how many couldn't get into the park, but there must have been plenty. Robin Roberts, who was just coming into his own as one of the great pitchers in baseball, was Philadelphia's hope to give them their first championship in thirty-five years. For us it had to be Newcombe. I don't know how many times they faced each other after that, but this game was easily the biggest one for both of them.

153

Each had an added incentive; each was shooting for his twentieth win.

Philly scored in the sixth inning, and we tied it up 1-1 on a great homer by Pee Wee Reese. He hit a lazy fly ball against the right field screen. Ordinarily the ball drops back on the field and is in play, but this time it slid down the screen and got stuck on the ledge of the wall about 15 or 20 feet above the ground. Pee Wee laughed all around the bases.

We had a chance to win the game in the ninth, but Cal Abrams was thrown out at the plate by Richie Ashburn when he tried to score from second on a single by Duke Snider. We still had men on first and third and only one out, but Carl Furillo fouled out and Gil Hodges flied out. The Phillies, given another chance, won the game in the tenth inning when Dick Sisler hit a home run with two on base.

I can still see that pitch now — a fast ball on the outside. As Sisler stepped into the box, I had called for time and walked out to talk to Newcombe.

"Looka here," I said. "You been pitching this guy outside all day, and he's been hitting you like he owned you. He's got three hits already. Now pitch him tight. Don't give him anything on the outside."

I walked back to the plate and gave Newk the signal for a fast ball inside . . . on the fists. As soon as I saw it coming, I flinched. It was on the outside. Sisler swung and the ball took off toward the left field stands — carrying with it about $7000 of what would have been my World Series share.

I buried my disappointment that winter by occupying myself with underprivileged kids in the Harlem YMCA. Together with Jackie Robinson, I spent a lot of time with these youngsters teaching them good sportsmanship and good citizenship, as well as supervising their sports activities. Jackie and I would make appearances in public schools all over the

154

city and speak to the youngsters. We had baseball clinics after school and on Saturday. I'd present trophies to youngsters for sportsmanship and character as well as for athletic ability. I've always thought a trophy or an award of some kind makes a youngster try harder. He knows he's getting something back by putting something into it.

While I was spending a lot of time with these kids, I made sure I didn't neglect my own. My spare hours at home were spent tinkering with model electric trains I'd bought for the kids on a large track setup in my basement. Another hobby I enjoyed was tropical fish and fish tanks.

I've been interested in electric trains since I was a kid. My Dad bought me a Lionel train set a long time ago. That started me on them. After we bought our own home in St. Albans, I really went in for electric trains and tropical fish in a big way. I had twenty-two tanks recessed in the walls of my basement plus two extra 30-gallon tanks. Upstairs on the sun porch, I had a 150-gallon tank plus another 30-gallon tank on the other sun porch. I had quite a collection of rare tropical fish. Among them were some Japanese Lionhead goldfish. Even as babies they'd run $100 apiece. When they become two years old, their heads resemble lions' heads. All these tanks and fish ran into thousands of dollars. I gave them all away when we moved to Glen Cove several years later. I have no basement in Glen Cove and there's just no other place to keep them.

I still have all my trains, though. I used to get quite a kick operating those trains. Of course, I don't do that any more, but my children love to operate them just as much as I do, even Princess, the youngest. I have one of the largest collections of electrical trains in the world. It cost easily over $5000. This track network has little cities, factories, stations, different little lakes running through it, and even people. It has the latest thing, too, rocket launching —

155

rockets that shoot straight up in the air. I have hundreds of trains of all kinds and description.

Later on I took up other hobbies, such as boating, fishing, and playing golf, although I must admit I was never more than a duffer in golf. Like most ballplayers, I couldn't get rid of that baseball swing. I might have become pretty good at the game if I had more time to play it. I did shoot a 98 the first time I played a match game. It was against Junior Gilliam. And I beat him, too.

Getting back to the winter of 1951. It was a bitter cold night early in January of that year when I returned home from the "Y." Ruthe was in the kitchen and she looked upset.

"What's troubling you, honey?" I asked. "The kids getting on your nerves?"

"No," she said, "nothing as trivial as that. It's the hot water heater. It's gone out."

"Okay, I'll fix it. In the meantime, get dinner ready, I'm hungry."

I took off my coat and went down to the basement.

"Honey, you gotta come down here and hold the spring door open while I light the pilot."

With Ruthe holding the metal door open as far as she could, I struck a match and stuck my arm into the opening. There was a muffled explosion, then a blinding flash. The water heater had exploded and blew both of us clear across the basement. Ruthe screamed. I felt a burning sensation across my eyes and everything went black. I wasn't hurt except for my face and eyes. I couldn't see a thing. Ruthe jumped to her feet and rushed over to where I was laying, my hands pressed to my face.

"My face, my face," I moaned. "It's burned."

Ruthe's mother, who was staying with us, came running down the steps.

156

"What's the matter? What happened?" she asked.

"His eyes!" Ruthe cried. "Roy can't see."

Ruthe and her mother hurried upstairs and got some butter which they smeared all over my face. My eyes were burning something awful.

Suddenly Ruthe let out a shriek. The skin on my face was peeling off as she rubbed it.

"Get a doctor," she ordered her mother. "And hurry."

They were both so nervous they couldn't drive, so they had a friend, Ray Vaughan, who lived across the street, drive me to Dr. Hill's home, a few blocks away.

"The cornea in each eye appears to be blistered," he told Ruthe after an examination. "I advise you to take him to a hospital immediately."

Dr. Hill bandaged my head and I was taken to Jamaica Hospital where I was put in a private room. An eye specialist, Dr. Arthur Minsky, was called in. I complained of a terrible stinging pain on my eyes and face, and he had the nurse apply some kind of a salve which made me feel a little better. After my eyes had been covered with black patches and my face was bandaged, Dr. Minsky said:

"It's not as bad as it looks. No operation will be necessary. The application of eyedrops should dissolve the blisters on the eyeballs. The face burns are superficial. I'm sure there will be no scars."

"My sight, Doc," I asked. "What about my eyesight?"

"It'll be all right," he said. "Don't worry about that."

Those next few days were horrible . . . lying there with my face all bandaged and those black patches on my eyes. For three days and nights I lay wondering whether I would ever see again. I prayed constantly. I kept thinking of my family. I had five children now. Five children and no business. The oldest was eleven years old, the youngest five months.

Am I going to be blind, I kept thinking. The thought

157

wouldn't leave me. The Doc said my eyes would be all right, but suppose he was wrong? Or maybe he was just trying to cheer me up? Or even if I didn't go blind, would my eyes be good enough for baseball? Gee, what else could I do?

If only I'd had a business of some kind. Something that would provide an income for my family in case anything happened to me.

I prayed to God again and made Him a solemn promise that if He allowed me to see again, I'd do my best to get into some kind of business that would give my family some security after my baseball days were over. And I kept that promise.

On the fourth day, the bandages and patches were removed. A lot of things were going through my mind then. First off came the patch on my left eye. I saw very faintly. Everything was blurred. But I thanked God. At least I could see. Then the other patch came off. It was the same. All blurry.

Dr. Minsky then bathed my eyes and applied some more salve to them. He told me the blur would be even worse but not to worry. For the next fifteen to twenty minutes, I couldn't see a thing. Then little by little it began to clear. Pretty soon I could see the same as before. I was lucky. My eyesight wasn't affected. I looked in the mirror. My face was still a little discolored, but it didn't look bad. The scar tissue over the eyebrows had cleared up. I took a deep sigh of relief and gave my thanks again to the good Lord.

I didn't waste any time looking for a business. With the help of Walter O'Malley, owner of the Dodgers, who advanced me the money, I went into the package liquor business, opening a store in Flushing. Eight months later, on September 6, 1951, to be exact, I was to move the store to Harlem, at 134th Street and Seventh Avenue, with my name in big neon lights, and four clerks, and three shiny new cash registers. I was to have a gala opening with a number of my friends there including Jackie Robinson, Don Newcombe, Nat "King" Cole, Sugar Ray Robinson, Archie Moore and a flock of others.

It was about this time that Mr. Rickey sold his interest in the Dodgers and moved on to Pittsburgh, to try to derrick the Pirates out of the cellar.

I had lost a friend.

After all, it was Mr. Rickey who put me in organized baseball. And it was nearly two years after I signed my first contract in the Dodger organization that he told me of the first time he was ever conscious of me. This is how it was. The Baltimore Elites were playing the Newark Eagles in Jersey City in 1945. Clyde Sukeforth had been sent over by Mr. Rickey to take a look at a big pitcher named Newcombe.

Sukey came back and said, "Mr. Rickey, I looked at that pitcher, but I also saw a catcher. I made a report on him. He can hit, throw, and for a big man, he can run fast."

"Like Gus Mancuso?" Rickey chuckled, referring to the Giant's great receiver who was such a slow man going down to first.

A week later, Mr. Rickey himself and his wife went over to Jersey City to watch me. He went incognito and watched me catch a double-header and later, back in Brooklyn, told his assistant, Bob Finch, to sign me.

For the record, I was the fourth Negro signed into organized ball. Jack Robinson, John Wright, and Don Newcombe came before me. After us came Roy Partlow and Dan Bankhead — both pitchers.

Mr. Rickey was forever preaching to me about spending more than I earned. I remember especially when Ruthe and me were interested in a house in St. Albans. The price was pretty stiff, and when I mentioned to Mr. Rickey that I was thinking of buying, he sent John Collins, then the Dodgers ticket manager, out there to check the property.

"You're always going to be in debt, Roy," he said, shaking his finger at me. "The day will come when we'll have to hold an exhibition game for you! You won't live within your income."

The story is that Mr. Rickey can squeeze a dollar. Not in my book. He was pretty free with me. I particularly remember the day after the 1949 season when Mr. Rickey called me in to discuss my contract for the next year. When I entered his office, he looked at me for a moment, took a piece of paper, folded it and handed it to me.

"You write it, Roy," he said. "And bear in mind you're a fine catcher. As long as you stay out of the insane asylum, you can write in the figure."

I was bowled over.

"Mr. Rickey, " I protested, "don't put me on the spot. You pay me what I'm worth."

Mr. Rickey insisted that I fill in my own terms. Finally I did. I handed the paper back to him, and he put it on the desk.

"Aren't you going to look at it?" I asked.

"I don't have to. I've got the best bargain in baseball," he said.

The figure I wrote was $12,500. I had given myself a $3000 raise.

That winter of 1950-1951 I was so busy setting up my new business that I had no time to go to a gymnasium for a workout, and my waistline showed it. So when Buzzie Bavasi, now the Dodgers general manager, told me that Newcombe was going to Hot Springs, Arkansas, in advance of spring training to take off some weight in the mineral baths, I jumped at

160

the chance to go with him. I wasn't only thinking of my weight but of my eyes. I had to know as soon as possible if my vision was normal.

The day Newk and I arrived at Hot Springs we made tracks for the ball park. After Newk had warmed up for a few minutes, I grabbed a bat and told him to throw me a few. We had no trouble getting some kids to shag the balls. Newk lobbed a few to me until I was able to get my timing. Then I hollered:

"All right. Now put something on it. Don't try to do me any favors. Gimme all you got."

The big fella put a little mustard on his pitches, not too much but fast enough. He threw about twenty pitches and I hit five of them out of the park. I hit some of the others pretty good, too. Finally, Newk walked off the mound.

"That's enough. You can see all right."

I was happy when I reported to the Dodgers training camp at Vero Beach at the end of February. But Charlie Dressen, the new manager, didn't feel the same way when he saw me.

"You're too heavy," he barked the minute he laid eyes on me. "I want you to run a little extra every day and I want you to do extra calisthenics."

I was in real fine shape by the time the team went to Miami for its exhibition games. Then it happened. In a game with the Athletics, Eddie Joost tried to duck out of the way of a close pitch. The ball glanced off his bat and caught me on the right thumb, the same one that was fractured six months before. Doc Wendler drilled a small hole in my thumb nail to relieve the pressure of the blood clot underneath it and sent me to the hospital for X-rays, which showed a chipped bone in the thumb. I'd be out for about two weeks, I was told.

To make sure I didn't pick up any extra weight because

161

of the inactivity, Dressen ordered me to go on a diet. The next day he handed me a typewritten sheet of paper. It read:

ROY CAMPANELLA DIET

MONDAY: Breakfast: Grapefruit, 1 or 2 eggs, coffee black (breakfast exactly same every day).
Lunch: Eggs, tomatoes, coffee.
Dinner: Eggs, combination fruit salad, 1 piece toast, grapefruit.

TUESDAY: Lunch: Eggs, grapefruit, coffee.
Dinner: Steak, tomatoes, celery, olives, cucumbers, coffee.

WEDNESDAY: Lunch: Eggs, tomatoes, spinach.
Dinner: Lamp chop, celery, cucumbers, tomatoes, coffee.

THURSDAY: Lunch: Eggs, spinach, coffee.
Dinner: Eggs, cottage cheese, spinach, 1 piece toast, tea.

FRIDAY: Lunch: Eggs, spinach, coffee.
Dinner: Fish, combination salad, toast, grapefruit, coffee.

SATURDAY: Lunch: Fruit salad (nothing else).
Dinner: Plenty of steak, celery, tomatoes, cucumbers, tea.

SUNDAY: Lunch: cold chicken, tomatoes, grapefruit.
Dinner: Chicken, tomatoes, cooked cabbage, carrots, celery, vegetable soup, grapefruit, coffee.

I looked up from the paper and into Dressen's grinning face.

162

"I'll be cackling like a hen when I get through with this," I said.

"And no beer," the little son-of-a-gun said.

"What a year this is starting out to be," I moaned.

And what a year it was. It was to be a great year, and a terrible year; a year of joy ending with sadness; a year of achievement, ending with nothing; a year that I can still recall almost day by day, and a year I still can't believe. It was a year full of pain.

EIGHTEEN

THE DODGERS JUMPED INTO THE LEAD RIGHT at the start of the season and the Giants lost something like eleven straight. In a two-game series against the Braves in May, I got seven hits including a home run in each game. We beat them 4-3 and 5-3. By July we were so far out in front, it looked like no contest. Everybody was having a good year, including me. I was lucky enough to come through with clutch hits in the eighth and ninth innings that won games for us. Even a spike wound in my left hand by Eddie Miksis when I slid into second base in a game with Chicago didn't stop me. After two days I was back behind the plate although I had to bat with a sponge in my hand for about a week.

By mid-July, I was hitting around .340 and was near the top in home runs too. By August we were ten full games in front. Then on August 5, during a game with the Giants at Ebbets Field, Whitey Lockman tried to score from first on a double by Willie Mays and crashed into me, sending me sprawling into the dirt. I landed on my left elbow. It was the hardest I've ever been hit in a ball game. I continued to

163

play for several days, but the elbow became very sore. Finally, I had to go to the hospital for X-rays. Bone chips. They told me to rest for a week, but I was back in four days.

On August 11, we were leading the Giants by thirteen and a half games. Then the impossible began to happen. The Giants went on a sixteen-game winning streak that brought them within six games of us. All of a sudden there was a pennant race. Not that anybody thought the Giants would catch us. After all, there was only a little more than a month left to the season. We were in Chicago and Turk Lown was pitching for the Cubs. It was the second inning and I was the batter. His first pitch was low and away, and his second pitch was high and inside. I started to duck away, but I never had a chance. The ball hit me right in the ear and I dropped to the ground like I'd been shot. I lay there on home plate with blood gushing from my ear and knocked half-unconscious.

They carried me from the field on a stretcher, put me in an ambulance and rushed me to Illinois Masonic Hospital. Ralph Branca, one of our pitchers, went with me to the hospital, where they X-rayed my head, bathed me and put me to bed. I found out later that we lost the game when Gene Hermanski — the Dodgers had traded him to the Cubs only a few weeks before — hit a home run in a late inning.

When the team entrained for St. Louis, I was left behind. I couldn't sit up to eat. They had to feed me through a glass tube for four or five days. I got sick every time I tried to sit up. I was discharged after the fifth day and put on a train for New York. What a trip that was! Every time I'd sit up I'd get dizzy and I had to go right back to bed. The dizziness lasted a long time. It wasn't until the team got back home the following week that I was able to join them. I had trouble for a while with pop fouls, especially when they were

164

hit directly over my head; but the dizziness eventually cleared up.

The Dodgers' lead over the Giants had been cut to four games when I got back into the lineup. There was pressure on us now. A month ago, we were a free and easy bunch, breezing to an easy pennant. Now we were playing tight and nervous baseball, looking back over our shoulder and watching the scoreboard to see how the Giants were doing.

During the last week of the season, we fought desperately to keep the pennant from slipping through our fingers. Everybody was grim and silent. There was no horseplay on the field. Tempers were short. We stayed out of each other's way. We were playing the Braves in Boston on September 27, and the score was tied in the eighth inning 3-3. Bob Addis was on third and Sam Jethroe on first for the Braves. As Earl Torgeson, a left-handed batter, stepped up to hit, I motioned for the infield to creep in close to cut off the run.

Preacher Roe, who already had won twenty-two games for us, came in with a good curve and Torgy rapped a slow grounder to Jackie Robinson at second base. Robby swooped in, grabbed the ball and fired to me. Addis came charging into the plate, but I had the ball waiting for him. He slid hard and bowled me over, but I held onto the ball. I had him cold, but Frank Dascoli, the plate umpire, called him safe.

I exploded. I got in front of him and shouted, "No, no, Frank, he's out!"

But Dascoli had turned his back on me. That got me even madder.

"I had him! I had him!" I shouted. "It wasn't even close. Man, I had him, I tell you!"

"He was safe!" Dascoli yelled back, and he turned his back again and began dusting off the plate with his little whisk broom.

165

Then I really let him have it. I stormed around him and flung my mitt on the ground. I really told him off. By this time practically the entire Brooklyn team was surrounding Dascoli. Big Frank straightened up, put the whisk broom back in his hip pocket and raised his right arm.

"You're out of the game!" he shouted at me, and I think everybody in the ball park heard him. Then he heaved out Coach Cookie Lavagetto. Before the game was resumed, Dascoli had chased the entire Dodger bench, leaving only Manager Dressen and Coach Jake Pitler in the dugout.

That was the first time I was ever thrown out of a ball game. I was thrown out two or three times since, but I've never been as mad as I was that day. What made it worse was that I was due to hit in the next inning, with men on first and third and only one out. And a left-hander, Chet Nichols, was pitching, too. Instead, they put in Wayne Terwilliger and he hit into a double play. We lost the game by one run. I'll always believe I could have gotten that run in from third.

What happened on the field was mild compared to what took place in the runway outside the umpires' dressing room, after the last out. The umpires' door in Braves Field was right next to the visiting team's clubhouse. As the Dodger players went by, they banged and kicked that door, shouting names you don't hear in no church. Preacher Roe, still fuming over the defeat, kicked at the door. So did Jackie and one or two others. The next thing I knew someone had kicked the panel out of the door.

Of course, we didn't get away with it. The umpires handed in a report to the president of the league. The upshot was that Jackie and I were fined $100 apiece and Preach got smacked for fifty bucks.

On the morning of the last day of the season, the Dodgers and Giants were in a flatfooted tie. The runaway had developed into a photo finish. In Boston the Giants were winning; in Philadelphia the Dodgers were losing. At the end of the fourth inning, the Phillies were ahead 6-1. We made it 6-5 in the fifth, but they got two more runs in their half.

By that time my left thigh was hurting like the dickens. In the inning before, with Roberts pitching, I hit a ball off the right field fence. There was only one out and I tried for three bases so that I'd be in position to score on a fly ball or grounder. I felt a sharp stab of pain as I rounded second, but I continued to third. As the game progressed, the pain grew worse. It didn't feel any better when the scoreboard showed that the Giants had won 3-2. Now we had to win, too, or it was all over for us. Faced with elimination, we fought back and in the eighth we scored three runs to tie the score at 8-8.

It was getting dark when the ninth inning ended with the score still tied. Both teams went scoreless in the tenth . . . then the eleventh . . . and the twelfth. In that inning the Phillies had the winning run on third when Eddie Waitkus, their first baseman, hit a low line drive that appeared headed over second base. How Jackie Robinson caught it, I'll never know, but he did, with a flying belly-whop catch the likes of which I never saw before or since. It was so dark that not too many of the 31,755 fans at the game even saw the catch. As a matter of fact, the Western Union operators were so sure that Waitkus's hit had gone through that they sent out a flash on the wires:

"Phillies win! Dodgers lose pennant!"

After saving the game, Jackie wasted little time winning it. The next time he was up, with two out in the fourteenth inning, he blasted a pitch by Roberts into the upper left field stands for a home run. Bud Podbielan, who had replaced Newcombe on the mound for the Dodgers, retired the Phillies in order in their turn at bat and preserved the victory.

The 1951 pennant race had ended in a tie. The Dodgers and the Giants would have to battle it out in a three-game playoff for the National League championship.

I was lying on the rubbing table in the Dodger clubhouse in Ebbets Field the morning of that first game with the Giants. Charlie Dressen sat dejectedly on a stool looking at me.

"How's it feel, Roy?" he asked.

"I walked in here today, Skip," I said with a grin. "That's more than I was able to do last night. Don't worry, I'll play. I prayed to God last night I would be able to walk this morning, and I can. If I can walk, I can play."

The night before, I wouldn't have given a plugged nickel for my chances to play. I had to be helped into the house.

"My leg is killing me," I told Ruthe.

Ruthe rubbed alcohol on it before I went to bed, and the next morning it felt better. As soon as I arrived at the park I made a beeline for the whirlpool. Now Doc Wendler was working on me, as Dr. Dominic Rossi, the club physician, stood by.

Dressen looked skeptical.

"What's the verdict, Doc?" he asked.

Dr. Rossi pushed his thumb into the muscle tissue. "It doesn't look too good," he said. "We'll try freezing it with ethyl chloride, and hope for the best."

I never should have played. "The best" wasn't good enough. I couldn't swing, I couldn't run and it even hurt when I threw. I not only hurt myself, I hurt the team. We lost 3-1 to Jim Hearn, but we might have won if I hadn't been in there. We had a chance to get Hearn out of there in the fourth inning. The Giants were leading by one run, and then singles by Duke Snider and Jackie Robinson put runners on first and third with one out. But I tapped weakly to the shortstop and, unable to run, was easily doubled up to end the threat.

168

It was a gloomy Dodger clubhouse after that first game. Dressen came over to ask me about the leg.

"I can't make it, Skip," I said. "I shouldn't have played today. I hurt the team. Why not let Walker play tomorrow at the Polo Grounds? Rube is a good catcher and he'll do a good job. Certainly better than me."

Rube did do a good job in that second game. He rapped three hits, one of them a home run, and he did a great job handling that curve ball of Clem Labine. The Dodgers won 10-0, tying the series.

Now came the showdown game in this last-of-three series. I had played in 143 games, catching 140 of them, hit 33 home runs, drove in 108 runs and batted .325, but those figures didn't mean a thing that day. It didn't matter what you did or didn't do during the regular season. As far as the 1951 pennant was concerned, only this game counted.

Since "freezing" that Charley horse hadn't helped, they shot it with novocain. I took my batting practice and jogged around the bases. I stopped halfway between second and third and walked the rest of the way to the dugout where Dressen was waiting.

"Well . . . ?"

"It's all right, I guess," I said with a shrug.

"I don't want you to guess," Chuck growled. "I want to know. Can you or can't you play? And I don't mean on one leg, either. Can you play so that you can help the team?"

"Well, truthfully, Skip, I don't know. In Ebbets Field, maybe. But here at the Polo Grounds, with all that foul territory behind the plate, I don't think I can catch up to those foul pop-ups."

That was enough for Dressen. He patted me on the rear and turned his face to the end of the bench. "Hey, Rube," he called out, "you're catching today."

And so I sat on the bench as Don Newcombe faced Sal

Maglie in the most important game of the year. For six innings my roomie was really firing that ball. I'd said a prayer for him from the first inning on. When the Giants came up in their half of the seventh, they were losing 1-0. Monte Irvin doubled, went to third on an infield out, and scored on a fly ball by Bobby Thomson. When Newk returned to the bench in the eighth with the score 1-1, I asked him how he felt.

"Tired," he grunted.

The boys gave him a pretty good rest that inning, scoring three runs for a 4-1 lead. Newk set the Giants down easy in the bottom of the eighth and for the first time I began to breathe easy. It looked like we couldn't lose. That's how the others felt, too. They were laughing and joking now, whereas, before, it was all business with nobody saying much.

The fans were drifting toward the exits as the Giants came up in the ninth for their last at bats. They kept walking even as Al Dark opened with a single to right field. But they stopped when Don Mueller followed with another single. Newk bore down and got Irvin to foul out but Whitey Lockman doubled to score Dark and send Mueller to third. The score was 4-2 now, with men on second and third. A base hit would tie the score.

Dressen came out to talk with Newcombe. He turned to the bullpen and waved his right arm. Ralph Branca, who had been throwing, put his warmup jacket over his right arm and came in to pitch to Bobby Thomson. The tension was building up. As Ralph was taking his warmup pitches, I suddenly remembered that two days earlier, in the first play-off game, Thomson banged a home run off Branca. I felt a chill come over me.

Ralph wound up deliberately, even though there were runners on bases, and let the first pitch go. Thomson looked at plate umpire Lou Jorda but didn't say a word. The next pitch was in the same spot. Thomson swung and the ball took off in the direction of the left field stands. The Dodger bench rose like one man.

"Sink, you devil, sink!" I begged.

But the ball didn't sink — not until it had reached the seats in the lower deck.

Never before or since have I seen such a commotion on a ballfield. The Giants went wild with joy. They were all out on the field even before Thomson reached third. By the time he crossed the plate thousands of fans had poured onto the field. Our guys just stood, dumfounded. As for me, I stood at the edge of the dugout and stared at the spot where the ball had disappeared.

It's strange the things you remember about something like that. Three pictures are still fresh in my mind. One is Andy Pafko standing with his back propped against the left field wall, waiting for the ball to come down. The other is Toots Shor, the restaurant man who is an incurable Giant fan, jumping out of his box behind third base and trying to get across the field to shake Durocher's hand. He never made it, but it was the first time I saw fat Toots run. The third is Branca sitting on the steps leading to the visiting team's clubhouse in the Polo Grounds crying his heart out.

It was a distressing end to what should have been a real happy year for me. Except for the injuries, I had enjoyed every minute of it. I don't think anybody ever had more fun playing ball. Catching, they say, is hard work and not a rewarding job. That's why they call the mask, protector, and shin guards the tools of ignorance. The idea is that if a man had any brains, he'd be a pitcher, an infielder, or an outfielder. I never looked at it that way. I could have been any one of those three, but from the start catching appealed to me as a chance to be in the thick of the game continuously. I never had to be lonely behind the plate where I could talk

171

to the hitters. I also learned that by engaging them in conversation I sometimes could distract them.

When Willie Mays first came to the Giants in 1951, he was one of my pigeons. Willie was so busy answering my questions with "Yes, Mr. Campanella," or "No, Mr. Campanella," that he was hitting practically nothing against the Dodgers. Then one day, realizing what was happening to him, he stamped his foot angrily and yelled:

"See here, Campy! You let me be!"

Later, whenever Willie stepped into the batter's box, I'd ask, "Willie, are you married yet?"

Willie didn't say a word. I kept asking him the same question every time he came up. But he never even looked at me. Finally, I said to him, "Willie are you mad at me?"

He stepped out of the box and motioned to Durocher in the coaching box. Durocher hurried over and asked what was wrong.

"He's bothering me," Mays said.

"Pick up a handful of dirt and throw it in his face," Leo said.

"Leo," I said, "Willie's got better sense than that."

One day, when Larry Goetz was umpiring back of the plate, he asked, "Don't you talk to Willie any more?"

"Larry," I said, "that boy's hitting too much for me to talk to him. Besides, ain't I got enough to do just taking care of my job? I can't spare the time, words or ideas from it."

The only consolation I got out of that year was in winning my first Most Valuable Player award. It was some time in November that I got the news. I was in Houston, Texas, with my barnstorming team. I had just come back from a shopping trip in downtown Houston buying some presents for Ruthe and the kids. I picked up the phone to put in a long distance call to Ruthe and the operator said, "We have a long distance call on here for you, Mr. Campanella, a Mr.

Dick Young in New York. Do you want to take it now?" I said sure, and Young, the fellow who at the time wrote about the Dodgers for the New York *Daily News,* told me I'd been voted the Most Valuable Player in the National League. I could hardly believe it, honest. I called Ruthe right away and she said she had already heard about it, but was waiting for me to call her. That was some night.

The next day I got a nice telegram.

CONGRATULATIONS. YOUR SELECTION AS THE MOST VALUABLE PLAYER WAS WELL EARNED. BEST WISHES FOR MANY MORE GOOD SEASONS. WEIGHT 200. HA HA.

CHUCK DRESSEN

NINETEEN

NINETEEN-FIFTY-TWO WAS ANOTHER YEAR OF injuries for me. On our first Western trip, I tried to pick a runner off first base and instead tangled with the bat of Toby Atwell, the Chicago catcher. I sprained my right thumb, but I didn't tell anybody and I kept on playing. In Philadelphia, a few days later, I went to my mother's house and Mom concocted her potion, a "miracle cure," she called it, a poultice of vinegar and clay. It did the trick too.

Then in Pittsburgh, Ronnie Kline nicked me on the left hand with a pitch and this time I couldn't hide it. I was out for five days. Just two days after I returned to the lineup, Jack Mayo of the Phillies banged into me at the plate, and somehow I caught my thumb in his shirt. That time I got a cut toe and a bruised right thumb. Again I was out for five days.

These injuries came before the season was two months old.

173

Then in July came the most crippling injury. A foul tip smashed into my left elbow and chipped a bone. Again I didn't tell anybody. I played that way for ten days, until the swelling and the pain became too much. The doctor put the arm in a cast and I was out for nearly two weeks. Right then, they tried to get me to agree to an operation, but I refused.

So, all in all, 1952 wasn't a good year for me personally, but I didn't feel too bad. After all, we won the pennant and that was more important than any other single thing. Truthfully, I say that I never felt too bad going 0 for 4 if the Dodgers won that day. The victory itself made it a good day for me. But I couldn't feel so hot about the series that fall. The Yankees beat us again, four games to three. I got but six singles in the seven games, no extra base hits and didn't score a run.

It was late that month (October of 1952) that I got a phone call from the Dodgers office, telling me to report to the Long Island College Hospital for X-rays on my arm and hand. When I got there, I was greeted by a nurse.

"Good morning, Mr. Campanella," she said. "Let me see now . . . you've been assigned to room —"

"Room? What for?" I asked.

"For your operation."

"What operation?" I shouted. Man, I didn't linger. I hurried right out of that hospital. "I'll be back Monday," I yelled over my shoulder.

The following Monday, a car rolled up in front of my house and out popped Lee Scott, the Dodgers traveling secretary.

"I ain't gonna go, Scotty," I greeted him.

"Don't tell me," he groaned. "Tell the front office."

So I phoned our VP, Buzzie Bavasi. Buzzie was mad. But I was stubborn. I flatly refused to have the operation.

Later that day, I was in the liquor store when the phone rang. It was Walter O'Malley.

"Listen, Mr. O'Malley," I pleaded. "This is all new to me, this operation stuff! I just don't go for them knives. The arm isn't that bad anyway. Honest. If it bothered me that much, I'd have the darn operation."

"Okay, Roy," he chuckled. "It's your arm."

About a week later I got another call from Mr. O'Malley asking me to come to his office. As I was driving over the Manhattan Bridge on that clear fall day, I thought of my first visit to the Dodgers office. I had to grin. Campy, I thought, seven years ago you took a subway down there and were afraid you'd get lost. Now you're driving a new Cadillac. Man, baseball has sure been good to you!

Naturally, I wondered what Mr. O'Malley had on his mind. Maybe he wanted to talk about the past season. Maybe he wanted to cut me down from the $23,000 I'd earned in '52. For me it hadn't been a great season — not even a good one. My batting average had dropped down to .269. I'd hit only twenty-two homers and had batted in ninety-seven runs in 128 games. If I'd known how close I'd been to those 100 RBI's, I wouldn't have rested that final week when Dressen told me to save myself for the series. When a slugger bats across a hundred or more, he's safe! But less than that and he's got to worry some.

Mr. O'Malley greeted me warmly. After he'd settled me back in a leather chair he asked about the hand.

"Good as new," I said.

"Really, Campy?"

"Really, Mr. O'Malley."

"Good," he said. "We're counting on you for a big season next year."

He opened a humidor on his big walnut desk, took a cigar

from it and handed it to me, then he took one for himself and lit it, blowing a smoke ring toward the ceiling before he spoke again.

"What are your plans for the winter, Roy?"

"Well, tomorrow I'm leaving on a barnstorming tour through the South, with Joe Black, Monte Irvin, Larry Doby, Luke Easter and a few other guys."

"And when you come back?"

"I got the store, Mr. O'Malley, and I'll be spending lots of time up at the Harlem YMCA working with the kids."

Mr. O'Malley nodded. "That liquor store of yours. You figure to devote all your time to it when you leave baseball?"

I looked up at him. "Me leave baseball?"

"Oh, you know what I mean — six, seven years from now."

"Mr. O'Malley," I said, "I don't ever want to leave baseball. Why, I've been in baseball all my life. What would I be doing if I wasn't in baseball? It's more than just a game with me. It's like a religion. I'd be lost without it. I'm never going to quit baseball voluntarily. When the day comes that I no longer can wear the uniform, they might as well bury me. Until then, I'll try to hang on as a bullpen catcher, as a scout, as a . . . well, as anything, just so I can stay in baseball."

Mr. O'Malley smiled. "That's what I thought," he said. "As a matter of fact, that's what I wanted to talk to you about. Would you be interested in remaining with the Dodgers as a coach when your playing days are over?"

At first I thought I hadn't heard him right.

"A coach?" I asked.

"Why not? You're intelligent, levelheaded. You're experienced. Nobody knows more than you about catching and you know more about pitching than most of the pitchers. Besides, you have a way with you. You're popular with the players. There's no question in my mind but that you'll

176

make a fine teacher. And I'd like to have you working for me as long as you care to."

"But . . . but — well, you know. Me, a coach in the major leagues?"

"You mean you're wondering how it would be for you, a Negro, coaching white players? I don't think you need worry about that. No, I see no problem in being the first Negro coach in baseball," O'Malley went on, "except for one thing."

"What's that, Mr. O'Malley?"

"Your weight. And I don't mean only from the physical point of view. You always put on too much weight in the winter and report out of shape. Now if you want to coach, you have to set an example for others. If you want to handle men, you must first be able to handle yourself. You think you can do that?"

"Mr. O'Malley, I told you how I felt about staying in baseball," I said. "I meant every word of it. I promise you right now that from now on I'll watch myself real sharp."

"I know you will, Roy. That's why I offered you the coaching job. You love baseball too much to stay out of it."

Next spring, I reported to training camp weighing 205 pounds, eighteen pounds lighter than the year before. And that weight included a mustache. I always grew a mustache in the winter just to have a little fun in spring training. I would go out and play in practice games with the mustache and then, the day before we'd begin our exhibition games, Pee Wee Reese would shave it off. It became a ritual.

One reason I was in shape was because I had spent ten days at Hot Springs taking the baths and doing lots of running. Larry Doby and Don Newcombe had gone with me. I also took along Ruthe and the two youngest kids. In the evenings we'd go out to watch a basketball game at the local high school. I became interested in one of the players. He

177

had the makings of a great basketball player. One particular night, I didn't see him and I asked the coach about him.

"Oh," said the coach. "You mean Bobby Mitchell. The boy had to quit sports — he has to work after school to make ends meet in order to graduate."

I asked the coach to have Mitchell come to my hotel for a talk. He told me the boy worked as a bus boy in my hotel. I had a talk with him there and the upshot of it was that before I left Hot Springs I made arrangements with a doctor friend of mine to take care of his clothing, books, and other expenses and to give him a weekly allowance, and to bill me.

Well, when Bobby Mitchell graduated from high school, he was given an athletic scholarship to Illinois University where he starred in basketball and football. After graduating from college, he was drafted by the Cleveland Browns and became one of the outstanding rookie halfbacks in the National Football League. I didn't see him again until the 1958 All-Star game in Chicago when the All-Stars, coached by Otto Graham, defeated the professional champion Detroit Lions. Mitchell was voted the Most Valuable Player in that game. I liked that.

Nineteen-fifty-three was the best year I ever had in baseball. Free of injuries for the first time in several years, I hit everybody and everything. I even banged a couple of home runs off Robin Roberts, the Phillies' great pitcher. The year before I batted exactly .089 against him. At the end of the first month, I was hitting .359. And I was doing all right behind the plate, too. But late in May, Billy Bruton of the Braves, the fastest runner in the league, stole a base off me.

On August 8, I hit two homers and drove in six runs against the Reds. Five days later I drove in four runs against the Giants. On August 28, I hit two triples in a game for the first time in my big league career. Three days later, on

178

August 31, I drove in my 124th run. That was a big RBI for me. Before the game a sports writer had told me I needed two RBI's to break the record for most runs batted in by a catcher in one season. It had been set by Walker Cooper of the Giants. So I knew. The RBI's came late in a game against the Cardinals. I hit a double off the left field wall, driving in two runs.

Another important day for me that year was September 6. Nobody had to tell me then that I needed one more home run to break Gabby Hartnett's record for catchers, for thirty-seven in a season. I had been reading for days how close I was. I got my thirty-eighth in Philadelphia. A week later the Dodgers clinched the pennant and by the time the season was over, I had set three new catching records: 42 home runs, 142 runs batted in, and a fielding mark of 807 putouts. My batting average for the year was a solid .312.

Steve O'Neill, the manager of the Phillies, called me the best catcher in baseball. "There isn't a thing he can't do better than any other catcher in the game, and when you put them all together there haven't been more than half a dozen catchers as good as Campanella in all the years I've been around." Considering that O'Neill was a fine catcher himself, probably the best of his day, that was sort of lovely to read.

Perhaps my greatest compliment came from Ty Cobb, two years later. We were playing in Chicago during the middle of the 1955 season when I had the pleasure of meeting him for the first time. That evening I saw an article in the papers. He was quoted as saying that I would be remembered more than any other player of my time; that someday I would be rated with the greatest catchers of all time. I appreciated that coming from such a man. One of my biggest regrets is that I never saw Cobb play. He must have really been something to watch.

Again, looking back, I feel proudest of my 1953 year, when I was the only catcher ever to lead the major leagues in home runs and runs batted in. I've always been a great admirer of Bill Dickey, Mickey Cochrane and Gabby Hartnett, and being able to accomplish something that they never did certainly is quite a thrill. I am proud of all my trophies but truthfully when I was playing I never thought of records. I just tried to do all I possibly could to help the team win. As long as I knew I did my best, I never felt too bad. Except maybe in the World Series. We just couldn't beat those Yankees. We all wanted to beat them so badly, we could taste it.

In the second inning of the first game of the series, I was hit in the right hand by a pitch from Allie Reynolds, and that just about washed me up for the series. The Yankees beat us in six games. I got a pop fly single in the first game, but I didn't hit a ball out of the infield in my other seven times at bat through the second game.

I was so discouraged because I couldn't grip the bat that I thought of benching myself for the good of the team. I told that to the sports writers after the second game. The morning of the third game Chuck Dressen came over to me while Doc Wendler was working on the hand. "I read in the papers where you said you can't play today," he remarked.

"I didn't say that," I replied. "I said I'd see how my hand was after I got here today and worked out."

"How does it feel now?"

"Pretty good," I said, taking my hand out of the whirlpool. "I'm going to play."

"Okay, but I don't want you to catch if you can't catch. And you'd better tell the writers it's your own idea. I don't want them to think I forced you to play."

Force me? Nobody had to force me to play, especially that afternoon. That night I was going to be Ed Murrow's guest

180

on his brand-new Person-to-Person television show. It was his first show. He had talked to me a month earlier and told me then that he had picked me as his first guest. The date was October 2, 1953.

"Now, Roy," Mr. Murrow told me, "all you have to do is hit a home run in the ninth inning. That will make the show a success."

Well, I wasn't up in the ninth so I hit the home run in the eighth. It was a big run, too, because it broke a 2-2 tie between Carl Erskine of the Dodgers and Vic Raschi for the Yankees, and gave us our first victory in the series, 3-2. That was the game when Erskine struck out fourteen Yankees to break the old World Series strike-out mark of thirteen set by Howard Ehmke of the Athletics against the Cubs in 1929. Neither Carl nor I knew anything about the record until the writers told us about it in the clubhouse after the game. It was the fastest I ever saw Erskine. He struck out Mickey Mantle four times that afternoon.

I won the Most Valuable Player award for the second time that year. I felt real good about that, especially when I was told that only three other men in National League history had ever won the MVP award more than once: Rogers Hornsby, Carl Hubbell and Stan Musial.

Even though we lost to the Yankees, that '53 team was both game and great. I regard it as the best I ever played on — even better than the 1955 world champions. We didn't even have Newcombe, who was in the Army that year. But we had Gil Hodges, Jim Gilliam, Pee Wee Reese and Billy Cox in the infield; Carl Furillo, Duke Snider and Jackie Robinson in the outfield, me behind the plate, and a pitching staff of Preacher Roe, Joe Black, Carl Erskine, Billy Loes, Johnny Podres, Clem Labine, Russ Meyer, Erv Palica, Jim Hughes and Bob Milliken. We had a good bench with Wayne Belardi, Dick Williams, George Shuba, Bobby Morgan, Don Thompson and Bill Antonello. Shuba was a great pinch hitter that year. The club as a whole hit 205 homers. Three men — Snider, Hodges, and me — each hit forty homers or better. Each of us drove in more than a hundred runs.

For the sixth straight year, I got a raise. My new contract called for $35,000, a boost of $5000. In January of 1954, the B'nai B'rith Association gave me a plaque for "High Principle and Achievement in Sports" during 1953. Then the New York writers at their dinner presented me with a plaque as the Player of the Year.

I don't remember much of what I said that night when I stood up to accept that honor, but one thing still stays in my mind — for it's true of every player I ever knew in big-league baseball. "You have to be a man to be a big-leaguer," I told them — "but you have to have a lot of little boy in you, too."

I don't believe many men have ever been happier than I was that night, but I knew even then that a baseball player can't go on forever, and the next day I got to thinking that I'd maybe never again have as good a chance to really lay something away for Ruthe and the kids. Finally I took my nerve in hand and went to see Buzzie Bavasi, and I told him I didn't think I had signed for enough money.

"How much do you want?" asked Buzzie — and he didn't bat an eye.

"I think I should get another five thousand," I told him.

Buzzie didn't say a word. He took the contract from my hands and tore it in little pieces. He asked his secretary to bring a blank contract, filled it in and told me to sign it. I looked at it. It was for $40,000.

That's the kind of man Buzzie Bavasi is.

TWENTY

BEFORE REPORTING FOR THE 1954 SPRING training season, Ruthe and I decided to take a cruise down South America. We visited all the Caribbean countries. The day we arrived in the Virgin Islands, they declared a holiday. School was let out and they had a big parade. It was my first visit to the Virgin Islands, but I had played in nearby Puerto Rico so many years. Puerto Rico is only half an hour away by plane.

Ruthe and I had a wonderful time on that cruise, getting back to New York in plenty of time for me to take off for Vero Beach.

Practically the first person I walked into when I arrived at the Dodger training camp was Walter Alston. My first skipper, Alston had replaced Charlie Dressen as manager of the Dodgers. I had heard about it before, of course, and in a way I sympathized with Dressen. Charlie had been very popular with the players, and he had been successful. All he did was win two pennants in a row; only he neglected to win a world championship. Now, all Walter had to do was to beat the Yankees in the World Series. No one even thought in terms of winning the pennant first. That was a foregone conclusion.

It was a tough spot for any manager, let alone a fellow who had never managed or even coached in the major leagues before. In fact, Alston told us later that his big league career consisted of only one time at bat — and he struck out.

"It's been a long time, Skip," I said, shaking Alston's hand.

"Yeah, sure nice to see you up here," said Don Newcombe, who had driven with me from New York.

"It's nice to be up here," Alston smiled. "Hey, Newk, you still taking orders from Campy?"

Newk chuckled. "He's something awful, Skip. Getting worse all the time. Treats me like a kid. Fusses over me like a mother hen."

Alston laughed. "Talking about hens, Campy, your folks still have that chicken farm you started for them by hitting those homers back in 1946?"

"Naw," I said. "Pop kept it a couple of years, but he sold it. Pop always said he was a vegetable and fruit man, not a butcher."

Alston nodded. "What else is new, Campy? How's the family?"

"Great, just great. Got six kids now. And own my own home out in Queens, in St. Albans. Ruthe will be glad to see you. She's coming down a little later with her mother and the kids. Wait'll you see our new baby. She's a girl. We call her Princess. But already she's the queen of the Campanella household."

"Sounds like you've been doing all right — as if I didn't know," remarked Alston.

"I've been lucky. And the good Lord's been good to me."

There are two kinds of luck, I've found — good and bad — and every person should expect a little of each. I've had more than my share of the good, so when some of the other kind began coming my way I couldn't very well moan about it.

On Sunday afternoon, March 21, we were playing an exhibition game against the Yankees, and Miami Stadium was jam-packed with people. I read the next day where more than 21,000 people were there, and I believe that's still a record crowd. I singled to open the third inning. Duke Snider, the next batter, hit a ground ball to Billy Martin at second base. He flipped to Rizzuto, the shortstop for the force-out. I hit the dirt and slid in hard trying to break up

184

the double play. My spikes got caught in the dirt, and as I fell, I jarred my left wrist. It throbbed as I trotted back to the dugout, but I continued to play. I didn't say anything — bruises were nothing new to me.

It was our last game in Miami, and Ruthe, her mother, and the kids were flying back home that night. My hand hurt so much by then that I couldn't hardly pack the luggage, and Sandy Amoros, a boy with Montreal the year before, had to help me.

"This hand of mine is really hurting now," I told Ruthe.

"Maybe you broke a bone," Ruthe said. "Why don't you go to a doctor and have it X-rayed?"

I told Doc Wendler about it the next morning, and he put the hand in the whirlpool. That didn't help much. I could hardly swing in batting practice without pain shooting up my arm up to the elbow.

"It's real bad, Doc," I said. "I think it's broke."

"We're playing in Tampa tomorrow," Wendler said, "and I'll take you to an X-ray technician out there. He's one of the best."

I wasn't too surprised when the pictures showed that the bone on the heel of my left hand was broken and that a piece of it had chipped off. We decided not to say anything about it to the newspapers. When we came to Birmingham, on the way up north, Buzzie Bavasi was waiting for us.

"My hand is broken," I told him. "I wouldn't mind it so much, but it's bothering me. I can hardly hold a bat. I can't even swing it good in batting practice."

After watching me for a couple of days, Bavasi called me up to his room and said, "Roy, it looks serious. Let's have the hand operated on."

I'd always been afraid of doctors and knives and I didn't want no one operating on me.

"No," I said, "let's wait. It'll work itself out."

185

But it didn't work itself out. It kept getting worse. We opened the season against the Giants and I hit two home runs off Sal Maglie. Everybody thought the hand would be all right now, but I knew better. I got another home run off Max Surkont in the third game but I didn't get another for three weeks. I got only one hit in my next twenty times at bat, and in May I was hitting .163.

The Dodgers played in Cincinnati on April 29, and I gave in to Buzzie to have the hand X-rayed again. A specialist at Christ Hospital advised that the chips be removed at an early date. "I don't see how he is able to play," the doctor said. He estimated an operation would keep me out ten weeks.

"What do you say, Roy?" Bavasi pleaded.

I shook my head. "No. It's my hand and I ought to know whether I want it cut — and I don't. Besides, I don't want to be out of the lineup that long."

I kept playing, hoping it would get better. But it didn't. The pain was right in the part of the hand where I gripped that bat. Padding didn't do any good. Every time I hit the ball solid, I'd have to go right back to the dugout and stick the hand in the bucket of ice water. Finally, on May 3, while we were in Milwaukee, I gave in.

"Okay, let's get it over with," I told Bavasi.

I was put on a plane and sent home, but the plane had to land in Philadelphia because of a heavy fog in New York. I telephoned Ruthe and told her that I was going to spend the night with my folks. When you're in trouble, no matter how young or old you are, the people who can give comfort are your mother and daddy. Mother said she'd pray for me and for the operation to be a success.

Ruthe met me at Penn Station in New York and we went right to the Long Island College Hospital. I was on the operating table for over an hour. Dr. Herbert Fett performed the operation. He had to make a five-inch incision before the damaged bone could be reached and the chip removed.

"Your case was one of the rarest of its kind," Dr. Fett told me. "There have been only eight such cases on record. The bone chip had become so entangled in the nerve that if you'd waited much longer, your hand might have become paralyzed. You're lucky. You might have lost the use of your hand."

I asked him when he figured I'd be back in action, and he said I'd be lucky to be back in two months. On May 30, less than month later, I was back in the lineup. I hit a home run the next day and another a few days later and it began to look like the operation was a success. Then, suddenly, I began to feel a numbness in my hand. My fingers got stiff, and I had no feeling in some of them. It was then I discovered that there was no muscle where my thumb joins the back of my left hand. Hold your five fingers out, close together, and you'll find a thick lump of muscle standing out along the back of your hand, below your index finger. On my left hand, instead of a lump, there was a depression.

The hand didn't hurt so much; I just couldn't grip the bat tight. When I swung hard, I had to let go with my left hand.

They took me back to Dr. Fett. After examining my hand, he said that the nerves had been irritated during the operation, but I didn't have to worry; it was only a temporary condition of paralysis that would disappear in time.

The paralysis didn't disappear; the hand got worse. Then it began to hurt like a toothache. The pain came from a bone in the palm of my hand. That was from the steady pounding the hand had absorbed from those fast balls.

The doctor said the pain was a good sign because a certain amount of stimulation was necessary for scar tissue to form around the nerve when the bone chip was taken out.

All I knew was that it hurt like the dickens each time I caught a ball, and I couldn't grip the bat properly when I came to bat. The rest of the season I played scared baseball. I was scared because it looked like I was coming to the end of my career. I didn't see how I could keep on that way. Not with one hand, anyway. Baseball was no longer fun; it had become a drudgery. Each morning I'd leave for the ball park wondering if it was my last day. I prayed every night before I went to bed. I was only thirty-two years old and it looked like I was washed up. What was I going to do if I couldn't play ball?

It was my worst year. I caught only 111 games, the fewest in my eighteen years in baseball. I hit only .207 and had nineteen home runs. That was the first time in six years that I hit less than twenty homers. The Dodgers finished third and the Giants won the 1954 pennant easy.

On October 20, I went back for another operation. Tests at the Neurological Institute had shown that there was no nerve reaction in the third and pinky finger of my left hand. I still didn't like the idea of anyone cutting my hand open, but it was a case of curing the hand or being through with baseball.

This time the operation took four hours. It was performed by Dr. Samuel Shenkman, a neurosurgeon, at Queens Memorial Hospital. Scar tissue from the first operation was removed and the nerves were freed.

I had a lot of time to recuperate, four months to be exact. The club sent a whirlpool bath to my store in Harlem and I had it hooked up in the basement so I could bathe the hand every day. Inside of a week I was beginning to have feeling in the hand. I was able to move the fingers that I couldn't

188

move at all during the season. The hand became stronger every day and pretty soon I was able to swing a bat. I swung it every day after that for about twenty minutes a day to strengthen my grip.

Getting feeling and movement back was like a tonic. One day I felt so good that I telephoned Buzzie Bavasi in the Dodgers office, and when he didn't recognize my voice I said, "You're talking to the Most Valuable Player in the National League for 1955."

He laughed, and I laughed, too, but that's how good I felt.

What a difference that 1955 season was. I was a new man; baseball was fun again. I didn't even mind — well, not much — when Alston, still not sure of my hand, I guess, dropped me to eighth in the batting order. That didn't last long, however. I was hitting as well as anybody on the team and pretty soon Walt moved me back to fourth. We won the first ten games that year and something like twenty of our first twenty-two. The pennant race was over soon after it began. The only question was how soon would we mathematically clinch it.

I was on my way to my best year. Actually, I still couldn't move my third and little fingers too well, but I could grip a bat and I could catch the ball in my glove without it hurting me. That's all that counted. By mid-June, I was hitting around .350, and I was leading the league. It was just about then that a foul tip struck my left kneecap. I shook it off and went right on playing, but after hobbling around for a week I agreed to have the knee X-rayed. The X rays showed that I had a loose bone spur, broken off from what they call the patella.

A rest was prescribed. The knee was put in a cast. I was out from June 28 to July 14, and I missed my first All-Star game in seven years, even though I was picked for it. From

189

1949 I had caught fifty-five consecutive All-Star innings, a record.

I came back to the lineup and kept right on hitting. In fact, I was still leading the league until the last few weeks. On September 8, we clinched the pennant, the earliest such date in National League history. Milwaukee was seventeen games behind us. My hitting fell off a little in those last few weeks, but I still managed to finish fourth. Richie Ashburn of Philadelphia won the batting title with .338. Stan Musial and Willie Mays were tied for second with .319, and I was a point behind them. Although I missed more than thirty games, I had thirty-two home runs and 107 runs batted in.

I was disappointed in not winning the batting title since it was about the only thrill I never got in baseball. This may sound like sour grapes, but I always felt I would have won it if my hand hadn't started going bad again that year. I didn't say anything at the time, but the numbness gradually returned in the summer months and the hand became misshapen due to the steady pounding on the nerves. Every time I caught a ball or hit one, there was a shock to the nerves in that hand. I had to use a sponge. That didn't help much, so I began wearing a regular dress glove underneath the mitt. It wasn't so bad when the weather was warm, but on cold days it was miserable.

This was no time to worry about a hand though. We had won the pennant, but there still was a World Series to be won. As always, it was the Yankees we had to beat. The Dodgers had played the Yankees five times in the World Series since 1941, and five times the Yankees had come out as world champions.

"This time," I swore, "it's gonna be different."

It sure looked like we were going to be bridesmaids again when the Yankees beat us in the first two games. We were really down after the second defeat. The fellows had their

190

heads hanging as they dressed in the clubhouse. Then Jackie Robinson spoke up.

"We gotta win this one. If we lose again, they'll be calling us choke-up guys the rest of our lives. Do we want that?"

"Jackie's right," I said. "Let's go out and give 'em hell tomorrow."

It was Bob Turley for the Yankees and Johnny Podres for us as the series switched to Ebbets Field for the third game. In the first inning, after Turley walked Pee Wee, I got my first hit of the series, a home run into the left field stands. I got a double and a single later in the game and we won 8-3.

The fourth game was almost a duplicate of the third. We licked the Yankees, 8-5, and I walloped a home run, a double and a single. I didn't get a hit in either of the next two games, but we won the fifth, 5-3, and lost the sixth, 5-1. That made us all even at three wins apiece.

More than 62,000 fans jammed Yankee Stadium for the seventh and deciding game. Yankee manager Casey Stengel named Tommy Byrne, the veteran lefty, as his pitcher; Alston called on Podres again. For three innings nobody scored. Then, in the fourth, after Duke Snider struck out, I hit a double to left. Carl Furillo grounded out, but Gil Hodges singled and I crossed the plate with the first run of the game. In the sixth, we got our second run. With Reese on first and Snider on second, I laid down a sacrifice bunt and Hodges hit a sacrifice fly to score Reese and make it 2-0. In the Yankees' half of the inning, Billy Martin walked, and Gil McDougald beat out a bunt. Yogi Berra sliced a fly just inside the left field line. Running at top speed, Sandy Amoros made a gloved-hand grab of the ball for the most spectacular catch of the series. A sharp relay from Amoros to Reese to Hodges doubled McDougald off first. Had the ball fallen safely, the Yankees would have tied the score and the winning run would have been on second with none out.

We were still leading 2-0 when Podres left the dugout for the final inning. The players on the bench, getting more nervous by the minute, began telling John how to pitch for the last three outs.

"Leave him alone!" I hollered. "Don't everybody tell him how to pitch. He did all right by himself for eight innings."

Podres got three in a row. Bill Skowron popped up. Bob Cerv struck out. Elston Howard — the last man that stood between the Dodgers and their first world championship in history — swung at a 2-2 pitch and sent a routine grounder to Reese who threw him out at first; and we finally beat the Yankees.

The boys celebrated a little bit in the clubhouse and later that evening Mr. O'Malley threw a victory party at the Bossert Hotel in Brooklyn. The streets were clogged with cheering fans and it was difficult to get into the hotel. Fans were milling around the hotel, dancing and singing in the streets. All of Brooklyn was celebrating. People were cruising around in cars, honking horns, throwing confetti, and really letting their hair down. I never saw anything like it before or since.

In November, with the World Series excitement all over, I got still another thrill. I was voted the National League's Most Valuable Player for the third time. In baseball history, only four others have ever won the MVP award three times; Stan Musial, Jimmy Foxx, Joe DiMaggio and Yogi Berra. It's quite a thing for a fellow like me to be in such company.

At contract signing time, Mr. O'Malley and Buzzie Bavasi called me to the Dodger offices where Buzzie handed me a contract. I took one look and put my name to it as quick as I could. The figure was a round $50,000. Imagine that! Only eight years ago, I had sat in the same office and signed a contract for $185 a month. Now I was earning more than twice as much as that a game. I don't remember ever feeling more proud. Buzzie must have been aware of what I was thinking.

"You know something, Roy," he said. "This contract makes you the highest paid player in the club's history. Nobody, not even Robinson, or Reese, or Snider, ever got paid as much." Then he added, with a little grin, "If you keep on having these kind of years, there won't be enough money in the bank to pay you."

Nineteen-fifty-five stands out in my mind for still another reason which had nothing directly to do with baseball. It was early in the season and the Dodgers were making their first western trip. On the train leaving Penn Station, Lee Scott, the club's traveling secretary, came over to the end of one of the cars where Joe Black, Junior Gilliam, Sandy Amoros, Jackie, Newk and me were sitting and talking and told us that the management at the Chase Hotel in St. Louis had had a change of heart. The bars against Negroes staying at the hotel were down.

Scott said the Chase Hotel was inviting us to stay there the same as the white players, except for a couple of restrictions. Number one, no Negro could eat in the hotel dining room. Number two, no Negro could sit in the lobby of the hotel. Except for those two conditions, we would be treated the same as the white players.

"Those are the rules, boys," Scott said. "You can accept or reject them. That's up to you to decide. Think it over. The front office will go along with any decision you make."

I already had made my decision — even before Scott had finished talking.

"Scotty," I said. "I'm not talking for anybody else; only for myself. It's got to be whole hog or nothing for me. As long as there's any kind of discrimination, you can leave me out. Besides, I've been coming to St. Louis for seven years

193

and if they didn't want me all this time, then I don't want them now."

All the others with one exception nodded their heads and said they'd go along with me. The exception was Jackie Robinson.

"I feel just as strongly about it as anyone," he told Scott, "and I certainly can't go along with the hotel management's so-called change of heart. But this at least is a step in the right direction. It's something our people have been fighting for. Because I believe that getting a foot in the doorway is better than being locked out altogether, I'll accept the invitation to stay with the club at the Chase."

The Chase in St. Louis had been the only hotel along the National League circuit that refused to accept Negroes. We were permitted to stay at the Netherland-Plaza in Cincinnati but had our meals in the rooms.

My first year with the Dodgers, I had stayed at a hotel in St. Louis called the Mid-City. Later, we colored players stayed at the Hotel Atlas which is owned by a friend of mine.

Finally we did agree to stay at the Chase. But that was almost a year later in 1956. This time all bars were down. The management agreed to wipe out all restrictions. We would eat in the dining room and could sit in the lobby if we wished. All of us accepted.

Although I'd had a real successful season in 1955, I was plenty worried when the 1956 season came around. The numbness in my left hand had begun to return. It pained, too, when I gripped the bat. In the early weeks, I had to be taken out now and then because I wasn't helping the team. One afternoon in June, we were playing the Cubs and I tried to pick a man off first. Instead, I hit the batter's bat and broke my throwing hand. My right thumb was double its normal size and the fourth and fifth fingers were broken. The left hand was nearly as bad.

194

"Why don't you ask out?" a newspaperman asked me. "Why don't you get some rest and maybe your hands will heal?"

"Why?" I repeated. "There's no answer to that question. We're trying to win something."

Finally the hand became so painful that I was sent to a doctor. He examined me and said he'd have to operate on the right thumb. He said it would keep me out six weeks or so. When I relayed that information to Bavasi, he said, "We can't afford to lose you for so long. You just got to play if you can."

So I played . . . until the pain became unbearable. They sent me to Dr. Fett again and he had the finger set and the right hand put in a cast. I was out fifteen days and it hurt the rest of the year. I dropped 99 points, hitting only .219, but I was satisfied because we nosed out Milwaukee for the pennant on the final day of the season. I hit twenty home runs that year, practically with no hands.

You can play just so much baseball on sheer stubbornness and will power, and then you've had it; nature takes over. I won the Most Valuable Player award in 1955 playing part of the season with crippled hands. But in 1956 they were too far gone for me to ignore them. The chips in my right thumb jabbed me every time I swung a bat and I knew I needed another operation.

It was just before the World Series with the Yankees, and I was having dinner with my family at home. "Whose turn is it to bless the table?" I asked.

"It's David's," said Ruthe.

We all bowed our heads while David intoned the blessing that begins each meal at the Campanella home. "We thank you, O Lord, for the food we are about to receive."

"Amen," said the children, Roy, Jr., Tony and Princess. "Amen," said Ruthe and me.

Later, after the children had gone off to bed, Ruthe turned to me and said, "There's something bothering you, Campy. Want to tell me what it is?"

"It's the hands, Ruthe, they hurt something awful, especially the right one. I'm afraid . . . well, I'm afraid this might be it. But I can't quit, honey. I'm not through yet."

"I know you're not, Campy."

"A lot of people think I am, but I'm not. I fooled them last year, and I'll fool them next year, too. I'm going to have my thumb operated on, and I'll be okay again."

"Campy! . . . Another operation?"

"Got to. I just can't swing a bat with those bone chips in my hand."

Ruthe sighed. "When do you plan to have the operation?"

"Soon after the World Series. Mr. O'Malley wants me to go with the team to Japan right after the series. But I want to have that operation over with as soon as possible."

"Do you have to go to Japan?" Ruthe asked. "Wouldn't it be better if you stayed home and rested instead of playing more?"

Truthfully, I didn't want to go to Japan. First of all, I was anxious to have that operation on my right thumb. And then, Ruthe couldn't go. She had to stay home with the children and I didn't want to stay away from her for six weeks. Mr. O'Malley kept insisting that I go. He said the people in Japan wanted to see me. Besides, he said I owed it to Uncle Sam. The State Department was sponsoring this good-will trip.

You know who it was made up my mind? President Eisenhower. It happened during the World Series which in 1956 opened in Brooklyn. The President was driven into Ebbets Field in a bubble-dome car. I guess it was bullet-proof. Anyway, a motor convoy came in, with other men running alongside. They opened the center field gates and

196

let them in. Ike stepped out of his car near a first base box and waved to the crowd. Then according to instructions we ballplayers lined up, the Yankees on third base line and the Dodgers on the first base line. In turn, we moved forward to shake his hand. When it came my turn, I said: "Hello, Mr. President," and put out my hand. I was about to move on, when he said, "Campy, you just have to go to Japan."

I was startled. I had no idea that Mr. O'Malley had told the President that I didn't want to go.

"We have to impress these people that we do have democracy here and we have to show them that we are not such bad people because of that atom bomb we dropped on Hiroshima," the President said.

I knew the President was right. There's nothing like sports to cement good will and make better friendships between countries. That's why I wish some day they'd send a team to Russia. Rafer Johnson, the decathlon champion, told me how the Russian boys would come to him when he was there and ask him questions about track and about the United States. They admired his ability to excel in all those events and he made a lot of friends for us in Russia.

That's democracy speaking for itself through sportsmanship. Politicians can't do it. Better understanding is created through competition on the field than over conference tables. Give people of different nations a chance to meet in athletics and you'll find they come to understand each other better.

Getting back to the World Series, the Dodgers started this time like we were going to roll over the Yankees in four straight. We whipped them 6-3 and 13-8 in the first two games. But they came back to win four of the next five. One of those victories was a perfect game by Don Larsen, the first in World Series history. It was the greatest game I ever saw pitched.

The day after the series, the Dodgers flew off to Japan.

We packed every park in every city we played in. They seemed to know nearly all of us by sight. The Japanese people don't have any letter in their alphabet like our "L," and they called me "Campanerra."

"Banzai, Campanerra!" they would yell.

I really enjoyed that trip to Japan. The Japanese were very friendly and great hosts. Their cities were fascinating, especially Tokyo, which is ultra-modern. I did a lot of shopping there and bought a load of stuff such as silk kimonos, pajamas, handkerchiefs, pearls for Ruthe and the older girls, field glasses, cameras, ivory figurines, toys and all sorts of trinkets for the kids, and silk shirts and lounging robes for myself. I even bought some Japanese furniture.

Hiroshima was quite an experience. We played a game there and those Japanese fellows wanted to win that game more than any other game we played in Japan. And they almost did. A little fellow hit a three-run homer in the third inning off Don Drysdale and put them ahead. We couldn't catch them until the eighth when I hit a home run with two aboard and that won the game.

We saw the direct center where the atom bomb exploded. The Dodger players had a group picture taken inside the tremendous crater, next to the tomb of a Japanese soldier. Mr. O'Malley placed a wreath and the fellows laid flowers on the tomb.

They were then building up another city in Hiroshima. Most of the houses were brand-new, but shells of a few old houses remained. Across the street from our hotel, which is called the New Hiroshima Hotel, a museum and shrine contains records and pictures of the bomb shellings.

The records give the time of the bombing: August 6, 1945, at 8:15 A.M. The U.S. B-29 dropped a bomb from an altitude of 8500 meters. It exploded about 570 meters above the ground level and caused a fireball about 60 meters

198

in diameter. A total of 260,000 people were killed and 163,-000 were injured. The whole central part of Hiroshima was completely paralyzed. The fires raged until 10 A.M. the next day. More than 70,000 homes were destroyed. It was impossible to believe that one bomb could do all that damage. I saw quite a few people with scars left over from the bombing. Most of those with more than twenty per cent of their bodies burned either died on the spot or later. Radioactivity killed thousands more. All the bombed buildings had been torn down except two. They were left there for people to remember.

The Memorial Shrine stands in a place they call Peace Park. They have a great big stone there containing the list of all the people that perished in the bombing. There's an inscription on it which reads:

> Repose ye in Peace,
> *For the error shall never be repeated.*

Each August 6, the people of Hiroshima come to this stone to hold memorial services for the dead, and renew their pledge to the cause of world peace.

I remembered then the words of President Eisenhower, and I understood now what he meant that day at home plate.

One thing happened in Hiroshima that should be told. Five of us Dodgers were standing in a group looking at a picture of some of the victims of the bombing. There was Clem Labine, Don Bessent, Ed Roebuck, Don Drysdale and myself. Then a Japanese fellow came over to us and asked, "You're Americans, aren't you?"

We told him we were.

"How do these pictures make you feel?"

For a minute we were all taken aback. Then Labine said

199

very low and deliberate, "Well, we just left Pearl Harbor and we saw the *Arizona,* too. There are still fourteen hundred men entombed on that ship."

Admiral Stump of the U. S. Navy had taken us on a tour of Pearl Harbor while we were there. Seeing the *Arizona,* with part of the hull still sticking out of the water, sent a chill down my spine. They had built a platform on the hull with a plaque and an inscription with the date when the Japanese sank it. December 7, 1941. That long-ago Sunday when I was playing ball at Caguas, and thought that beating Santurce in a double-header was important. I learned for the first time that each day the flag flies over the derelict ship because it is still in commission.

"The American flag," the Admiral told us, "will fly over the *Arizona* and its crew forever."

TWENTY-ONE

LOOKING BACK, I THINK THAT TRAGEDIES LIKE those we saw at Pearl Harbor and Hiroshima helped me later on to appreciate how good it is just to be alive! And to tell the truth, I didn't think I was going to live during those first few days in Glen Cove Hospital following the accident.

Old Campy had made headlines before, but never like this. I guess nothing like this had happened before to anyone in baseball, and that made it news. The lobby of Community Hospital at Glen Cove was bulging with reporters from the New York and Long Island newspapers and the wire services.

Mr. O'Malley had come to the hospital during the morning while the operation was on. An hour after it was over, he and Dr. Sengstaken had a talk, and then they met the reporters.

O'Malley said: "It was a long operation. Dr. Sengstaken and his staff did a fine job. Roy stood it well. The prognosis is hopeful. The spinal cord is not severed, but there is a definite fracture of the neck."

"How about Campy's chances to play again?" a reporter asked.

"I'm more concerned with his physical welfare at the moment than whether he can play ball again," O'Malley answered.

"What about you, Doctor? Can you make any prediction about Campanella's chances of playing again?" the reporter persisted.

"It's really too early to predict. However, if it will help you, I can make some rather general comments," Dr. Sengstaken said.

"First, while Roy's condition is satisfactory, he must still be considered on the critical list. His life was in definite danger. It cannot yet be determined whether the paralysis is permanent.

"There is no guarantee that it will ever heal completely. The spinal cord is affected. It is possible he won't fully recover from the paralysis. He is paralyzed from just below the shoulders to his toes. He cannot push out his arms or grasp, but he can pull in his arms if they are held out for him."

A reporter asked: "How long is the recovery period in cases like this?"

"Anywhere from two months to years before he ever walks again," the surgeon answered. "But remember, I said there is a possibility that he won't fully recover."

"Isn't his age a factor too, when we add in the period needed for recovery?"

"He won't be able to play ball before a year; and, in my

201

opinion, he would be foolish if he tried to continue playing baseball."

Those first hundred days after the accident were the worst in my life. In all that time at Glen Cove Community Hospital, I was strapped in bed, unable to move any part of my body except my arms — and those only a little.

For seven weeks, up to the end of March, I lay there in one position, with the Crutchfield tongs still coming out of my head. They held my broken neck in place in order for it to heal. For three months, I had a tube in my neck.

I thought I was going to die . . . and I nearly did. Honestly, I didn't much care.

Three days after the operation, I caught pneumonia. From then on, my only thought was to keep breathing. I guess I got panicky. That's when I thought I was a goner. They had to cut a hole in my throat so that I could breathe. My lungs were congested and the doctors put a tube in my throat to bring up the mucus from my chest. The medical term for this is a tracheotomy. My left lung had collapsed — though of course I didn't know it then. They had to give me oxygen to stimulate my breathing — like the artificial respiration they give to people who have been nearly drowned.

I was a real sick man . . . real sick. Nobody knows how sick. Not even me. I was hanging between life and death — first a broken neck, then pneumonia.

I was a sight. I was full of tubes. They also had a tube in my nostrils, which was part of the tracheotomy. That tube was to bring up the water from my stomach. Also, I couldn't eat, so I had to be fed through my veins. This was done through tubes in my arms which nourished me with sugar and water solution, glucose.

I had constant headaches because of the Crutchfield tongs and the pair of ten-pound sandbags which held my head in place.

202

The tubes in my nose and throat gagged me. I was lying on an inflated mattress with a motor under it, and it kept pumping in and out. That was to keep my body in motion and keep away bed sores which I would have gotten if I had been lying perfectly still. I couldn't move myself on the bed, so they had to have the bed do the moving.

God was good to me. He spared me. I beat the pneumonia and pulled through. But it was close. That was the second time I thought I was very close to death. The other was when I lay helpless there in the automobile with the motor running and the gasoline flooding underneath the car from the broken gas tank. One spark then, and I would have been burned to death.

By February 5th, a week after the accident, they took the tubes out of my arms and I was able to eat solid food. Not that it tasted good. Nothing was good. I began to think that maybe I'd be better off dead.

I was a helpless cripple. I had to have constant attention, like a baby. I had three nurses around the clock and they were wonderful . . . Mrs. Thelma Sputhard, Mrs. Evelyn Murphy, and Mrs. Florence McAuliffe. They couldn't do enough for old Campy, and I am very grateful to them. They kept my body in wonderful condition. I also had a therapist who came in every weekday, and he would massage me for four or five hours a day. He exercised my arms and legs to prevent the joints from stiffening and also to retain and strengthen the muscles that I could use.

I was strapped to a bed which turned upside down. Every two hours it was turned so that I was alternately on my back and on my stomach. This was to help circulation and prevent skin breakdown which might lead to infection.

The suspension frame of that bed was my prison. My world alternated between floor and ceiling.

Across my bed was a chrome bar with a mirror that could

be turned any way, so that I could see around the room. The first day I looked in it and saw myself was my worst day, in my mind, that is.

I never felt so low as when I looked at myself and saw those tubes and that shaven head.

I cried, "Lord, have mercy on me."

I prayed.

I didn't want to see anyone. I didn't want to have any of my friends see me, the way I looked. Above all, I didn't want my children to see their Daddy in this condition. I begged Ruthe not to bring them. I told her that I didn't want to see nobody but her.

I didn't even want any light on me. I made the nurses keep the blinds closed. I didn't want to be a part of the world. I felt I no longer belonged to it and hoped that it would remember me as I was — as a ballplayer — not like this.

But it was in the darkness that the worst thoughts . . . and fears . . . came. I couldn't chase them. I couldn't stop thinking when I was alone. It was all right when Ruthe was there, talking to me, or when one of the doctors came in and encouraged me. Ruthe brought me meals which she cooked at home and fed me. Not that the hospital food was bad. I just didn't have much appetite, and I wanted her cooking.

But at night, during those long hours when I was alone, I couldn't help thinking bad thoughts. I hardly ever had a full night's sleep. I just couldn't help myself, I couldn't fight off fear.

What will become of me? Am I going to die? If I live, will I be paralyzed and never walk again? Will I always be like this — helpless, unable to move? To have to be fed and bathed and watched over constantly! Will I ever be able to do anything for myself?

And what about my family? Ruthe and the kids? What kind of life will it be for them with a cripple for a husband and a father? Why should they have to suffer too? How will they live? Who's going to support them? Six mouths to feed — seven, counting Ruthe.

Over and over, those thoughts kept gnawing at me. The days were as black as the nights. I lost interest in everything. I was filled with self-pity, with despair.

No matter how hard I tried to think of other things, my mind always came up with the same question: What good will I be to anyone?

I wasn't getting any better.

The doctors and nurses tried to cheer me up. They talked kindly with me and tried to get me interested in other things. They'd turn on the radio and read me the sports pages. They even brought in a TV set; but I didn't want to look at it — which I could have, through the mirror on the bed bar.

I just lay on my back, my brain full of panic. There were times when I felt close to hysterics. I know I cried myself to sleep many a night.

One day Dr. Sengstaken came in, asked the nurse to leave, and closed the door. I couldn't move my head, of course, and couldn't see him. But I could tell by the tone of his voice that he wasn't just coming by to pass the time of day and jolly me up.

He got right to the point. He said he was disappointed in me. He said he expected me to put up more of a battle. He told me to stop feeling sorry for myself, that I wasn't the only man who'd ever been hurt.

"Roy," he said, "you've got to fight. We can only help you ten per cent. The other ninety has to be your effort."

His lecture shook me up. He talked a while longer. After

he left, I began to think. I knew he was right. I had to start thinking right thoughts. I had to get hold of myself.

All my life, whenever I was in trouble, I had turned to God for help. I remembered my Bible. I asked the nurse on duty to get it out of the drawer of the night table and open it to the Twenty-third Psalm.

The Lord is my shepherd. I shall not want.
He maketh me to lie down in green pastures; He leadeth me beside the still waters.
He restoreth my soul; He leadeth me in the paths of righteousness for His name's sake.
Yea, though I walk through the valley of death, I will fear no evil; for Thou art with me; Thy rod and Thy staff they comfort me . . ."

From that moment on, I was on my way back — and I knew I was going to make it. I no longer felt sorry for myself. This was a little tough break that happened to me. But it was something I knew I could handle with the help of the good Lord.

It's quite a nice thing to have God on your side — and I know He is on mine. Three times since the accident, He pulled me through. I'm a lucky man. I thank God that I'm alive.

This was a challenge, the greatest I ever faced. I was determined to lick it. I knew I would have a long, tough fight in front of me. But I was no longer afraid. I knew that He would help me if I helped myself. I was willing to do whatever was necessary, as much as necessary, to beat this thing.

I compared it to baseball. When you're in a slump, you don't feel sorry for yourself. That's when you have to try harder. You don't quit. You have to have the faith, hope, and conviction that you can lick it.

206

Without faith, you don't have much chance. I pray every day now, as I have every day of my life. I used to say a prayer before each game, just before the National Anthem. I didn't pray for victory. The good Lord's not out there to win a ball game for you. You shouldn't ask Him for that kind of help. I prayed that I would stay healthy and not get hurt. I don't think the Lord has turned his back on me.

For a while my condition remained unchanged. There were no reports from the hospital for nearly a month. But on February 19th, three weeks after the accident, the first bulletin was issued. It was not encouraging: "There is no change in the patient's paralysis. His muscle strength has not shown any improvement since his admission to the hospital."

Then came some progress, though very slow. My lung infection had cleared. Then came that wonderful day when they removed the tongs and sandbags from my head. They put on a neck brace instead. But it was then that I found out I had claustrophobia. Imagine that. Here I'd worn a catcher's mask for twenty years without ever having a closed-in feeling.

But they put a plastic mask over my head and shoulders to hold my neck rigid. The face part of it had little holes, like a screen, for air and to be able to see. I only had it on a few minutes. I couldn't get them to get it off fast enough.

"My God, it's choking me. Get it off!" I screamed. "I'm choking, I'm choking!"

They pulled it off quick and had to put me back in traction until they could arrange a substitute. They went to a surgical supply house and this time rigged up something which was more like a catcher's mask.

It had leather pads which held my chin and temple but was open in front where my eyes and mouth were. With that one, I didn't feel like I was all closed in and smothering.

On March 7th, the first encouraging bulletin was issued.

Roy Campanella's general condition shows some improvement. His muscle strength has improved, and he is now able to move his wrists and straighten out his arms. His sense of feeling improves slowly and is now down to the upper abdomen . . .

His general medical condition remains satisfactory. The previous lung infection has cleared completely. The tracheotomy tube is still in place, used chiefly for removal of mucus since his cough-reflex is not strong enough yet to assure clearing of the bronchi.

The traction applied to his head has been removed but he is not permitted any motion of his neck. The vertebra remains in good position and shows the expected healing. A body-turn frame is being used to facilitate nursing care as well as to change his position periodically. Physiotherapy has been started, assuring exercise to his arms and legs.

He enjoys television and radio and will be having visitors in the near future. He is following the activities of his team closely.

I began to do my own exercises for the first time. A special steel bar was placed across the bed, above my head. My hands were strapped to the bar, as I couldn't grip it. But I was able to try to chin myself. It was very good exercise for my chest and arm muscles. I was able to do twenty to twenty-five a day. These exercises restored strength to my arms. I did the bar exercises on my back. Then, they'd turn the bed over and I'd lay with my face in the mask which held my neck and I'd be on my stomach. That's where I would do my reading, and another exercise for my hands, trying to squeeze a small rubber ball.

In the beginning, I couldn't do a thing, and the nurses would read the sports pages to me. But when I was able to

208

be turned over, I could read a newspaper by myself. I could keep in touch with baseball a lot better that way. And I learned to turn the pages. It was hard but I didn't have any help. I wanted to do it myself.

One day, something happened that made me feel very proud. I was rolling that rubber ball with my hand and trying to squeeze it, although I still didn't have any movement in my fingers. Then suddenly, I was able to pick it up with one hand. Then the other. Actually, I was able to do it with my wrist muscles and thumb. The four fingers on each hand are stiff and I cannot move them. But I picked it up — and it was the first time since the accident that I ever picked up anything.

It was the day before the baseball season started and it meant a great deal to me.

Thinking about baseball was both good and bad for me. During spring training, I'd think of how I should be there in Florida instead of lying here in this bed for a hundred days, and I'd wish how I was back down there bullin' with the fellas in Campy's Bullpen. That's a bench outside the kitchen in Dodgertown at Vero Beach. I used to sit there after lunch and talk with anyone who felt like talking. They painted right on the outside wall of the building, above the bench, a sign: CAMPY'S BULLPEN.

Being able to pick up that ball was wonderful, and I kept trying to get more movement in my arms and legs. While I was trying so hard to help myself, I was encouraged by others. Letters poured in from all over the world. I never thought that many people knew old Campy. Famous people and just plain folks. I appreciated that. It gave me a lift. Every letter I received helped.

I had one from Red Skelton, quite a long one. At that time, his son had trouble, too. That was Richard, who later died of leukemia. Perry Como, Art Linkletter . . . they sent telegrams. I received so many. Even from President Eisenhower and another from Vice President Nixon. Think of that!

The Dodger players sent me a very beautiful card. It was a funny one. "If you don't hurry up and get up, we'll come up there and go to bed with you!"

And then I got a kick out of one from the Cleveland Indians. Each player wrote me an individual card saying he hoped I'd get well and signed his name, and I thought that was very nice of them. Being in the American League, too. And Frank Lane, the general manager at Cleveland, also wrote me a nice letter.

I also received one from the Baltimore Orioles. "Although you aren't in our league, you're still a champion in baseball," they wrote.

I got a fine card from the Yankees, and Dan Topping, their owner, sent me one of the most beautiful azaleas I ever saw. I had it replanted outside my home.

Branch Rickey, my old boss, wrote me a wonderful letter, too. So did Lou Perini of Milwaukee. I guess I heard from just about every club. Jackie Robinson and Eddie Stanky wrote, too. And Junius Kellogg got in touch with Ruthe and offered to give me all the help he could. Kellogg has been through this, too. He advised me on quite a few things. He's the basketball player from Manhattan College who was paralyzed from the waist down in an auto accident while traveling with the Harlem Globetrotters.

I still couldn't have any visitors, but in the middle of April, after they took the tracheotomy tube out of my throat, I asked Ruthe to bring the children. I waited until then because I didn't want them to see me looking like that with a thing in my throat.

But when they came, I felt terrible. I had tears in my eyes. I was afraid of facing them. But they seemed to cheer me

210

up. They never did say: "Gee, Daddy, why are you in bed?" or "Daddy, why can't you move?" They never once mentioned anything like that. Not once.

I realized then how silly I was to have been scared to have them see me. I was happy to see them. It wasn't only that deep-down feeling of just seeing your own children. Every father has that. But I guess you feel it more when something happens to you and they are so wonderful about it.

A week later, my mother and daddy came all the way down from Philadelphia to spend a Sunday with me there in the hospital. I know they felt pretty bad at seeing me that way, but they were calm and gracious and I enjoyed their visit.

The one thing I don't want is for people to feel sorry for me.

TWENTY-TWO

During most of the three months I spent there at Glen Cove, I made steady progress. Slow but steady. Each day the therapist came to massage my body, trying to revive what muscles remained, trying to restore life to those that had quit. He even exercised the muscles in my fingers and ankles. Mostly I lay in bed, a tube in my throat to help me with my breathing. Every two hours, nurses would turn me face down to help my circulation and limit bed sores, and massage my back. I still wore a heavy corset around my body and there was a bulky metal frame over my head. Naturally, I had to have someone feed me, wash me, shave me, even turn me over. I began to get some feeling lower down in my body after the first month. The doctor told me to try always to move my legs, regardless. I tried but couldn't. I still can't. But I started feeling little sensations running down my legs. I kept trying. I'd talk to myself. I'd say, *Campy, raise that left leg!* I'd try. At first I didn't feel anything. Then I'd feel a sensation in my hips when I tried to move my legs. It was as if my legs were trying to transmit something to my brain, but there's a block in my vertebrae and it stopped right there. At first, I'd get spasms. My body used to shake something awful, and I could hardly catch my breath. That stopped after a while.

Later I watched baseball games on television every chance. For a long time I couldn't even talk about baseball, I felt so sad. Now I couldn't wait for the games to begin. Talk about a bedside manager. I was calling the pitches, second-guessing the manager and disagreeing with the umpire.

The most depressing thing about watching the Dodgers play was seeing them lose. I couldn't understand it. I knew they weren't that bad. While watching TV, I wore special glasses because I was flat on my back. They were weird-looking things, but they proved to be a godsend. They're called prism glasses. The nurse would slide the TV set on a roller right over my stomach and I'd be looking through these glasses at the ceiling, but I'd see the TV screen. The best way to explain what kind of glasses they are, is that if a person was to look through them from a standing position, he would see his feet. I looked straight up at the ceiling from my bed and saw the TV screen right over my stomach.

I began taking more of an interest in the world outside the hospital. I still wasn't allowed to have any visitors outside of my immediate family except for a few close associates. Mr. O'Malley was one of my first visitors after my operation. My mind was still not clear at the time. I couldn't see him, but I heard him say: "Campy, this is Walter O'Malley. Don't worry about a thing. I'll be back when you feel better."

He didn't come back for about a month. He had a little trouble of his own. He had to go to a hospital for an operation but he visited me as soon as he was discharged.

"Campy," he said, "all I'm interested in right now is for you to walk again. I don't care whether you ever play ball for me again. Walk and I'll be satisfied. Another thing — you'll never have to worry about a job. You have one with the Dodgers the rest of your life. If you can walk, you'll be a full-time Dodger coach. If not, you'll work for the organization in the front office. That's a promise."

All the time I was in the hospital, every two weeks I got my Dodger salary check. I still do.

By early May of 1958, I had reached the stage where the doctors at Glen Cove Hospital could do nothing more for me. I needed more advanced treatment.

Dr. Charles Hayden and Ruthe had been considering several hospitals, even one in Italy. But Dr. Hayden finally decided on the New York University — Bellevue Medical Center's Institute of Physical Medicine and Rehabilitation at 34th Street and First Avenue in New York City. He contacted their head man, Dr. Howard A. Rusk, who came out and examined me. He examined every inch of my body — legs, arms, fingers, toes. That was May 2.

"Roy," he said finally, "you're not quite ready for our Institute. As a rule, a patient must be in a more advanced stage before we accept him. But your physical makeup is so excellent that we will make an exception. But remember this, Roy. It's going to be a lot of tough work. You're going to have to work harder than you've ever worked before. At times, you're going to become discouraged, discontented and maybe disillusioned. But in time, if you work hard and

213

faithfully, you may leave the hospital under your own power. Do you think you're ready for it?"

All I said was, "Doc, when can we start?"

On Monday, May 5, with no publicity at all, I was taken down the back way in the freight elevator, lifted into a car and delivered to Rusk Institute. The following day, a press conference was held with Dr. Rusk in the Dodger offices at Montague Street in Brooklyn. Dr. Donald S. Covalt, assistant director at the Institute, described my condition to the newspaper boys. It was not encouraging.

"Campanella remains a quadriplegic case," Dr. Covalt said. "He can move his shoulders very well, but he has only weak movement in his wrists and there is no muscle function below his arms.

"It is not a good sign. We would like to have more continued progressive movement. At the present time we feel rehabilitation should be started in order to guard against softening of the bones. Eventually we will get him in a wheel chair. He is in great spirits and he is anxious to get started.

"How much movement will return or how long it will take is conjecture. Before World War II, such cases remained in bed the rest of their lives. Since then, however, much has been accomplished. We have treated nearly 400 severely disabled cases and about 75 per cent, though still paralyzed, were able to return to productive places in society. Campanella has the drive, he has the spirit. However, the longer a quadriplegic remains without movement, the less chance he has for recovery."

A reporter asked Dr. Rusk for further comment. "He has to get more function from his triceps muscles. If he gets back no more movement than he has now, he won't be able to walk. His progress has been slow; too slow in fact for me to give you much encouragement. But one thing is very

214

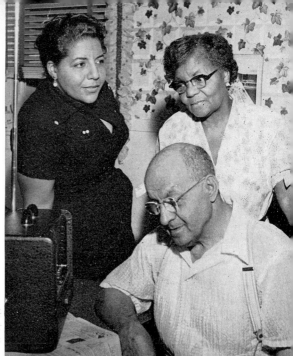

Three of my favorites—Sister Doris, who stood her ground with me in plenty of childhood battles, my mother and dad. Pop said they were listening to a Dodger game when this was snapped. By their looks, we must've been losing.

Photo by Malcolm Poindexter

ORIOLE PARK
1939.

Photo by Paul Henderson, Baltimore, Md.

By 1939, I was feeling my oats with the Baltimore Elite Giants. This is the team that afforded me a solid background for catching that stood me well later on. Almost eighteen when this was taken, I'm third from right in the front row. Ten years later I caught my first game in the major leagues.

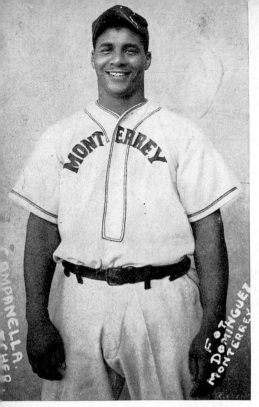

In 1942, I went south of the border to catch with the Monterrey team. I liked everything about Mexico including the wages. Actually, this is a postcard I sent home to the folks. Not as exciting as one of a bullfight but I thought it was just fine.

The Fotomart, Nashua, N. H.

In '49 I had my first job in organized baseball, as catcher for the Nashua team in New Hampshire. The other Negro with that Dodgers farm team that year was pitcher Don Newcombe (center, rear row). On Don's right is Walter Alston, our manager. Alston and I joined forces later at St. Paul and finally with Brooklyn in '54.

Honors, scrolls and things like that mean a lot to a fellow . . . but even more to his folks. Mom seems pleased as punch here, and Dad, Doris and Ruthe look sort of proud too.

Wide World Photos

Contract signing with Mr. Rickey was always reported as a cat-and-mouse game — with the player supposed to be the mouse. But for me, it was always a fine, warm experience. Looking back, I guess I owe more to Branch Rickey than he ever paid me. This was in 1950, my second full year with Brooklyn, and I got a good raise.

A good catcher should be a jealous mistress of home plate. Taken in a '55 game with the Phillies, I like this shot because it has a bit of everything. But what I like best is that I've made the tag on Eddie Waitkus. We won the pennant that year but the Yankees took us in six games.

Brooklyn opened the 1954 season at the Polo Grounds and I opened with a home run off Sal Maglie. Here, Junior Gilliam and Jackie Robinson offer greetings and salutations. But '54 was the season the Giants stormed back to win the pennant ... yes, and beat Cleveland four straight!

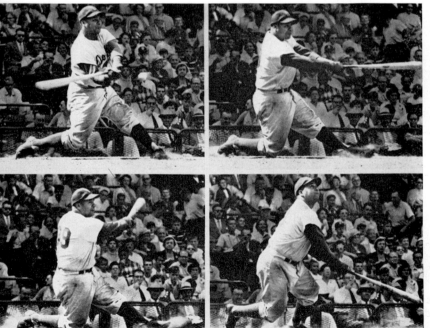

Ever since the beginning, I had a hitch in my batting swing. Here's a good sequence showing how my right knee dips as I take a full cut. It looks like I hit it a mile — straight up. That's like blowing a 3-foot putt.

On January 19, 1959, I had my second scrape with death almost within the year. A big air compressor tore loose from a truck on the Long Island Expressway, jumped the divider and rammed us nearly head-on. Strapped in the front seat beside my driver, all I got was a shaking around.

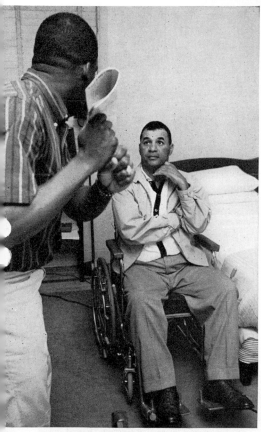

Robert W. Kelley — courtesy LIFE Magazine.
Copr. 1959 Time Inc.

the Institute in New York, my convalescence s hastened by everybody. Dr. Rusk, his rkers and the patients themselves — they were just great! Here, one of the therapists nonstrates his batting technique. Those arms, ists and hands, I got to admire.

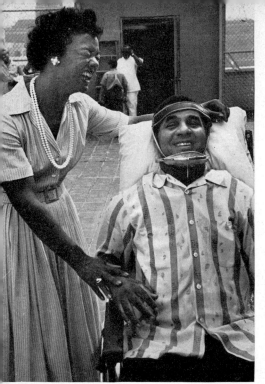

Any man with a family is never out of touch very long. On good days, just being on the roof at the Institute with the sun shining, blue skies above and Ruthe by my side . . . well, I could start counting my blessings again.

There's a bit of clown, or maybe it's ham, in most of us—and our youngest, Princess, sure wasn't short-changed! Here, Roy Jr. isn't buying what Princess is selling. As for Tony, Ruthe and me — we dig her the most!

There's so much more to catching — or living — than just going through the motions. Here, in fielding practice, Roseboro works on the quick peg to second as Pignatano observes.

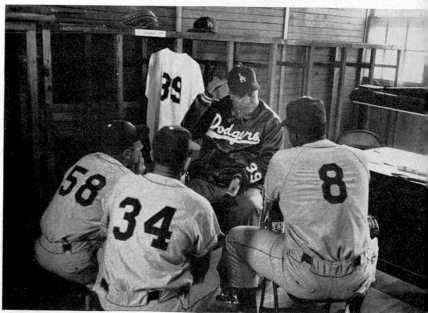

Just being back with the Dodgers at Vero Beach in '59 was a wonderful tonic for me. My main duties were to help the young catchers all I could. Here, I'm stressing a point for John Roseboro as Norm Sherry (34) and Joe Pignatano (58) listen.

It's good to be alive! Man, it's the mostest thing there is, and any time you feel different, don't be afraid to get down on your knees and talk things over with the Lord.

much in his favor. His spirit, morale and attitude are very high. He is eager to help himself. That's bound to be a big factor toward any eventual recovery."

Dr. Rusk told the reporters that he expected me to stay at the Institute about a year. In ten days I was to start exercises to increase movement in my arms and to induce movement in my legs and other parts of my body.

It didn't work out that way, though. The day after I was brought to the Institute, I caught cold and that set me back quite a bit. I ran a fever for nearly three weeks. I still had difficulty breathing and I was susceptible to any kind of cold. My lungs weren't working right and I had headaches from those prongs and sandbags that had been used after the operation.

I didn't leave my room for nearly two months, and I was in bed all that time. Those patients who had been admitted with me were mostly wheel chair cases by now. After classes, they were allowed out in the corridors, in the recreation halls — even outside on nice warm days. But mostly they would sit in the halls and chat.

My nurses said that the other patients kept asking why I remained room-ridden. They thought I didn't want to mingle, that I was brooding and was angry with the world. They didn't realize I wasn't as advanced as they were to start with. Normally a patient can begin exercise classes his first day at the Institute.

Well, I couldn't get out of my bed, let alone my room. To tell the truth, I was feeling so blue then that I didn't want to come out. I welcomed the solitude of the four walls.

I didn't start to go to exercise classes until August, three months after I was admitted. Before going to classes, I had to learn to sit up. Believe me, that took some doing. Remember, I had been lying flat on my back on a Stryker frame bed for nearly six months.

At first, they put me on a "tilt board," a ten-foot board, supported by two wheels, that is just like a sliding board. They strap the patient on it so as to support his back and they wind it up gradually so many degrees at a time until you are in an almost vertical position. That is to get blood circulating. It also pushes the weight down on the feet and legs to strengthen them.

The first time they put me on the tilt board I lasted about fifteen minutes. That was considered very good for a first try. You see, all the blood rushes down from your head and the upper part of your body and usually you black out. I didn't black out, but I got very dizzy and I asked the attendant to let me down. At first, the board is tilted at about a 60 per cent angle; then they raise it to about 75 per cent, then 90 per cent, and finally straight up and down. I felt funny at first looking at people from a tilt board. When you're on your back for so long, people look different when you stand again.

I was on the tilt board twice a day for over a week, fifteen minutes at a time. I'd get tired at times, but I wouldn't feel it in my legs because I had no feeling. Usually after getting off the tilt board my neck would ache. That's because I was still wearing my bulky neck brace.

The next step was sitting in a wheel chair. That was quite a feat in itself. It was a good feeling, sitting in that chair. For the first time I felt that I was really making progress. If I could sit, I could learn to manipulate the chair. If I could move around, there was no telling what I could do next. Then I got a setback. A muscle knotted up in my buttocks from sitting and I developed some kind of an abrasion. I just couldn't sit without pain. Back to bed I went. It bothered me a lot.

Finally, when I began to feel better, I sat up again in the wheel chair for fifteen minutes at a time. Then came the

216

most difficult thing of all — feeding myself. I had eaten lying down for so long that I found it impossible to eat sitting up! It was hard learning how to eat lying down, but it was twice as hard learning how to eat sitting up. For some reason the food didn't taste good and I couldn't swallow it.

At first they tried to teach me to feed myself without mechanical help. They placed food in my hands and I'd try to lift it up to my mouth. I could lift my arms, but they weren't strong enough to go all the way. And the times I managed to lift it that high, I had no sense of direction. I'd get the food on my nose, in my eyes, sometimes even on my head. Once in a while I'd hit my mouth. You see, I had no control of my fingers — I still don't, just my thumbs. Spoon-training followed. They put the spoon handle between my thumb and index finger. But it sure was slow work. I wondered if I'd ever be able to feed myself. I'd ask the nurses if there was anybody else like me in the Institute who could feed himself. "Don't worry about it," they'd say, "you'll feed yourself." But I did worry.

Then one day they attached a gadget to my right wrist. They'd fit a spoon or a fork in it, and it made eating easier. I was still in no position to eat in the hospital dining room — the goal of all quads.

I never asked for help in feeding myself. The only thing is that when I was having too much trouble and my arms would get tired, I'd ask to be laid back down. Come to think of it, I don't think I ever asked the doctors, all the time I was in the hospital, how long it would be before I could walk again, or even if I'd *ever* walk again. I just prayed to the good Lord for help and guidance and I read the Bible every chance I had. When the day comes that I'll take my first step, I'll get on my knees and thank God for keeping me alive. I'll thank Him for giving me the will power that wouldn't let me quit, for making me fight on when things were real black. This is all God's will, and I put myself in His hands.

By the middle of August I was able to get straight up and down on the tilt board; I was able to sit in the wheel chair for an hour at a time; and with the help of the gadget I was able to feed myself without being embarrassed. All in all, I was feeling quite a bit better and I began to get the urge to get out of the room. I wanted to talk to the other patients. I felt it would be good for me. It's bad to be confined in one room for so long, but it's worse when you have no one to talk to — I mean someone of your kind, one who's stricken as you are.

The doctors said I could have as many visitors as I wanted, in fact seeing and talking to outsiders would do me a lot of good. Ruthe urged me to let people come visit with me. Finally, she asked Dr. Rusk to talk to me about it.

"Roy's afraid they won't accept him," Dr. Rusk said. "But they will — when he accepts himself."

He was 100 per cent correct.

I simply didn't want visitors because I was afraid they'd pity me. And the last thing I want is pity. That's what I like about Dr. Rusk. He doesn't believe in pity. Work — that's what he believes in! His theory is that no matter how sick a person is, no matter how handicapped, there is something he can do, both mentally and physically.

I never met a man like Dr. Rusk in all my life. I never saw a man more dedicated to his work. It's a privilege to have a man like that living in this country. Thanks to him and his dream, and his ideas, and his perseverance, thousands of persons live today who would have been dead fifteen or twenty years ago. It's Dr. Rusk's belief that as long as you can breathe you should hope.

As soon as I was ready for it, they rolled me around to see the other men and women who were in the same boat with

218

me. It was part of the program that is always used at the Institute. Every once in a while, when I'd get a little blue and slack off in my work, Dr. Rusk or one of his assistants would say:

"Who do you think you are, Campanella, somebody special?"

That would shake me loose from myself, and then I'd smile and get back to work.

There was one morning, though, when I really felt about as low as you can get. This was aside from the four or five months when things were at their roughest — especially those first few days when I didn't know for sure whether I'd live or die. And didn't care! I've got to tell you about that most miserable of all mornings for me.

What week or month it was isn't important. Because when you're coming back from a far ways off, the days and nights become one drawn-out piece of eternity.

I was attending class in the hospital. We were up on the fourth floor and the nurse this day was a young lady named Carol Cole. She had been working with us quads for weeks. A quad cannot push with his arms. Scoop and pull, yes, but not push. This day, undergoing "range motion" with four or five other quads, I had finally turned myself over on a floor mat. Later on, I'll explain to you what those classes are — what is involved, such as pushups, weight lifting, range motion, breathing, stretching and all the rest of it. But up to that point turning over on that mat was about the most important single accomplishment in my entire life. I thought I'd left an arm on that mat. But *I had* turned myself over — from my back to my stomach. And in time, those other pupils had done it too. In some of those exercises it got so that I could lead the class. To hear me giving my buddies the encouragement from my "coaching box" must have sounded pretty funny.

219

This day our instructor, Therapist Cole, had propped us all up with our backs against the wall. I had asked to try to sit up on my own. Without support. I toppled over a few times. In fact, twice I fell hard. Talk about awkward falls! I never saw — or felt — anything like it playing ball. And I've been hit plenty hard in my day. You topple with the thud of a sandbag, because even if your arms may *want* to break your fall they can't.

But finally there we all were, propped against that wall in a sitting position and waiting for our next instruction. Miss Cole brought out a soft white volley ball.

"Now," she said with a big smile, "I'm going to teach you how to catch a ball."

It didn't hit me at first. I didn't get the full meaning of it all at once. But then it came through to me. She was talking to me as well as the rest of us. She was gonna teach me — Roy Campanella — how to catch a ball!

It hit me a wallop.

There I was, a guy whose claim to fame — such as it's been — had been built on my ability to catch a ball. Cripes. Roy Campanella. Campy — Number 39 with the Brooklyn Dodgers — a fellow who had risen from a $45 a month Negro league performer to a $50,000 a year man, a three-time Most Valuable Player, a member of a world championship club — all because of his ability to do one thing better than most: catch a ball.

The pitchers I had caught tumbled through my mind like a big parade, Swimmy White, the first pitcher I handled in Negro ball — Swimmy and his scuffed-up emery ball. Dave Barnhill . . . Terris McDuffie . . . Johnny Podres . . . Rex Barney . . . Don Newcombe . . . Don Drysdale . . . Preacher Roe . . . Ralph Branca . . . Ewell Blackwell . . . Robin Roberts . . . Sal Maglie . . . Carl Erskine

. . . Joe Black, and so many throwers and pitchers in and out of the country.

"You're going to teach me to *catch?*"

I said it so loud it startled her and the class. And then, I guess, she must have understood the look on my face. It must have been pathetic because she turned away and busied herself with something else for a moment or two. She acted like she had a speck of dirt in her eye. I also had something in my eye, but it wasn't a speck of dirt. The pretty little nurse standing before me, poised to toss the volley ball to me — and me trying desperately to keep from toppling over. I knew what I had known for months. That I had a long, hard fight ahead of me.

"Okay, Nurse, let's go," I said after I had got hold of myself. "This should be very interesting."

Actually, this was something I'd known about and had been dreading. But I hadn't brought myself around to think about it. I knew that this step was part of the exercise designed to help bring a person back by getting him to use his arm reflexes.

The nurse took turns lobbing that ball to each of us. I watched the others strain as they tried to "box" or cage the ball with their arms. They just couldn't manage it. When it came my turn, she lobbed the ball to me — gentle-like from only about seven or eight feet away. She threw it about chest high so I could catch it between my arms and wrists. I couldn't raise my arms quick enough. Sometimes she lobbed the ball higher than my chest and I couldn't get my arms that high to even block it. It would strike me in the face and shoulders. I felt terribly clumsy and I was really embarrassed. Gee, the way I used to catch standing up and now I can't even catch sitting down. Not only that, but when I would try to catch it I'd topple over. Not once, but several times. And each time she'd have to set me up again.

"That wasn't fair, Nurse!" I managed to stammer. "You're cheating. You caught me off guard."

We both knew it wasn't so. She wasn't cheating, and I was ready all right, but my body was not. Neither were my arms.

Man, isn't this something, I thought. Not to be able to catch a ball that size. Why, it's ten times bigger than a baseball. And she wants me to throw it, too. How can you throw it when you can't even catch it? I smiled weakly and tried to cover my miserable feeling with what I intended to be a wise remark.

"I'll get back at you some day. Just as soon as I get well, I'll *really* whip it to you. We'll see if *you'll* catch it."

She laughed at that. I didn't feel like laughing, really.

For a fact, I was starting all over again. It was true. I couldn't catch that volley ball then . . . You see, physically, it's like being a baby. Learning to crawl and then, maybe, walk — and then, maybe, catch.

TWENTY-THREE

ONCE I HAD GOTTEN OVER THE FEELING that I didn't want to see people, especially visitors, one of the first to visit me was Mr. Bernard Baruch. Mr. Baruch is one of the chief contributors to the Institute. We had a pleasant chat during which Mr. Baruch said that it makes him feel awfully good to be able to contribute to a cause that helps people like me. Averill Harriman, at the time Governor of New York State, was another caller. He offered me a job with the New York Boxing Commission.

"I talked it over with Julius Helfand, chairman of the

State Boxing Commission," he said, "and we agreed we'd like you to become a Deputy Boxing Commissioner."

He said it paid $8000 a year.

"What would I do?" I asked.

"We can go over the details later," he said. Then he said some nice things concerning my contribution to sports, what an example I'd be to young boxers and all. After thinking it over for a few days, I informed the Governor that I could not accept the job. I was a baseball man, not a boxing man. It wouldn't be right to accept a job that I didn't know anything about.

Then one day they told me that Bill Veeck, now head man of the Chicago White Sox, was downstairs. I said send him up. I had a special telephone in my room by then. All I had to do was reach out and press a button with my hand and that would connect me with the operator. Then I'd give her the number I wanted and she'd keep the line open. I'd just lie on my back and talk and the special microphone attachment would pick up my voice. I'd receive calls the same way.

I had an interesting visit with Bill Veeck. He told me about being a patient in the same hospital years before when he had a leg amputated after being wounded in the war. I couldn't see him because I was lying on the striker bed, face downward. All I could see were his feet. He told me about trying to get a big league team in New York to take the place of the Giants. He said he had come to New York to talk with Mr. Bernard Gimbel about that, and that if he ever did get control of a team in New York he'd want me to be connected with it in some capacity. He left after about a half hour and told me he would keep in touch with me.

I had a visit from some of my teammates one day. Reese, Snider, Furillo, Hodges and Erskine came over, when they were rained out of a game in Philadelphia. You know how

223

players gripe. I told them, "Fellas, don't ever gripe about nothing. If you've got to live like this, there's nothing else to gripe about."

I got a surprise visit from Ted Williams one day when the Boston Red Sox were in town. It was early one Sunday morning before he left for Yankee Stadium. We talked pitchers and hitters. Before Ted left, he asked me not to tell anybody that he had been up to see me. This Williams is quite a fellow. He's forever doing nice things for people, but he don't want anyone to know nothing.

Leo Durocher, my first skipper in Brooklyn, stopped by and we had quite a gabfest. Leo was good medicine. He's so full of life, so full of spirit, that he makes you climb up the ladder a little bit.

"When are you getting up, Roy?" he barked out with that big voice of his. Man, his whisper can jar a deaf man.

"I'm on my way up now, Skip," I answered. "Don't worry about me. I'm going to make it."

It was the day after Durocher visited me that I started going to classes. They took me up the elevator to the seventh floor where they have the exercises. There were about fifteen others in the big room that looked like a gymnasium. They were paraplegics, and quads, like myself, both male and female, ranging in age from sixteen to about fifty. An instructor attached an eight-pound weight to my arms, put gloves on my hands, and told me to try to lift it. I surprised everybody by lifting it. You have to raise your arms, with those iron weights, from your waist up to your chin. They judge you on the number of times you can lift those weights, and I was able to do twenty in a row the first day. That was considered excellent. Later I got so I could lift up to 35-pound weights, and I could do it as many as sixty times.

We had different kinds of exercises. We'd start with a half hour of weight lifting, then there'd be range of motion.

224

That's when they exercise your arms and legs in different ranges and stretch them. The purpose of range of motion exercise is to keep you loose. From being inactive, a quad's muscles draw and they tighten up and they've got to be loosened or else you can never use them. Then there was the mat class. We had to roll over from our back to our stomach and back again. That was the worst of them all. Those mat classes sure wore me out. That was about the only exercise that really hurt. Each time I'd roll over on my shoulders, I'd get pain. I had always stayed on my back and when they turned me over in the Stryker frame, the whole bed would turn over with me. So it took me a long time to get accustomed to do it without pain.

One exercise was called occupational therapy. They fitted plastic hands over mine and with them I would write on a typewriter and finger an organ. This exercise is to rejuvenate and strengthen the fingers that are still able to function.

The other was a breathing exercise. They fitted a gadget over my mouth for me to inhale and exhale oxygen. My lungs weren't collapsed, but there was something wrong with my breathing, and for the longest time I couldn't say a whole sentence without losing breath. I tired easily from talking. Also I had a lot of mucus from lying down so long, and this oxygen breathing helped me clear it up. I breathed that oxygen for half an hour a day for five of the six months I was there.

All in all, I was kept pretty busy from the time I woke up, around eight o'clock, until I went to bed, around nine or ten. At the end of the day, I was a pretty tired fellow. I remember one day Don Zimmer, Johnny Roseboro and Johnny Podres dropped in on me when the Dodgers were East. They went to a few of my classes. "Man," Zimmer said, "we never worked that hard in spring training."

With it all, I still found time to read my Bible every day. That was one of my pleasures. For a long time I couldn't turn the pages, and I had to ask Leroy Newsome, my attendant, to do that for me. He'd urge me to try to turn the pages myself, but I couldn't do it. Every day I'd try and finally I'd plead: "Come on, Leroy, I'll do it tomorrow."

Then one day Leroy walked out in the corridor after giving me my Bible. When he came back, he asked me, "Want me to turn the page?"

"Not today, Leroy," I said. "I've just learned to turn them myself."

He didn't believe me. He came over and looked. I had turned to the 101st Psalm: "I will sing of mercy and judgment: unto Thee, O Lord, will I sing . . ."

TWENTY-FOUR

SOON AFTER I STARTED SITTING UP REGU-larly, I wanted to get around in the hospital and visit with the other patients. I didn't want to be confined any more. Just sitting in your room and not talking to people is bound to make you sulk. I had had enough of that. Dr. Rusk was very eager for me to visit with the other patients who'd had similar accidents. He felt that I would help their morale, and they in turn would cheer me up.

I didn't know what to expect that first time I went out to mingle with the others in the hall, but it turned out to be very interesting. They were all friendly and we talked about lots of things. Nearly all of them were more advanced than I was and they helped me a lot with good advice. I asked them what could I hope to do, how long would it take for me to do it, and how much more movement I might get back in my arms and legs. Would I ever be able to walk again, and how much longer should I expect to stay in the hospital.

I suppose I could have asked the doctors all these questions, and it wasn't because I was shy or I was afraid of the answers. I knew right from the start that I was hurt pretty bad and I knew what the odds were against my ever walking again, but somehow I felt more at home with the patients. We were all in the same boat, we all had the same problems, we all had the same thoughts, the same hopes, the same joys and thrills when we accomplished something. We were good for each other.

During those first few months at the Institute I used to think about Mr. Rickey whenever I'd watch a TV game that Pittsburgh was playing. I'd heard that he had suffered a serious heart attack. So you can imagine my surprise when one rainy morning in August I saw someone coming towards me. He was carrying a cane and he stooped a little. But I didn't need a second look. It was Mr. Rickey. I had been sitting by myself in the hall and just thinking things over when there he was.

"Well, Campy," he said. "It looks like the two of us have been having our troubles. How you feeling, boy?"

I was flabbergasted. "How am I feeling, Mr. Rickey?" I said. "To tell the truth I wasn't feeling so good — until this moment. But right now I feel real good!"

He brushed off my question about his health. "Nothing much," he said. "Just a little flare-up with the old pump. Doctors —" he snorted — "they can be the very devil, can't they, Campy?"

I had to laugh.

I told him that they'd read me his wire soon after the accident . . . and it helped. He liked that. "Son," he said, "at that moment only a wire from the good Lord Himself could have meant very much to you. But I'm glad you received it and that you knew that I, along with the rest of the country, was thinking of you."

Then he broke it off and talked of the future. One thing, especially, I remember, was how interested he was in the little exercises I was trying to do with my arms as we talked.

"Constant exercise like that has got to help you," he said. "It's like a ballplayer having a bruised finger. He's told to soak it for long periods in hot water, but instead of soaking it a half hour at a time, he gives it five minutes and thinks he's done his part. The same applies to you, Campy. Don't ever do less then they ask. Continue to do more and the next time I see you, why, I'll bet . . . well, I'll bet you a quarter you'll grab my hand instead of the other way around."

We had a good bull session on baseball. He told me that before my accident he had picked the Dodgers to win the pennant. But in all his talks on the subject, he had added that the club had an Achilles heel. The Dodgers were deep in everything, he said, except catchers . . . if something should happen to Campanella, it would be tough.

He also told me about his mother-in-law. A broken hip — her second in eight years — along with pneumonia, had finally taken her when she was three months shy of her hundredth birthday. To hear Mr. Rickey tell about her, this lady had tremendous spirit and a sense of humor. But there were times after that second fall that she'd sometimes wonder out loud, especially when she was in pain, as to why the good Lord still wanted her around.

"She never stopped to consider what an inspiration she was for us all including her grandchildren and great-grandchildren," said Mr. Rickey. And then he added that silent inspiration is a tremendous thing.

It wasn't until sometime later that I realized that maybe there was something in what he had said that should apply to me.

While we were talking, I had another visitor, Red Barber. I don't know who was happiest when Red showed up for his first visit, Mr. Rickey or me. Just having the old Dodgers' "Voice" along with the gentleman who had brought me into baseball — well, it sure pushed a lot of sunshine into what was a rainy day.

Mr. Rickey had to catch a plane back to Pittsburgh. He's the hustlingest man there is, and I was sorry to see him and Red leave. Watching them head for the elevator, I thought what a tonic they had been for me.

Not until months later did Barber tell me how serious Mr. Rickey's coronary attack had been. After being flat on his back in a hospital for a time, he was sent home with the understanding that he remain in bed for at least three months.

"He'd been home only a few weeks," added Red, "when he read that you could see people again — have visitors. He wanted to be among the first, so he simply got up and caught a plane, just to see you."

How can anybody place the real value on a friend like Mr. Rickey?

I was cheered by the spirit of the other handicapped people I saw and talked with in the halls, and I hope in turn I was good for them. Being with them made me feel so much better. I felt ashamed now because I had wanted to exclude myself, to hide from everyone. Oh, there were days when I'd get to feeling moody again, when I'd get feeling a little sorry for myself because that particular day I wasn't up to doing certain things. But that was when I needed to be with my fellow patients the most. Being surrounded by all those wheel chairs made me realize again that I wasn't the only one. They taught me how to accept my condition and be grateful for all the little things I could do.

I don't think I had been sitting up more than a week when I was allowed to sit outside in the street. On nice sunny afternoons my nurse would wheel me out to the 34th Street side of the hospital, and I'd sit there for about fifteen or twenty minutes, taking in the fresh air. I really enjoyed sitting there. Every time a sight-seeing bus would come by, the driver would announce to the passengers, "This is the hospital Roy Campanella is in." I could hear him plainly. The passengers would see me and they'd wave their arms and yell "H'ya, Campy!" Sometimes cars would stop and traffic would become stalled. There's a Coco-Cola plant across the street from Rusk's Institute and the workers would come over and bring me Cokes. I always did go for soda pops. They brought me so many, I couldn't possibly drink them all.

I was sitting outside on 34th Street one day when a nurse came over and said, "Mr. Campanella, will you be here for a while?" I said I would and she came back with a boy who looked to be about eleven or twelve years old. He was a fine-looking youngster, but he had a cut from the top of his head right down between the eyes. He was wearing dark sun glasses. He was very friendly and spoke very intelligently and I liked him right away. He was a real little gentleman. He was very much interested in baseball, and we talked quite a bit about it. I was so impressed by him that I told him I had a baseball up in my room autographed by all the Dodgers that I wanted him to have. He was very happy about that, so I had the nurse wheel me to the elevator and we went to my room.

The baseball was on the dresser and the nurse took the ball and gave it to the boy. He held the ball in his hands

230

and told me he would say a little prayer for me that night before going to bed. I told him I would do the same.

"I'm sorry I can't put my name on it, too," I told him as he was about to leave. "I can't hold a pen in my hand yet."

"That's all right, Mr. Campanella," he said. "I can't see."

It was like someone hit me over the head with a baseball bat. It never had entered my head that he couldn't see. I didn't even know who he was. He told me his name was Timmy, but that didn't ring any bell. He was just a nice kid. It was not until later that I learned his name was Timothy Getty, the son of the oil and railroad tycoon Jean Paul Getty, who has been called the richest man in the world.

Timothy Getty, God rest his soul, was operated on for a brain tumor a few days later, and he never recovered. His death made me very depressed.

It was just about then that my business agent, Frank Scott, contacted me regarding a radio show. An advertising agency had interested a large brewery in sponsoring a five-minute daily broadcast featuring me. I was to interview different sports people each night. The idea appealed to me. During my entire career in the major leagues, I had been the one being interviewed. Now I would be on the other side of the fence. It figured to be very interesting.

We worked out a deal, and that's how "Campy's Corner" got started. At first they wanted to call it "Campy's Bullpen," but that title was limited to baseball. This show was to cover all sports. Therefore "Campy's Corner." Chris Schenkel, well-known sportscaster, was assigned to work with me and he proved to be a big help. He helped me over the rough spots when I was breaking in. In fact, the entire crew were wonderful. Having a show of my own proved to be the best therapy in the world for me. It gave me an incentive. More than that, it was the answer to something that had been bothering me for a long time. Here was a way

231

I could earn a living all over again; here was a way I could provide for my family in the future.

The first night we had quite a few guests. Phil Rizzuto, Ray Robinson, Pee Wee Reese, Archie Moore, Ford Frick, Branch Rickey, Yogi Berra. I was very nervous. I don't think I have ever been so nervous before. I was scared, but I was happy, too. Here I was still crippled, but able to work. What a lift that gave me!

My first few shows were carried over the public address system in the hospital. All the patients would hear them. At the end of the interviews, the patients would come to my room or we'd get together in the corridor and all the celebrities on my show would talk with the patients. I'll never forget the day I had Tallulah Bankhead on my show. She was the hit of the hospital. She cheered everybody up with her jokes and friendly kidding. She'd hug and kiss the men patients and they loved her. She visited me several times and she always had the place jumping. They wouldn't let her leave.

I had Mr. O'Malley on my show one evening. After our interview he offered me a job with the Dodgers, as a part-time coach and radio commentator for the club's home games. Accepting the job, though, meant moving my family clear across the country to Los Angeles. That meant I would have to give up my home in Glen Cove, sell my liquor store and property in Harlem. It was important, too, for me to continue my rehabilitation program at Rusk, and I doubted that I could find any other place as good.

"Take your time, Roy," Mr. O'Malley said. "Think it over for as long as you wish. The job will always be open for you."

Thursday, September 4, 1958, was a special day for me. On that day Dr. Edward Lowman came to my room and told me I could go home for the weekend. As long as I live,

232

I'll never be able to describe how I felt when I heard the news. I know I had tears in my eyes. And I couldn't speak. it would be the first time I'd been home with my family in nine months. Many nights — and days too, for that matter — I used to lie in bed and wonder if I'd ever see my home again. I used to dream of sitting in my own living room, with my family, looking out across Long Island Sound through that large bay window and see those big ships far off in the distance. Now it would no longer be just a dream.

The next day, Friday, I had Nat (King) Cole as the guest on my show. Nat and I are old friends, and when I told him that I was going home that evening for the first time, he invited Ruthe and myself to be his special guests at the Copacabana night club where he was entertaining. I asked Dr. Lowman what he thought about my going and he said, "I think it's a good idea. It will do you good to get out among people. The sooner the better."

That night, without any of the other patients knowing, I was sneaked out of the hospital and driven to the Copacabana where Ruthe and I had dinner with Nat. We drove home to Glen Cove after the show, where, for the first time in nearly ten months, I slept in my own bed, although I still had to wear my neck brace and I had to be strapped into the bed.

On Sunday night my attendant, Leroy Newsome, drove me back to the hospital. Of course the news that I had been in a night club made the newspapers and the reporters kept calling and asking for an interview. Until then, I hadn't wanted to see any of the boys, mainly because I didn't feel I was up to facing a barrage of questions and cameras. Also I didn't want my friends among the newspapermen to see me until I was in better condition.

Incidentally, I had been getting mail every day I was in the hospital, sometimes more than a hundred letters a day.

233

Every one of the letters were nice, wishing me well, encouraging me in my fight, and offering prayers for my recovery. Now, for the first time, I got some letters that were not so nice. These letters took me to task for visiting a night club on my first night out of the hospital.

Just three days after I returned to the hospital from that weekend at home, I had my first press conference. It was quite an ordeal. I posed for pictures for about thirty minutes, then I chatted with the reporters for another hour or so and finally I went through a number of interviews with radio and television commentators for an hour and a half.

I remember that day well. It was Wednesday, September 10. I was wearing a blue sweater, slacks and sports shoes for the occasion. I still wore the brace to support my neck and I had to talk into a microphone because my voice got tired and low if I talked too long. I recognized a lot of my friends among the hundred reporters, radio, newsreel and camera men who were there, many of them who had been with me from the start.

It was quite a thing. I told them of the progress I had made, about my different classes and the kinds of exercises I took each day, and I demonstrated to them how I could use my arms, touch any part of my body, manipulate my electrically controlled wheel chair, and even feed myself.

"I would have had you up here long before this," I said, "except that my sitting time has been limited. But now that I've made such tremendous progress in the last couple of weeks, with the help of my new radio show and my visit home, it's all right."

They asked me a lot of questions. My worst night? I told them a day or two after the accident when I got bronchial pneumonia. I was paralyzed, and I couldn't breathe either through my nose or my mouth. I was completely helpless and I thought I was done for . . . through. I told them

234

how the doctor had slit a hole in my throat, inserted a tube, and I could breathe again. Words couldn't express what a relief that was . . . and everything had been steadily better since that night.

I told them how after the accident I couldn't use my hands at all. I couldn't eat or drink by myself. "Now," I said, "I can feed myself, with the aid of a gadget. That's a big jump. I know it doesn't sound like much, but to me it's wonderful. I'm not concerned about my legs right now, but just my arms and hands. It isn't so bad if you have something wrong with your legs. You can get around in a wheel chair. But you can't put wheels on your hands."

How about relaxation, someone wanted to know. "I listen to the radio mostly days, watch TV at night, and read the papers and my Bible. I never was a comic book man. I keep up with baseball, especially the Dodgers, every day. And I've got my radio show. All these things, together with my classes, keep me busy from nine in the morning to nine at night."

My future? I told them how Mr. O'Malley had offered me a job with the Dodgers, but that I didn't know yet whether I'd be able to accept.

The boys then started directing their questions at Dr. Rusk, who stood at one side of me while Dr. Lowman stood on the other.

"We feel Roy's improvement has really been phenomenal," Dr. Rusk told them. "We have thirty-five other patients with similar problems and he is way ahead of the average. Although his legs and lower extremities still remain completely immobile, he has made great strides as far as his shoulders and arms are concerned.

"He has worked so hard to accomplish the things he has that he has been an inspiration to us all. This is hard to say, but I honestly believe that Roy's contribution to this life

235

has been far greater than anything he could possibly contribute to it through baseball. The way he has been able to combat this misfortune has given hope to so many, many thousands of disabled persons, not only in this country, but all over the world. I believe he actually has become a symbol to them. We know that from all the letters we have received. I'm sure he will be a part of our rehabilitation program as long as he lives."

Dr. Rusk was asked if he could say how much more improvement could be expected and he answered: "Only time will tell. You can't say yes and you can't say no up to a year. Campanella will remain at the Institute for some months to come at least. He will be able, however, to go home on weekends."

The conference lasted nearly three hours, and I was exhausted when it was over. At that time they allowed me to sit up for nearly two hours at a time. But after those reporters and photographers left, I went right to bed and I didn't leave it for two whole days.

When I got up and around again after the press interview, I went in to see a young girl of sixteen from Riverhead, Long Island, and another girl of seventeen who had been brought all the way up from Alabama. These girls were lying in Stryker beds. I told them I had gone through the same thing and knew how bad it was. I said they were more fortunate than me because they could be visited by people like themselves. In the hospital where I'd been at first, I was the only one in that condition.

From then on, I visited people every day while I was in the hospital. One day Dr. Rusk asked me to talk to a seventeen-year-old high school athlete from New Jersey. The youngster had suffered a broken neck in a football scrimmage. He was really downcast when I went to his room just before dinnertime. I sat by the foot of his bed and talked

236

with him. I didn't ask him how he got hurt or anything like that. I talked about baseball and other sports. After a while he volunteered to tell me what happened. Then I told him how I got hurt, how bad I felt at first, and how much I had improved. I told him that I had progressed to a point where I could go home on weekends.

"Just because you suffered this misfortune," I said, "doesn't mean the world has come to an end. You're young and you can lick it, but you have to be willing to fight. You still have plenty to live for."

When I left him I knew he was feeling better because he thanked me for coming to see him and asked me to visit him again.

There was another kid from Connecticut. He broke his neck diving into a shallow swimming pool. He was completely paralyzed and he was really low. He lay there just like I did with tongs in his head. He wouldn't see anybody, but he let me talk to him. I explained to him that it was no disgrace. He had nothing to be ashamed of. I let him see the things I could do. There were thousands like him and me. He just had to live with it and pray to God for help and courage to live with it. Seeing me getting around in my chair and feeding myself was a great tonic to him.

It was good for me to visit with these people like myself. I went to cheer them up and I always came away feeling better myself. I think I made it a little easier for them. The thing that worried these people most was that they would always be a burden to their family and their friends. There was one lady in particular, who had pressure on her spine. The upper part of her body was in good condition, but she could walk only with braces and crutches. And only for a couple of hours a day. The rest of the time she had to keep off her feet. Her husband was a good man and she had three fine sons. They visited her every day but she was

237

moody and brooded constantly. The doctors told her she could go home weekends, but she didn't want to leave the hospital. She was ashamed to go home.

Her room was only three doors from mine, and when her family came they usually would stop to talk to me for a while. They felt terrible about her attitude. I felt more sorry for her family than I did for the lady. I talked to her like a Dutch uncle. I explained to her how much good it would do her if she went home weekends and spent some time with her husband and children. At first she wouldn't even listen. She moaned about being useless. What could she do at home? She'd only be in the way, she was a burden to her family, she'd be better off dead, and things like that.

"Look at me," I said to her. "Do you think I'd be better off dead? You at least are able to do things with your hands and fingers. I can't move mine at all. You at least can take a step or two with your crutches. I can't even stand up. Yet I go home regularly on weekends. That's one of the things I look forward to all week . . . being in my own home with my wife and children.

"I can hardly do anything, but my family is glad to have me home. They don't think I'm a burden, and I know yours don't either. They want you home, they need you home."

I finally convinced her — but it took her three months to make up her mind.

There was a middle-aged man who lost a leg in an automobile accident. They fitted him with a wooden leg, but he would never try to walk on it. He just sat in the wheel chair, refusing to even try to walk. And every once in a while he would cry. One day I wheeled over to him in the corridor and spoke with him.

"You think you're the unluckiest man in the world because a little thing like that has happened to you," I told him. "But you're wrong. You're a lucky man. Just think of

238

how much worse off you could be. My goodness, I'd give a million to be in the condition you're in. You can walk. Man, how can you sit there in a wheel chair when you can just get up and walk is beyond me. Why, you can walk right out of here if you've a mind to. All by yourself without having to depend upon anybody else."

I kept after him for two weeks and finally one day I saw him outside the hospital with his family. He was walking on his wooden leg. He left the next day and he walked out of the hospital with a cane.

The inmates listened to me because I had something to offer that no one else at the hospital had — baseball. I would tell them baseball stories, stories about the Dodgers, about the games I played, about the players I played with and against, about Stan Musial and Jackie Robinson and Pee Wee Reese and Joe DiMaggio and Ted Williams. I'd tell them funny things that happened to me, and to others on the field. I got their confidence and their friendship and they knew that the things I asked them to try to do were only what I tried to do myself.

Not everybody in the Institute was depressed and gloomy. One of the most cheerful fellows I saw was a steel executive who got both his legs mangled and had to have them cut off below the knees. He was always gay, always smiling, always trying to cheer up the other patients. His biggest concern was that he had just bought a new home with a great number of steps and he wondered how he would manage to get up to the front door.

There was a boy on our floor who didn't have the use of his arms and legs. He learned to paint at the Institute, holding the paintbrush with his teeth. He painted beautiful pictures. To give you an idea how good some of these pictures were, Mrs. Sophie Gimbel, wife of the department store executive, and a steady contributor to the Institute, held an auction at Palm Beach one day and all of the pictures were bought. The boy and I became good friends and he presented me with one of his paintings that I kept in my room. It was a beautiful painting of a farmhouse scene in New Hampshire, where he came from.

We were like one big family in the Institute. We'd sit in the corridors every evening after dinner and discuss such things as our families, the jobs we used to have, the people we knew, what we'd do when we got out. We became a sort of community. The inmates usually stay there six months, although some stay longer. Some have stayed as long as two and three years.

On Sundays we'd all go to the chapel in the hospital and as soon as I was able to, I'd go too. That is until I was allowed to go home weekends. They have Catholic, Protestant and Jewish chapels at the hospital. Father Thomas Carroll, a patient who suffered from paralysis of the hip, was in charge of the Catholic chapel. He said Mass every morning. Rev. Oliver T. Chapin conducted the services I attended. I finally got to be a member of the choir, although I was the only member wearing a brace on my neck.

I tried to get together with these people as much as I possibly could; I even began to eat in the hospital restaurant just to get accustomed to eating in front of other people. I knew I would be going home soon for good, instead of just for weekends, and I would have to eat in front of other people if I went out to eat in a restaurant, so it was best to get used to it as soon as possible. The majority of the people in the hospital restaurant were patients, but they had their friends and family with them. I was the only quad there. The others were all paraplegics.

I couldn't feed myself then, even with the gadget. I just didn't have the strength in my arms to get the food up that high. Ruthe had to feed me. Before I left the hospital, though, I was able to eat by myself. I could hold a hamburger and I was even able to eat soup with a spoon without spilling too much of it. I was able to eat fish, and chicken, and lamb chops, and steaks, but someone cut up the meat for me and took the bones out of the fish.

Just a month before I went home for good, something happened that gave me a tremendous lift. The Hearst people asked me to write a syndicated column on the World Series! The Yankees and the Braves were meeting again. Not only that, but they provided a box for my family and me. It was for the third, fourth and fifth games. Now it was the third game, the first in the Yankee Stadium. It was on a Saturday, and I was home for the weekend.

We left the house at around noon, and arrived at the Stadium about an hour later — just a few minutes after the game had started. I admit I was a little nervous, as it was the first time I was out in public and in a real big crowd since the accident. The nervousness almost turned into panic when it came time to put my wheel chair in the aisle and they found the aisle wasn't wide enough for the chair. Before I knew what was happening, a couple of husky firemen lifted me out of the chair and carried me down the aisle. For just that first minute, I felt like some sad freak. It was the most embarrassing thing that ever happened to me. I felt ashamed. It was awful. I don't think I would have gone to the game if I had known what was going to happen. If I could have run, I'd have been out of there in two seconds flat. But there I was, being carried in somebody's arms, like a helpless child. As the firemen, with the help of my attendant, were getting me to my seat, I could hear the buzzing of the crowd. Then came a tremendous roar, and following that a great deal of cheering and clapping and whistling. At first I thought the people were cheering some play on the field. But when I was finally seated — there between my wife Ruthe and my boy Roy, Jr. — and looked around, I saw that everybody around me had their eyes in my direction, and I began to realize that it was me they were cheering. It's hard to explain the feeling that came over me. I don't believe any home run I ever hit was greeted by so much cheering. At first I thought, "I don't want this!" But what could I do? I couldn't get up and leave. And then I accepted the cheers, in my heart. Just like they were meant. I knew that they came from the heart — and Lord, how they helped.

I wouldn't be honest if I said that I didn't hear the people's comments as I was being carried down that aisle. Sure I did. But while I might have felt a bit happy at the recognition they were giving old Campy, it hurt too that I had to be seen that way.

As I sat there behind home plate, tears rolled down my cheeks. I remember Roy, Jr., looking up at me kinda funny. "Daddy, are you crying?" he asked. He had never seen his daddy cry before. Then I looked hard at Ruthe. She also had tears in her eyes. I could see the players looking my way leaning out of the dugouts and all. And I remember several of the Braves players waving at me. Yogi Berra, the Yankees' great catcher, who had been squatting behind the plate, stood and waved to me and smiled. I could see he wanted to come back to the screen and talk to me, but I think he was too embarrassed or maybe he didn't want to embarrass me.

That regular box seat was in the first row in back of the screen behind home plate. It was the first time I had sat in anything but my wheel chair. I was worried whether I could sit in the seat without a belt or some other means of support. When you're paralyzed, you worry about everything that's new. You don't know how you're going to cope with it. But

242

with Ruthe on one side and with Roy on the other, I made out all right.

And I took those next two Series games in stride.

TWENTY-FIVE

I WENT HOME EXACTLY NINE WEEKENDS BE-fore I was discharged from Rusk Institute for good. I remember the day, Friday, November 7, 1958. The day before, Dr. Lowman said to me: "Roy, tomorrow when you go home you don't have to come back. That is, not as a regular patient. You're going to be discharged. But we want you to come back to the hospital every Monday, Wednesday and Friday, for therapy treatments and exercises."

Hearing that I was going to go home and be able to stay home every night gave me kind of a funny feeling. In a way, it upset me sort of, because I had gotten used to being in the hospital, being with my fellow cripples, and I was a little afraid of being home without having the other patients to talk to; because, after all, they were as good for me as I was for them. But I soon shook off that feeling. Just like every step that's new, I first wondered how I would face it, but I always did. Thank God I had a home to come back to.

Home at last, I was tired but I was happy. I was sitting in the living room with Princess on my lap, and she was having a grand time driving my wheel chair. It felt good having her on my lap again, even if I had no feeling there. I could hear Roy, Jr., and Tony playing and quarreling in their bedroom, and in the kitchen Ruthe was busy preparing dinner. What a wonderful feeling it was to be home for real. "I've got to think I'm fortunate," I thought to myself as I looked through the picture window out onto the water of Long Island Sound. "Thank God I had a house to come back to and a family to come back to and the jobs I've been able to do all this time. How many people get hit like I got hit and have nothing to come back to."

I had just returned from the barbershop in Glen Cove. Leroy Newsome had driven me to the barber's and back. I still wore the neck brace and I had to be strapped in the front seat, with a safety belt holding me erect. And I had to be lifted in and out of the car. But once in the house, I needed no help. In my chair I could get around the house without anybody having to help me. You've no idea how much it means being able to do things for yourself.

I realized that I still had the toughest job ahead of me. My schedule at Rusk called for three therapy visits a week, six classes a day from 10 to 3. One called for range of motion exercises of the arms. A second was for weight lifting and pulling sandbags and pulleys. A third would be occupational therapy, helping me to write with the aid of the plastic hand. The next would be typing, which is meant to put life back in my fingers. Then I'd go to the mats where I would practice balancing myself in order to sit up. Then, of course, there would be that volley ball game, for reflexes and such things.

Except once, when I was involved in an automobile accident in January '59 — almost a year to the day after the first one — I went to classes religiously without hardly ever missing a visit. I remember the first time I went back to the hospital, I stopped at the snack bar downstairs for a hamburger and milk. I didn't want anyone to help me. I struggled and had quite a time with it, but I ate the hamburger all by myself and I felt very proud.

While I was there, an elderly man about sixty or sixty-five, wheeled over and began talking to me. He told me he had been invalided for ten years. For most of that time, he said, he felt so ashamed he didn't want to leave the house. He

244

didn't want people to see him. Then he read about me and the things I had said in a magazine interview. That gave him the courage he had lacked, he said, and he decided to enter the Institute. Now he was sitting in a wheel chair.

I explained to him that when you're paralyzed you just can't take a pill and expect to walk. There is no such thing as a walking pill. It's all work, and you have to have something right there in your heart to do it with.

A few months later, this man was able to leave the hospital on his own two feet, wearing braces.

On another visit to the hospital, an elderly lady pulled up to me in a wheel chair and asked whether I was Roy Campanella. When I nodded my head — I could do that by then — she said: "Mr. Campanella, you are the cause of my being here. I had no more interest in life. I felt I was useless, a burden to everyone. Then I read the story of your accident and how you refused to give up. From you I gained new hope. I decided to give it a try, so I'm here."

"As long as you try, you've achieved something," I said. "Don't give up no matter how hopeless it looks. You never know. Have faith. Trust in the Lord and yourself. If you keep trying, you may wake up one day and find you're able to walk again."

On December 10, 1958, I took my first night trip from Glen Cove into New York. We were driving into town, to Toots Shor's, where I was to receive an award from the Kiwanis Club.

It was a bitter cold night. In the car were Ruthe, Leroy Newsome and me. Leroy was driving. We'd gone about a mile or so from the house when I saw the pole. It was standing there on that S turn on Dosoris Lane not far from the school the three youngest — Roy, Jr., Tony and Princess — attend. It stood straight and tall and cold in the bright glare

245

of the street light. There wasn't even a dent or a gouge in it to show where I had hit it. This night, nearly a year later, as I passed it by, I thought of a lot of "ifs." If I had started home earlier; if they hadn't postponed my TV guest appearance; if I had been driving my own car; if the road hadn't been icy in that one particular spot . . . if, if, if. What's the use of looking back? It ain't gonna turn back the clock. It ain't gonna wipe out those last eleven months. It ain't gonna bring back my legs. Wishing ain't gonna do nothin' for me. Fighting and working will, though, and that's what I aim to do until I walk again.

This night I had wanted to be dressed in my best clothes. I had thought of the tuxedo which I hadn't worn since the night I wore it to the Baseball Writers Dinner in New York — the last time I was voted the Most Valuable Player award — and had to say a few words. Yes, I had thought of the black tie but I'd finally settled on my brown business suit. I didn't know whether this was to be a formal affair or not. I was to be honored by the Kiwanis Club, a powerful civic organization which annually picks the "Man of the Year" for achievement, character, courage and devotion to his fellow man. Two years before they had awarded the honor to Thomas E. Dewey, former Governor of New York State. The next year the honored man was Keith Funston, president of the New York Stock Exchange. Now it was to be me.

Why? For what? I didn't know, but that didn't prevent me from being a touch proud and a bit humble. But when I stop to think of it — why me? Because I was a ballplayer who had an unfortunate accident? Because I broke my neck and was lucky to be alive? Because I was back home with my family after nine months in the hospital? Because I fought to live and start a new life when I suddenly lost the old one? Was that a reason for being selected "Man of the Year"?

This was a little too much for me. I appreciated it, but I

246

couldn't understand it — and I still don't. Most Valuable Player of the year? I knew what that meant. I had earned that award three times, as many times as any man in the history of baseball. I knew what that was for. But what was this for? Courage? Does it take courage to fight to live . . . to get back home to your family . . . to battle to be able to provide for your wife and children . . . to try to live a useful life even though you're a quadriplegic and cannot use your hands and feet?

The most thankful man of the year? Yes! The luckiest man of the year? Yes! But *the* Man of the Year? I couldn't buy that. But it was a wonderful feeling to be placed in the same category with such distinguished persons and great public figures as Tom Dewey and Mr. Funston.

It must have been around 7:30 when I was wheeled into Toots Shor's and taken up the elevator to the third floor. The first person I met was Nelson Rockefeller, then Governor-elect of New York. He had been there an hour or more and he was about to leave. He had waited as long as he could but he had a list of other engagements that he simply had to keep. He was behind schedule as it was.

But he stayed a while longer after I got there. He had already made his speech and I was told later he had said some wonderfully complimentary things about me. Now he was saying those things to me in person. What a warm feeling that man and his quiet words gave me. Imagine, a Rockefeller putting his arms around me, a broken-down ballplayer, born on the other side of the tracks, telling me how proud he was to call me his friend.

Then he had to leave, but before he stepped into the elevator, Mr. Rockefeller gripped my shoulder and said:

"Campy, I hope you don't want for anything. But should you ever want something from me, no matter how big or small, I want you to get in touch with me without hesitation.

If there's anything at all in my power to do for you, I will. The front door of the Governor's Mansion in Albany will always be open to you as long as I am there. Remember that. Goodbye, Campy, and God bless you."

Thinking back on that night, a lot of nice things were said . . . things I hope I'll come to merit. That big third floor room was filled with important men from many walks of life.

What did I tell them? Only what was in my heart. Ruthe was sitting among friends, at one of the tables directly in front of the dais. I raised my hand in her direction and said, "If it were not for my wife, I wouldn't be here tonight. It's because of her faith, her comfort, her encouragement, her spirit, her loyalty and devotion and above all her tireless care and consideration that I came back from a helpless cripple to where I am today." I told them how appreciative I was to be living in such modern times. Just fifteen years ago, a fellow in my state could have done nothing but lie in bed and die away!

Actually, I take therapy treatments practically around the clock, even when I'm at home. I spend an hour a day on the tilt board at home. Jim Williamson, who has replaced Leroy Newsome as my attendant, straps me on the board every day without fail. The reason for this is to strengthen your bones. Otherwise, the bones dissolve into calcium, and if that ever gets into your bloodstream, there's nothing anybody can do for you. You're a goner.

I'm fed antibiotics each day. I practically live on pills. The kidneys are my greatest concern. I drink only prune or cranberry juice. Prune juice is helpful to the bowels; cranberry juice helps prevent formation of stones in the urinary tract.

Ruthe sees to it that I take my medicine on schedule. She is the one who dresses and undresses me. I have to be padded around the middle and around my shoulders, and she is expert at it. She also sees to it that I'm taken care of in a sanitary way. The only thing I don't let her do is carry me. My attendants handle that.

Some people say it takes courage to live like that. Me, I just want to live. The doctors used to remind me that the one thing I must do is keep fighting, keep trying, keep thinking all the time about getting better. I know there are people like me who have given up. I have too much to live for to think of quitting. Like I told all those people, when the Philadelphia chapter of the Baseball Writers Association of America gave me an award as the most courageous athlete of the year in 1958:

"All of us like to live, and I'm one of them. And I hope to continue to live. And to live you have to battle, and be courageous, just like this plaque says."

I was invited to lots of affairs during the winter of 1958, many of them as guest of honor, and I went to nearly all of them. I learned you have to get around. If you just sit and worry and not go any place, it's bound to worry you. You have to keep your mind busy. The best medicine I had when still in the hospital was getting out to see those three World Series games between the Yankees and Braves at Yankee Stadium. I also attended a couple of professional and college basketball games at Madison Square Garden, as well as trotting races at Yonkers Raceway. Also, I went to my store in Harlem once or twice a week, and every Monday and Wednesday afternoon I taped my radio show.

Since leaving the hospital, I have been astonished at the number of places I've been able to go to where the wheel chair is no handicap. Going to all these places has not only helped me, but I think helped quite a few others afflicted like me. They look upon you for encouragement. You sort of set the example for them and you can't afford to let them down. Because as a ballplayer many know me, everything I

249

do gives hope to others. That's why I try a little extra hard when sometimes things don't look too bright.

You see, the biggest trouble with quadriplegics is that they're ashamed to have people see them. There were a couple of fellows in the Institute who didn't want to leave even when there was nothing else that could be done for them there. In the hospital, you feel at home because you have a lot of company. Everyone else is like you, and it makes it easier. Most of the others are in wheel chairs and you don't feel like a freak. No one stares at you. In the dining room, everybody feeds himself with the aid of a gadget, or someone else is feeding him. You think nothing of it. No one pays attention. But in public you're afraid to face normal people in a wheel chair. You feel that you don't belong. When you go to a restaurant and have to be fed, you become self-conscious. You think everybody in the restaurant is staring at you. You feel ashamed; you want to hide. You become even more aware that you're a helpless cripple.

I know that feeling; I went through it. I went through a lot of other tough things, too, but nothing that can touch this. The worst part is when people feel sorry. They recognize you and come over and you can see the pity in their faces. It's true they're all sincere but they're not doing people like myself any good. That's the kind of feeling I've been fighting against ever since I got out of the hospital.

I don't want people to feel sorry for me. I don't need pity. I feel I'm doing very good. The best therapy for a quadriplegic is keeping his mind occupied, having some kind of a job. Funny thing, people feel sorry for quads, but not many are sorry to the point where they give them jobs. Quads need help, not pity. They need a job. That's the thought in every quad's mind . . . if I only could get a job.

Sure they can't walk and maybe they can't use their hands. But quads can do lots of other things. Rusk Institute is full of quads who study all types of IBM machines — they learn typing, shorthand, secretarial work and how to operate calculating machines. There are lots of jobs they can fill, but few of them get jobs. Why? Because people won't grant them a real interview on account they are in wheel chairs. It's hard to make people realize that with proper training they can do as well at some jobs as any other person.

These people can still be useful even if they can't move their legs or their hands. If only they were assured they could get a job when they got out of the hospital, they would lose that useless feeling that they are only a burden to everyone else.

I'm not exactly in the worst position in the world. If you don't believe me, just take a look around. You'll find lots of people worse off than me. True, I'm still paralyzed from the neck down, and I have no feeling at all in my legs, but I can move my arms and shoulders and I have a little movement in my hands. I've learned to make the most of everything, and I'm grateful for the little things I can do. You don't know what you can do until you try it. You'd be surprised what you can do when you have no choice.

I get around almost as much as I used to. The only inconvenience is when I have to be carried in and out of my bed, my chair, and my car. Otherwise, I live like I used to. I've sort of gotten used to the fact that I have no movement in my legs. I manage to get wherever I want to in my wheel chair, which has become my home.

I may have to live with this a long time . . . maybe all my life. But I've got so much to live for — my family, my job, myself. I've always enjoyed life and I'm going to continue to enjoy life even if I have to do it in a wheel chair for the rest of my life.

TWENTY-SIX

ANY PARENT WHOSE SON HAS GOT HIMSELF messed up with the law, for one reason or another, will understand how I felt the day I learned they had picked up my boy David. Of all days, it happened to be on Washington's Birthday. That's one holiday I don't think anyone in the Campanella family will ever celebrate no more. It's a day that brought us all misery and more misery.

In 1959, Washington's Birthday fell on a Sunday, so it was celebrated February 23. Monday was a busy day for all of us. Ruthe had a dentist's appointment for our three youngest — Princess, Tony and Roy, Jr. The office is in Harlem at 152nd Street and St. Nicholas Avenue.

Jimmy Williamson, my attendant, drove us down to the dentist's office where we dropped off the brood at about one-thirty, and he and I drove on to my store on 134th Street. We were supposed to pick them up at an aunt's house near the dentist's office at five o'clock, then go to Ruthe's mother's house up in the Bronx for dinner. The only one who would be missing at the family dinner, aside from my two oldest daughters who were in Philadelphia, was David. The fifteen-year-old was spending the holiday weekend at a friend's house in Flushing, not far from the Queens Day School which he attends.

I had a number of things to take care of in the store. Usually my secretary, Miss Cynthia Mason, handles those things for me, but since this was a holiday it was her day off. Miss Mason is one of the most efficient girls I've known. When I was laid up for so long she really kept things going at the store.

Harry, one of my clerks, was working. He kept me com-

252

pany as I checked the books and bills. At five, we picked up Ruthe and the children and drove to her mother's. We had an early dinner and were just about finished when the phone rang.

It was for Ruthe. She took the call in another room. She returned after a few minutes and said, "I have to go out."

She said it like she was going out for a pack of cigarettes, so I didn't question her. Somehow I sensed that something was wrong, but I figured that she didn't want me to get worked up about it.

The thought still bothered me after Ruthe had left the house so I called the store. I thought maybe it had been robbed. Harry answered.

"Is anything wrong down there?" I asked.

"Not in the store," said Harry. "But they got David locked up."

"Locked up? For what?"

"I don't know, boss. But after you left the store, a police car came by. They were looking for you. It seems they got David in jail for some street fighting. I didn't know where I could reach you, so I called Miss Mason."

I told Harry to call my secretary and have her call me back at my mother-in-law's immediately. Miss Mason called in a few minutes.

She told me all she knew, which wasn't very much. Harry called her after the police had left and then she phoned the house for Ruthe. I asked her why she didn't ask for me and she said she thought it best not to disturb me. That beats me. They're always concerned about "disturbing Campy." Like I was half dead, or something. They forget that I'm no longer a hospital patient. I'm up and around and I'm living the same life I did before the accident. I'm still the man of the house, but I've got to admit, though, that Ruthe is always calmer than me and is more likely to do the right thing,

253

especially in an emergency. With her it's a kind of reflex. With me it's practically a campaign. I'm apt to get excited and mad at myself when things go wrong and I can't do nothing about it. Chew on yourself and you only wind up sore.

According to Miss Mason, David had gotten involved in a street fight around Queens early in the afternoon and the police had picked him up and hustled him off first to the neighboring station house in Flushing, then all the way to the Youth Shelter House in the Bronx. Now I knew where Ruthe went, and it wasn't for cigarettes.

All I could do now was wait until I heard from Ruthe. But the hours passed and no word from her. I was worried half to death. I kept thinking that maybe there was more to it, that they didn't want to tell me everything because again they didn't want to disturb "poor crippled Campy." The hours dragged on and I was about to call up the Bronx police on my own when the doorbell rang, and it was Ruthe. It was now around midnight, five hours after she had put on her hat and coat and said calmly, "I have to go out."

Ruthe wasn't calm now. She was so nervous, she looked like she was about to jump right out of her skin.

"Where's David?" I asked right out.

She realized right away that I knew.

"He's still in the Shelter House," she said. "They won't let him out. They released the other two boys they picked up with him, but they're holding David overnight. They wouldn't even release him in my custody. They said they want him to appear for a hearing in the Youth Court in Jamaica tomorrow. And we have to put up thirty-five hundred dollars bail to get him out."

"Youth Court? Hearing? Bail?" I cried out. "All that for having a street fight?"

Suddenly Ruthe began to cry. I felt something break in-

254

side of me. I didn't remember ever seeing her cry before. Not even all those days she came to visit me in the hospital. Oh, I was sure she cried every now and then, but never in front of me. Ruthe is a strong girl with full control of her emotions. Now she was sobbing and she couldn't control herself. I realized what she must have been going through, what she had gone through during the past thirteen months.

Finally, she got hold of herself. I listened as she talked. The police were accusing David of breaking into a store in Queens — a drugstore. He was supposed to be the head of a big gang. The cop that arrested him admitted he didn't even see David in the fight but they were sure he had been in one and that he was the leader of the gang. They charged him with being a juvenile delinquent.

Ruthe said she had a chance to speak to David and that he admitted he had a fist fight but he swore he never broke into no store. He told her the police made him sign a confession. He said they told him that if he didn't sign a confession, they would make it tough on him. He said he had pleaded with them all afternoon to let him call me on the telephone, but that they only laughed at him.

I was getting madder by the minute. I was mad at David, at the police, and at myself. The first charge — the one for street fighting — was bad enough. But the second one — for breaking in and burglary — that was more than I could take.

"David's no thief!" I yelled. "David's a good boy. He never stole a nickel in his life. My boy is being framed. Confession or no confession, he never done anything wrong. I'm gonna get him out of there right quick."

I was all for getting into the car and going over to the Shelter House right then, but Ruthe convinced me that there was nothing we could do until tomorrow. She said she'd get in touch with our attorney, William (Pat) O'Hara,

255

the first thing in the morning and he'd put up the $3500 bail. I knew she was right, as usual, and we decided we'd go home and try to get some sleep.

Sleep for me and Ruthe, though, was a million miles away that night. I kept thinking to myself as I lay in bed, "David a thief? Impossible." I didn't believe it for a minute. How? Why? What reason would he have to do a thing like that? He had everything he wanted. He lacked for nothing. His mother and I always saw to it that he had money in his pocket. I was sure even if he did break into the store, as they claimed, he wasn't after no money. Why did he do it then? For kicks? On a dare? I had to find out.

David in a fight? Yes, I could believe it. Not that he was a bad boy, or that he couldn't get along with people. But sometimes a youth maybe gets himself mixed up with the wrong kind of boys, and before he realizes it he's in deep and he thinks he's got to prove he has what he thinks is guts. Two such crowds get together and before you know it they wind up in what they call a "rumble" which is supposed to prove which crowd is tougher.

That was bad. I didn't have any idea that David hung out with a gang. He's a very quiet boy, never says much. But he's always been a good son; he never before had given us any kind of trouble. I wasn't thinking so much of myself, though. I was thinking of Ruthe, who was lying in her room, without sleep like me, her mind all mixed up and her heart heavy with fear. And I was thinking of David, too, all locked up and scared to death, and ashamed and worried over what he must be doing to his mother and father.

Later, at the hearing, it came out that David is not my own son, but my stepson. I was sorry it came out. Not that I had anything to hide. I'm proud to have David as my stepson, but I figured what's the difference? As far as Ruthe and I are concerned, he is my real son, just like Roy, Jr., and

256

Tony. He's been a part of my home and my life ever since he was about a year old. He's called me "Dad" ever since he first learned how to say the word, and he's been just as important a part of my life as my three younger ones and my two older daughters by my first marriage.

I was still trying to figure out this crossword puzzle when I noticed it was light outside. I could hear Ruthe already walking around the house. As soon as she realized that I was awake, she came into my room and told me she was leaving for the Children's Court in Jamaica. I was too broken up to go. I lay in bed all morning and afternoon, listening to the news reports on the radio. Sure enough, there it was. "Roy Campanella's son picked up as a juvenile delinquent . . . Campy's son facing burglary charges." That's all I kept hearing all day. You'd think these announcers had nothing else to talk about.

There in the room by myself with nothing to do but worry and fret, I suddenly thought, "My gosh, what about Florida?" I was slated to leave that next Saturday morning and fly down to Vero Beach. Mr. O'Malley had asked me to work with the young pitchers and catchers in Florida — yes, and later to be in charge of Dodger tryout schools during the spring and summer at Ebbets Field. In a real sense, I was about to go back to my job — baseball. I had thought so much about Vero Beach, and finally had convinced myself that I *could* do the job! However, a cripple just doesn't get up and take off. It takes planning. I had planned to the extent of having a lot of paraphernalia sent ahead. A spare wheel chair had been outfitted with balloon tires up front to make for easier going through sand. Also a spare tilt board had been shipped down there along with tubes and bottles and all sorts of stuff. I was to live in the camp hospital which would make things a lot easier for everyone. Talk about the best-laid plans of mice and men. Mine sure had been shot.

257

But honestly, those plans didn't count any more. Ruthe and David were all that mattered now.

I didn't hear a thing from Ruthe all day; I really didn't expect to. It was after seven o'clock when she finally returned, and she had David with her this time. It was the first time I had seen him in four days. He came in with his head down; he didn't say anything. He was more concerned with what I had to say. I looked at him hard. He was drawn and nervous and scared, but he didn't look like no criminal to me. He didn't look like no juvenile delinquent either. He looked like what he was: a normal, healthy, fifteen-year-old boy who is no different from most boys. Ninety-nine per cent of them are good boys.

David is tall and lean. Not skinny, but wiry. He's rather small-boned, and he leans more to music than to sports, although he's not a bad athlete. I would have liked to see him take more of an interest in athletics, but I certainly don't hold it against him; and I respect and love him for what he is — a sensitive boy with more than an ordinary talent for music. As a matter of fact, David is part of a singing quartet, two colored and two white boys, who call themselves the Delchords. They form a close harmony swing group, and Martha Raye thought enough of the boys' ability to have them sing on her TV show. King Cole told me they have considerable talent for youngsters — and I don't think he'd tell me that if he didn't believe so.

I didn't say anything to David that night until we finished dinner. Then I asked him to come into the den with me. He got up without saying a word, as if he had been expecting something like this and knew it had to come.

We were alone in my den, father and son. We faced each other, me in the wheel chair, he on the couch. He sat up straight.

258

"All right, son," I said quietly, "here we are, just the two of us. This is me, your dad, talking. There's no cops here, no probation officers, no lawyers, nobody but you and me. We're going to talk man to man. I'm asking you to tell me what happened, straight out, everything. Right from the beginning. Don't hold nothing back. And I want the truth, no matter how bad it is, no matter how much it hurts. All right. I'm listening."

Then he told me. He told me about the boys he palled around with, about the street arguments. He told me about the fight he had. No knives, no weapons, nothing but fists. There were six of them in this fight, three against three. It happened early Monday afternoon. The fight had been arranged the day before after the boys began pushing each other around in a bowling alley. It was a stupid, silly thing to do but sometimes boys are known to do stupid, silly things. You know how it is . . . one dares the other, and the other has to accept the challenge, otherwise he's afraid they'll think he's yellow.

The boys made their own rules on this fight. When they showed up in the alley on Monday some of the bigger fellows searched the battlers for knives and other weapons. They didn't find any. Then the six kids were squared off and they started swinging.

"The fight didn't last long, Dad," said David. "Honest. There was a lot of wild swinging, but not many punches landed. Nobody won anything. The only thing we proved, I guess, was that we had the guts to be there. We all just got tired around the same time and we agreed to quit. I guess we were all glad that it was over and nobody turned tail.

"I had just come out of the bowling alley after washing up and was walking down the street, by myself, when a police car pulled up beside me. One of the two cops asked if my name was Campanella. I nodded my head and he began asking me questions. Then he told me to get into the car and they took me to the station house."

"What about the other thing?" I wanted to know. "Did you break into the store, like they say, and did you steal anything?"

"I didn't break into no store, Dad," David said earnestly. "Honest, Dad, I never stole anything in my life. Everything they say is a lie. I'm no thief. I got mixed up in a street fight, yes. I made a mistake and I'm sorry about that. But I didn't break into no store."

"What did you do, then? You must have done something. Did you break the window of the store?"

"Yes, Dad, I did. I broke the window and then I ran. I got away from there as fast as I could."

"Why did you do that? What possessed you to break the store window? Do you think, just because you didn't actually break into the store, that you're innocent? What sort of devil got into you? Tell me, what made you do a fool thing like that?"

"One of the fellows dared me to hit the window with my shoulder to see if I could break it. He said I couldn't do it."

"You foolish, silly boy. How dumb can you get? You're lucky I'm in a wheel chair," I said. "Wrong is wrong and you never were wronger . . . you were wrong and stupid in running around with kids that are no good for you, for getting into silly street fights and getting your name on the police blotter and opening yourself to other charges that can be made against you. You let me and your mother down, you let your brothers and sisters, your whole family, down. You let your church and your school down. You let yourself down and you let down everybody who knows you and your parents. You took advantage of my position. You took advantage of your mother, who couldn't give you all the time

260

you needed because of me. Do you realize what you've done? Your mother is sick over it. You've broken her heart. You've brought her shame."

There were tears in David's eyes. He looked at me pitifully, like he was asking for one kind word. But I wouldn't give it to him. I gave him the riot act but good. He took it all without saying a word. Finally, when I was through he said:

"I'm sorry, Dad. You got no idea how sorry. Nobody has. Not even Mom. I was plain stupid. But I learned my lesson. No police will have any more trouble with me. I'm going to keep my nose clean from now on. I realize what I did to you and Mother — and to myself. I'm going to make this up to both of you. See if I don't.

"But one thing I want you to believe. I swear I didn't steal a thing. No matter what they tell you, I didn't even go into that store. They said I'm a leader of a gang. That's not true. They said I committed robbery. That's a lie, too. Sure, I signed a confession, but I was so scared I didn't know what I was signing. They said I was in lots of trouble. They said I had stolen some money and then gave me a piece of paper and said I'd better sign it or things would be twice as tough for me. That was the first night. They wouldn't let me talk to you. I was all alone and I was scared to death. I never had been in trouble before. I never had been in a police station house before. That was before Mom came. I just didn't know what to do."

That was David's testimony to me, his Dad. And I believed him. It came from the heart. He couldn't lie then even if he wanted to. That didn't make him and what he had done right, of course. He was still wrong. He was still guilty in what he did. When I was David's age, and when I did something wrong, I caught it from my Daddy, and David would have caught it from me if I had been able to. David was guilty, yes, but what about me, his father? Where did I stand? Shouldn't I share part of the blame?

The good Lord knows I've always tried to teach all my children right from wrong, to respect other people and their property, to have respect for the law, to have faith and love of God.

David deep down is a good boy. Thank God he's a right-thinking boy and he realized his mistake before it went too far. I really didn't mind his fighting, at least not much, because he didn't use a knife or a gun, just his fists. But he was still wrong and I'd have given him a whipping if I could. I never before had to give him a whipping. Not that I don't believe in them. My Daddy used to give me one many times and sometimes kids learn the facts of life and citizenship by having it whaled into them.

David always did everything I wanted him to do, like cutting the lawn and keeping the garage tidy, and running errands, and taking care of his younger brothers and sister. I never had cause to treat him any different from the others. But this case is a little different from that of other children. You must remember that while David is a normal boy with normal interests, he has had to live in a goldfish bowl to some extent nearly all his life because his father happens to be in the public eye.

When we bought the house in Glen Cove in 1957, it was mainly because of the kids that we made the switch from St. Albans. Ruthe and I felt we were taking the right step. And it was, for everybody except maybe David. The other children were very young so it didn't matter. But David was thirteen and it was not easy to leave his friends and everything behind and start all over in a new community. In Nassau County he was not accepted for himself; he was always Campy's boy, and he wanted his own identity. So he turned to the friends he had made before and that meant that he

262

spent a lot of time away from home. That's where David and I began losing the close contact with each other that we always had before. And then when I was away in the hospital, we drifted even further apart.

That talk with David took place on Tuesday night. The next morning, and again on Friday, David had to go back to court. The result of Wednesday's hearing, on the street fighting charge, was that David was put on probation in the custody of his mother. But it was a different story Friday. This was the more serious charge, breaking in and robbery.

That was one of the longest days of the year for Ruthe, David and myself. Ruthe spent the whole afternoon in court with David. I was alone in the house sitting in the big living room and looking out over Long Island Sound. Man, at that point I was sure all twisted up — inside and out. Here I was slated to leave the next morning for the Dodgers training camp at Vero Beach, to begin working at my new job as a special pitching and catching coach. I should have been happy; but suddenly, for the very first time in my whole life, baseball didn't seem important any more. To be home, with my family, and to be of some help to the boy and to Ruthe . . . that seemed to make the only sense. It was a cold windy day, and the Sound was full of choppers with the tide seeming to run every which way. But that old Sound wasn't any more mixed up and full of turmoil than me. Bonnie, our Scotty (he's really an old gentleman now), was with me. He seemed to sense that something was wrong, he waddled over and rubbed his side against my leg. Like he realized I couldn't do that no more for him.

Sitting there, and thinking about David and the trouble he was in, made me realize how easy it is, today, for a boy to run off the track.

I realized then as never before that raising a teen-ager is no easy thing. You got to work at it. I appreciated more than ever before the feeling I've always had for those families in poor neighborhoods of big cities when their kids get into trouble.

Too often, trouble is waiting on 'em, right at their doorstep. All the boy has to do is to step around the corner and run smack into it. I've come to learn that the better neighborhoods in the suburbs are also having their troubles with teen-agers. Broken families have a lot to do with this trouble — a whole lot. And they tell me that during and after any big war the kids pass through a restless stage. What with cold wars and threats of more shooting wars, they feel what's the use of trying to settle down and grow roots with a job? So, you might say, the "climate" for trouble is there. Yes, and the fact that so many mothers, who learned they could earn good money in factories during wartime, haven't been able to quit. The families may grow, but the idea seems to be that two breadwinners are twice as good as one. So Mom is gone most of the day and she's just too tired to control her kids when she gets home.

Where do I, a father of six (and a grandfather now too), come into this picture? As a matter of record, I've been part of it for a long time. In the old days I spent many an afternoon with youngsters at the Harlem YMCA. The whole reason for me working in the gym with them, and in baseball clinics for kids, was to channel them into sports and off the streets. Why, it was only back in the winter of 1957 that I appeared on a national TV program. In it I appealed to kids not to be roughnecks and punks . . . to keep out of trouble by spending their energy in sports instead of getting themselves messed up in gang scrapes.

"Stay on the track," I'd said. "It's nicer that way — and much easier."

But suddenly, my own boy had jumped the track.

There are times when you got to do more with a boy than

just preach. When I talk to youngsters, I try to talk to them the way I liked to be talked to as a youngster. But it all hangs on the fact that if you're a good sport as a boy, the chances are you'll become a decent gentleman. Also, the good you do along the way comes back to you one day later on. I believe that and I try to impress my own children with that fact.

I also believe that with kids a firm parent is, more times than not, a kind parent. I don't mean "kind" in the way of being overindulgent. Being a pushover for your youngster is simply a form of laziness or selfishness. "Kind" to my way of thinking is trying to gain some understanding of the boy along with making the time to spend with him.

Since January 28, 1958, however, that relationship has been impossible in our home. Certainly there has had to be a letdown in supervision . . . and I guess that loose supervision can be as bad as no supervision at all. Like I said, a teen-ager today — yesterday too — requires rough physical handling, when he *needs* it; not from his mother, but from his father. For some time now, my association with David has been limited to talking "at him" from a wheel chair instead of getting "with him." That's important. Nobody knows better than I what a big job Ruthe has tackled and will continue to handle, trying to be both mother and father during all the months I was laid up and away.

I've spent hours by myself in the last year trying to think things out and get the answers. And since David's trouble, I can understand that the boy — any boy — at fifteen can get restless. Being at home with two younger brothers and a baby sister, and a dad who is an invalid, can get to be boring, maybe. Ruthe and I both took that into consideration when we let David spend occasional weekends at the home of a school friend of his in Flushing.

But the time had come for David to realize that, in some

ways, he's got to pinch hit for me when I'm not around — as the oldest male member of the household.

It was while I sat there thinking these things that Friday afternoon that our family physician, Dr. Marsden, dropped by. Apparently Doc hadn't come to look at me; he'd come to talk to me.

"Campy," he said, "I'm not suggesting what you should do. I'm ordering. I want you to be on that plane tomorrow morning for Vero Beach. There's nothing you can do here except grind yourself to bits. That's what you're doing right now. There's nothing more you can do for David. You can stay here and continue stewing like this — and you'll be back in the hospital. This isn't just a friend talking to you. It's your doctor prescribing for you! Be on that plane tomorrow and no nonsense!"

It was maybe a half hour after Doc Marsden left that the phone rang. I thought it would be Ruthe, with some news, but it was Lee Scott, the Dodgers traveling secretary. He was calling from LaGuardia Field. He had just landed with the Dodger plane and we would be taking off next morning at 10:00 A.M. — with a planeload of rookies.

"You ready?" he said.

"As a matter of fact, I ain't," I replied. "I don't know if I can go at all. Right now I'm waiting for Ruthe to call with some news on David. How about calling me at five o'clock?"

Scotty called at five and again at nine. But still I couldn't tell him anything. But around ten that night, Ruthe called that she was on her way home — with David. The woman magistrate had continued David's probation on the street fighting charge, but she had had to postpone his hearing on the other, more serious charge until a further check could be made. It would be three or four weeks before David would be ordered to appear in court again.

When Lee Scott called a third time, at eleven o'clock, I

266

said, "Scotty, I'll be at the airport by nine-thirty tomorrow morning."

TWENTY-SEVEN

Returning to Vero Beach with the Dodgers for their spring training was the best thing that could have happened to me. Mr. O'Malley had let me know some time before that he not only wanted me down there, he needed me. That in itself was a kind of victory. Have you any idea how much it means for a person like me to *know* that he's needed somewhere?

A month before I left for Vero, Mr. Rickey had phoned me at home one evening. "Roy," he had told me, "there's a job, an important job, for you in the Pittsburgh organization. Don't forget it . . ."

I don't need to tell you how much that call has meant to me. Mr. Rickey, who'd given me my first chance in organized ball, who'd really made possible all the wonderful things that have happened to me since, still wanted me. He still felt that I "belonged" — and that, even though I no longer could play the game I love so much, I can still do something for those who can.

When Mr. O'Malley asked me to come to Vero, he told me he expected for me to take the young Dodger catcher, John Roseboro, in hand. He wanted me to take Roseboro and try to teach him, in a short time, what I'd learned in a long time. That, and to take in hand the other catchers as well as the young pitchers. . . .

The next morning, I was up bright and early. My attendants, Jimmy Williamson and Danny Mackey, had me packed and into the car by eight o'clock. I'd hired a chauffeur to drive the car to LaGuardia airport and return to Glen Cove. That way I could say goodbye to my family at home without attracting any fuss at the airport. But Roy, Jr., insisted on going along just to give his daddy an extra send-off hug.

At LaGuardia the traffic cops were very considerate. They told us the location of the plane on the field. Then they sneaked the car onto the field, off to one side where we couldn't possibly attract any attention. That way we were out of everybody's way. Sitting there in the front seat and watching those big iron birds take off and land gave me a few qualms. After all, this was to be my first air trip since the accident. I didn't know how I'd take any bouncing around if we hit "weather." I didn't know how they'd manage to lift me in my chair and carry me onto the Dodger Convair 44. There were so many things I didn't know the answer to. I thought about that basketball team of paraplegics called the Flying Wheels. Don't those fellows practically fly all over creation to play their basketball games? I felt better.

It was easy to spot the Dodger plane by those big blue letters, LOS ANGELES DODGERS, painted along its silver sides. The letters looked handsome . . . almost as handsome as those other letters, BALTIMORE ELITE GIANTS, had looked on that big old bus in Harlem that morning over twenty years before. Campy, I thought, you're sure traveling at a different pace and in a far different way this time! But if the good Lord would have allowed me to walk, or crawl, to that old Elite bus, this day, I'd gladly have given most everything I own for that privilege.

We didn't take off until nearly 11 A.M. Lee Scott had to make sure he had all those Dodger farm hands aboard, safe and secure. Lee is quite a fellow. He's been the Dodger traveling secretary since 1952, and he's still as full of pep and bounce as he was the first day I met him in '49.

268

The pilot of the Dodger plane, Bump Holman, is the son of the man the Vero Beach ballfield, Holman Stadium, is named for. His co-pilot is a boy named Jim Curzon.

I was driven out to the loading ramp where Scotty greeted me. "Campy, we can use you — plenty," he said. He didn't have to say that. But he did, and it gave me that added confidence about returning to Vero Beach — a far different sort of fellow, physically, than I was when I last reported there in March of '57, two whole years earlier.

After the car drew up alongside the loading ramp, my attendants Jimmy and Danny — both good strong boys — lifted me, chair and all, and carried me up those steps into the plane. Then they unbuckled my straps and put me into an aisle seat and strapped me up again. I couldn't help but notice that there were a lot of eyes looking at me — eyes belonging to maybe twenty minor league kids that the Dodgers were taking to Vero. But nobody came over to me until half an hour later — after things had quieted down and we were up in the air.

The last person I said goodbye to was Roy, Jr. This time the tables were reversed a little. In Yankee Stadium, that first day of the '58 World Series in New York, it had been Roy who had seen his Daddy cry. Now the shoe was on the other foot.

"Take care of your mother, son, and Tony and Princess and David. By rights you all would be going to Vero with me, just like in the old days. But —"

"Daddy," he sputtered. "You do the job down there real good . . . and we'll all take care of each other real good. Don't worry about us, Dad."

And then he busted out with big tears rolling over his freckles. But he snapped right out of it and after giving me a kiss on the cheek, the boy marched out of that plane like a real trooper.

269

"How old is Roy, Jr. now?" asked Scotty.

"Ten last August," I said. "And in some ways, a mighty old ten he is, too."

The flight down was uneventful. The sky was calm, the sun brilliant above the clouds, and things were real smooth and pleasant. In twos and threes those rookies began to come to my seat introducing themselves and just letting me know they were glad I was aboard.

We landed around 4:30 P.M. Bump Holman put the big ship down like it was rolling on eggs. He didn't crack a one. I was the last passenger off. As Jimmy and Danny and Bump carried me down the gangplank, I got the surprise of my life. There on the ramp must have been the entire population of Dodgertown! Mr. O'Malley, Buzzie Bavasi, Walter Alston, Pee Wee, Duke, Carl, Gil . . .

Talk about a homecoming!

I didn't say much. What could I say with my heart and my eyes filled to brimming? But I think they knew I was happy, really happy, to be back at an honest to goodness baseball camp with the men I'd won with and lost with down the years.

I didn't sleep too good that night. My head was just too full of emotions to let me quiet down. My bedroom was in the infirmary, which gave plenty of room for Jimmy, Danny and me, along with my paraphernalia. This included two battery-driven wheel chairs, a tilt board, rubbing table, and all the other stuff that I require. A lot of it, including the wheel chair with balloon tires, had been freighted to Vero more than a week before I arrived. It was on hand and waiting for me.

The last person I spoke to before I turned in that first night was John Roseboro. He's a fine boy — a fine human being. Just how good a catcher he'll be only time can tell.

He's a big boy, much taller than me, at least six feet, 195 pounds, and he comes from a little town in Ohio — Ashland. In '57, my last year with the team, Roseboro opened with us but spent most of the year in Montreal. He was back with Brooklyn the tail end of the season. What he lacked more than anything else was confidence. That's understandable when, without any advance notice, he was thrown into the first string job in '58.

"John," I said that first night at Vero, "you and me are going to get to know each other real good down here. Not only that, but by the time we pull stakes and move West, you're going to know more about our pitchers than they know about themselves. Baseball isn't all base hits and strikeouts, and fielding. Above all that, it's a *personal* game. And the more you know about your pitcher, the better equipped you'll be to help him through a jam. You got to know your pitcher like he was your own brother. You understand what I'm saying, John?"

"I sure do, Campy!" he said, his voice deep and warm and smooth. "You know what, Campy?"

"No . . . what?" I said.

"I'm really looking forward to tomorrow. I really am."

That's all the prayers I needed that night.

Once my way of living at Vero had been sort of set up and smoothed out, my days down there were pretty much alike — but, for me, in a very wonderful way. Rolling over the green grass in my chair to the batting cage where I'd station myself off to one side was sure "going home." The sights and the smells and the sounds that I'd missed for so long came back to me in one big whiff. The thud of baseballs smacking into glove . . . the sharp crack of the bat against the ball . . . the hard work and sweat and the concentration of the pitchers and hitters and the sound of men's voices . . . the old and the new nicknames and the little jokes . . . but over and more important than all this, the quiet determination that this had better be a new and better Dodger ball club! These things I can't describe too good — but down there I felt it all through me.

Actually, before I got out on the field that first morning, I had a little visit with John (Senator) Griffin, the clubhouse man, and a Dodger trademark for many years. As I rolled into the clubhouse, there he was. Griffin, who has a different loony hat for every occasion, looked at me, took that dead cigar from his mouth and said, "Campy, welcome home."

Then he went over to a locker with my name on it — right beside Pee Wee's in the coaches' little room in back. He opened that locker and I saw my old mitt in there. It looked to be in good shape. Then he took out a brand-new windbreaker with No. 39 on the sleeve. He helped me on with it and then he fished into the locker again and took out my size baseball cap. "Seven and one eighth," he grunted. Then he put it on my head.

This was before the boys came in to change into their uniforms, but they trooped in pretty quick. I was outside, getting the sun and the feel of my new jacket when they came busting out of there with their spikes clattering on the wooden steps. At that moment, well, for a second I all but climbed out of my chair and tried to join 'em. It was at that instant that the realization hit me with a finality that jarred me. Because after that first moment when my mind wanted to "go" but my body couldn't answer the command, I realized as never before that I wasn't going to run or even walk with 'em . . . and I wouldn't, ever. These things you live with for a long time and you know, without being told. But that morning, man, I just felt awful all over again. It didn't last long — that wave of self-pity or maybe it was frustration. I remembered Dr. Rusk asking, "Who do you think you are, the great Campanella?" I shook myself back to reality and, right then, I said to myself, "Campy, you're down here to coach, not play. Now get on with it!"

Another thing. All the reunioning with old teammates is fine for the spirits. But it can be overdone from both sides. I tried to make sure I wouldn't overdo that "recollecting" stuff from my side, and the guys didn't, either. After all, those boys had something more on their minds than patting my head! They all had jobs to hold or jobs to earn. I thought of the years when I was in their shoes. Sometimes coming to camp too heavy, but more times wondering how my hands were going to hold up. But no more of that. No reason to wonder how my hands were going to hold up this time. After all, all they had to do now was rest easy in my lap. Frankly, I think I would have gone a little nuts if I hadn't had John Roseboro and those others to talk to and to worry over.

This association wasn't only on the field. It occupied a good deal of each working day. Naturally, I couldn't "show" Roseboro little things about catching, like blocking low pitches, but I could "tell" him. But the main thing was building up his confidence in his own ability to do the job that Roseboro really inherited from me. Thinking back, it's very possible that my usefulness to the Dodgers in '58 would have been limited. Because I'd reached a stage where my hands had been broken up so bad that they weren't about to bounce back much any more. And without his hands a catcher is almost as bad off as a boxer with damaged hands. An infielder or an outfielder can get away with that type injury better because he may not have to deal with more than a half-dozen chances in a game. But a catcher's got to be in there on every pitch, catching and throwing . . . catching and throwing. What I started to say was that young Roseboro might have taken over the bigger portion of the '58

273

season anyway, but had he had to, at least he knew I'd have been there and working with him in his corner. As it was, however, he was sort of *thrown* into the job.

It was during an intersquad game at Vero, the day before the Dodgers were to play Cincinnati in an exhibition game. I was up in the stands on the first landing behind home plate and I had John up there with me.

"John," I said. "How much do you know about Don Drysdale?"

"Well, when he's fast he's like a bullet, and when he's —"

"I don't mean his stuff," I broke in. "What I mean is something about his personal life. His hopes and his dreams and his fears, maybe. He's got 'em, you know — just like you got 'em. And the more you understand his nature, why he is like he is, the better you're goin' to handle him. That goes for every pitcher on the club . . . Johnny Podres, Clem Labine — the whole lot of them."

I let him think that over for a while.

"You mean I should pry into a man's affairs?" he questioned after a bit.

"No, but you can learn an awful lot about a man off the field that may mean a ball game on the field. How many times does the manager consult you when he's trying to make up his mind whether to lift a pitcher or let him stay in there? Plenty. That's when what you know about that pitcher as a person can mean an awful lot. If there's something worryin' him — maybe his wife, or his baby, or his father is sick — and that worry is robbing him of the hop to his fast ball or the break to his curve . . . well, a little or a big thing like that could mean a ball game if he's left in there for just one more pitch.

"You got to mix more, John. You got to go out with the pitchers — have lunch with them, sit with them, listen to them one at a time and learn their traits as well as their wor-

274

ries. It all comes down to something you and me both know — that a catcher is an awful lot more than a receiver. He's got to make snap decisions, not some of the time, but all of the time. And, more than that, he's got to take charge. You show me a meek catcher and I'll show you a nothin' catcher. A meek catcher is one that lacks confidence. That makes the pitcher's job twice as difficult! You've heard that a horse can tell when his rider lacks confidence? The same goes for the pitcher. He can tell when his catcher lacks confidence. Hittin' or catchin', you've got all the gear to make a real big score, John. If the Dodgers didn't know it, you'd've been back in the brambles long ago."

Nobody else but a coach can preach to a man about his position and make it stick. We started, John and I, going down the Cincinnati batting order, discussing the strengths and weaknesses of their hitters. Temple . . . Robinson . . . McMillan . . . Ennis, I was having a high old time reciting what to call for against such-and-such a hitter and why.

"Where do you keep all that dope . . . in a little black book?" asked Roseboro when I ran out of steam.

"No," I said pointing to my head. "It's all in there. I studied them all the time when I played against them — and I studied them more from the flat of my back last summer. Watching 'em play on television. They still got the same weaknesses they always had and that goes for any established player in both leagues."

During those weeks at Vero Beach, *Life* took a lot of pictures. One in particular I didn't think much of and I hoped they wouldn't run it. But they did. It showed me strapped to the tilt board in a vertical position. I spend more than forty-five minutes each morning strapped in this standing position, and it's no fun. Anyhow, that picture of me on the board, looking sort of sad, made me feel bad when I saw it. From the look on my face, you might think I didn't care no more. A lot of people wrote to me, not so much on the rest of that layout, but on that one picture. One man wrote, "Don't give up, Campy. Just remember, there's an awful lot of people who had your injury who didn't live to tell it."

He needn't worry. Old Campy realizes only too good how lucky he is to be alive and to be able to get back into baseball. Not so much, maybe, with my body, but at least with my mind.

At Vero, I came to realize that I wasn't the only handicapped fellow watching the games. Before the spring of '59, I hadn't noticed hardly any cripples, but this last time I noticed quite a number of them. At one time or another I talked with most of them. They had read or heard where I could make it back. It seems that that one thing encouraged them to come out too. Some of these folks told me that they never expected to see me at Vero again . . . and frankly, I never expected to be there again!

The nice things they said: Thoughts like "I just want to shake your hand" . . . "Good luck, Campy" . . . "God bless you, Roy."

What can you say to wonderful people like these, except "Thank you. Thank you so much."

One afternoon, when Mr. O'Malley was sitting with me high in the stands behind home plate, two small boys came up to me. One of 'em had a battered old baseball with half the stitches gone. Would I sign it?

"I can't work the pen," I said. "I just can't sign it."

Well then, would I just *hold* the ball for a little bit? I did that. When I gave it back to him, that kid's face was a wonderful thing to see.

It was about four or five days after my arrival at Vero that the radio gang showed up. Chris Schenkel, my MC, director Bill Mellor and engineer Frank Kaplan. Man, was I glad to see them.

276

"Chris, buddy," I yelled when he walked in that morning, "where you been?"

"Oh, here and there," he said. "We've just been waiting for you to get settled down and organized. You ready to work?"

I sure was.

The taped radio show that Chris and I have been doing since August 1958 has really caught on. It started small on one station in New York City, WINS, in the evening. Today it's in practically every major city in the country including Philadelphia. I say that because that way Mom and Dad and Doris and the two girls can listen to me. Just knowing that I'm coming through to them means a lot. The sponsors of this show are Ballantine beer, the "Three Ring" people, and the R. J. Reynolds tobacco company, which makes Camel and Winston cigarettes, is an alternate sponsor.

Back in New York, there were times when we would spend as many as fourteen hours a week on this show. That way we'd get a lot of programs in the can. Working ahead that way made it a whole lot less strain on all concerned. The show, as you know is called "Campy's Corner," but when we started it in the summer of '58 it was more of a mailbag type show. Chris would read letters from a lot of folks, including one from the President, from Joe DiMaggio, Frank Sinatra and all sorts of people who are well known. Looking back, those first shows were really rugged. I'd do them lying in bed, with Chris stretched out next to me and holding the mike for me to talk at. He'd get things going and then bring me in. At first it was hard for me to breathe right. That's because I'd done very little normal breathing on my own for too long a time. As for laughing, I'd all but forgotten how. Those boys had patience. There were days when it would take twenty minutes of retakes to get out a five-minute show. After the mailbag bit had begun to grow a little

277

thin, along with a built-in question and answer routine, we started to have guests. All these recordings were made down at the Physical Rehabilitation Center in New York — and with Dr. Rusk's blessing. You know, I think if I told that man I wanted to ride a horse tomorrow, he'd say, "Go right ahead, Campy. And while you're at it, have a real good ride!" In Dr. Rusk's book, there's no such thing as "can't."

Mostly, my guests were ballplayers. We'd rehearse what I was going to ask them and then time out the guest's answers so that we'd finish right on the button. And man, that can take some doing. But not one of them complained and not one of them looked for a fee of any kind — ever.

Down there at Vero, I had all the Dodgers I could use — from Walter O'Malley on down. These tapes, or rather shows, were air-mailed out to Los Angeles and New York and the other cities, so we held pretty good to the time factor.

Evenings at Vero Beach had always been something a little special for me and that's still the case. Back in the old days, after supper, I used to like that little corner outside the kitchen where I'd sit and bull with the chef or whoever happened by. That was the corner that came to be known as "Campy's Bullpen." There, in that little alcove with the evening sun slanting off the whitewashed clapboards, things were real pleasant . . . just chewin' the fat about anything that happened to cross our minds. But mostly it had to do with baseball. I think that some of the best old belly laughs I ever enjoyed came out of that little spot behind the main reception hall and mess hall at Dodgertown. From Pee Wee on down through the rawest rookie, everybody came to know that there was usually a discussion of some sort, and a few laughs too, to be had in this spot I'd come to regard as my own private bullpen.

Another "special" that was nice to come back to was a

278

little old eating place that Charlie Dressen introduced me to years before. It's called Sockwell's. All it is, really, is a shipping house for crabs. An old place, Sockwell's is a short drive out of town and back on the Indian River. When they're not packing crabs on ice for shipping, an old-timer there serves crab fingers. Trying to describe how they pull and prepare the claws wouldn't mean much. Just let me say that you got to taste these crab fingers to know how good they are. Some like them with shrimp sauce and drawn butter, but my preference is to eat 'em with a real hot sauce — Tabasco, Worcestershire and trimmings. The hotter the better.

Another thing I enjoyed was the fact that each day at Vero I had fresh fish for lunch or dinner. Do you know who caught them — for me, special? Carl Furillo. With the possible exception of Ted Williams, I guess there isn't another ballplayer who can catch more eating fish than Furillo. Even when the fish are sound asleep, he'll stir them up and get them on his hook. I've always had a special fondness for mackerel. Carl knows this, and so each morning early he'd slip away from camp and go catch me a fish or two. I never asked him; he just went and did it. Things like that you don't forget.

It was the second or third day at Vero and I was sitting behind the batting cage when something struck me as real funny. Off to one side, Pee Wee was hitting fungoes to the outfielders. I'd been complimenting him on how good he was batting those high flies. He never missed the ball. But this time, when he tossed it up, instead of batting it, he grabbed it again. Duke Snider saw this and he yelled, "What's the matter, Pee Wee, you still taking those called third strikes?"

I started to laugh, and the first thing I knew, I was laughing so deep in my belly that it hurt. Maybe I seemed a bit nuts to some of the players — but I wasn't. I realized then I was just overjoyed. After all those months of suffering, I had come home again. And being back and all, well, it almost made me forget my troubles.

Speaking of troubles, I've learned that nobody who is allowed the luxury of being alive has a right to get too worked up over trouble. Why? Because trouble is what makes a man put out and bring off a better job than he'd do without it. After all, we all have our built-in troubles and I think that maybe God put them in our path to make us toe the mark a little sharper.

I had troubles before this thing . . . and before David got himself tangled up with the law. I don't like 'em, these troubles, but sometimes I think how sort of flat life would be without a share of 'em.

Something else I've come to know, and that is that Ruthe is at her most wonderful best when we have trouble. I remember the night in St. Paul in '49 when I got the call back to Brooklyn and hurried home to tell her the good news. She was in bed, and Roy, Jr., then only a day or so old, was in a secondhand crib beside our bed. "Campy," she said when I told her. "I'm so happy for you . . . and for *us*, that I'm crying with the joy of it. It tastes awfully sweet, but you know, trouble isn't so bad either. Because when we're a *team* like we are — nothing can beat us down for too long."

Thinking on trouble, I know that when it strikes, if you can manage to meet it head on, smile at it and roll up your sleeves to beat it, God takes a hand. He gives you an inner strength. It don't show like muscles, maybe, but it's stronger and more lasting than muscles. I found that to be so. I don't really have much any more in the way of muscles, but I got something else that's better and stronger. God.

It was several days before I was slated to go home that I had a call from Ruthe. She and David had just come home from court. The woman magistrate believed David's testimony. She was convinced that he did not enter that store nor did he steal anything! However, she had put the boy on indefinite probation: a type of probation to make David realize that children are to respect property and be careful of their street associations. She had done what she considered best for David in the belief that his probation would help him to appreciate and respect the freedom which all boys in America have.

In the final analysis, the proof remains with David. And I'm willing to give most any odds that my boy will continue to respect the trust that that judge has placed in him.

TWENTY-EIGHT

AT VERO BEACH I HAD A LOT OF TIME TO think about things that happened to me and around me in baseball. For me, it was a time when a fellow could sort of add up the score of a game and a way of life he'd known. Down there, while sitting high in the stands and watching and studying the skilled labor of the Dodgers and the teams they played in exhibitions — well, I studied a lot of talent. That was part of my job. And the more I thought about the present, the more I reflected on the past. I got to thinking about the great athletes I'd played with and against and to rate them in my mind.

Especially pitchers. After all, a catcher's biggest concern behind that plate is to make his pitcher pitch a little better than he can. In that respect, one of my most pleasant memories was working with Sal Maglie. I always had wondered how it would feel to catch the Barber when he was with the Giants and was our No. 1 enemy. I had hit against Maglie quite a bit and I often wondered how he got us out so consistently. But after catching him, I found out. He threw the best curve ball I ever caught. He had amazing control of it and he could throw it at several different speeds. That no-hitter he hung on the Phillies in 1956 was a thing of beauty. And he was nearly forty at the time.

Maglie was not the toughest pitcher I ever faced, though, nor the best pitcher I ever caught. My vote for the toughest pitcher I ever batted against goes to Ewell Blackwell, the tall drink of water who hurled for the Cincinnati Reds. I think I got one hit off him in all the years I batted against him. He had a peculiar sidearm delivery and the balls seemed to come through by way of third base. They didn't call him the Whip for nothing. I've seen him chase batters right back to the dugout. His fast ball ran away from you and his curve ball was like a snake.

I got quite a kick catching him in the All-Star games. He was almost as difficult to catch as to hit. That's because his ball never went straight. I had to box a lot of his pitches. I'll never forget that game we played in Detroit. Vern Stephens of Boston was the American League hitter. He had a funny stance. His legs were spread out wide, one foot here and the other way up there. Blackie would let one go with that sidearm sweep of his, and Stephens would fall down. Many's the time he chased me back to the dugout. It was a pleasure to catch him, after having to hit against him all these years.

The best pitched game I ever caught was Carl Erskine's World Series victory over the Yankees when he struck out fourteen batters. He was really fast that day, but the pitcher who was absolutely the fastest I ever caught was Karl Spooner. Nobody ever threw harder than that kid did in those first two games he pitched in the majors. Both of them were shutouts. I think he struck out fifteen Giants and followed it up by striking out twelve Pirates.

282

The best pitcher I ever caught consistently for the Dodgers, both for knowledge and ability, would have to be Preacher Roe. Right behind the Preacher, I'd rate Sal Maglie and Don Newcombe. Newk had more sheer ability, but when it came to thinking out there on the mound, I'd have to hand it to Roe and Maglie. They were the only two pitchers I ever caught who knew exactly what they wanted to do with every pitch and could get the ball where they wanted nearly all the time. In 1951, Roe had the best year I ever saw a pitcher have. As bad as Ebbets Field was for left-handers, he won twenty-two and lost only three.

I mentioned Blackwell as the toughest pitcher I ever faced. That's true — but I should mention another fine pitcher who ranks right behind Blackie in my book. That's Whitey Ford of the Yankees. That little left-hander is clever, cocky, full of ability and has great control. He always gave the Dodgers fits in the World Series. Funny thing, he lived in Glen Cove, too, and we used to drive to World Series games together.

Poor Newk, on the other hand, never had any luck in the World Series. But nobody was a better pitcher than he was the year he won twenty-seven games. I remember the first game he pitched in the majors. It was in 1949. We were playing the Cardinals. He threw four pitches and there were four base hits. So I went to the mound. Before I had a chance to open my mouth, Newk asked me: "Roomie, do I have anything?"

"How do I know?" I answered. "I haven't caught a ball yet."

Picking the toughest hitter I ever caught behind is easy. That's Stan Musial. You couldn't fool him. There was no particular pitch he couldn't hit. You couldn't cross him up because he never guessed. He's the kind of hitter who waits until the last split second and he is always able to get good

283

wood on the ball, even when you get him out. The only way to pitch to Stan is to keep the ball moving in and out, never giving him the same pitch twice in succession.

I remember we were playing the Cardinals one evening. Musial, who always wore us out, was the hitter; so I thought up something that I hoped would stop him. I got together with my pitcher and told him: "When Musial leans over in his crouch, I won't give you a sign. You make believe you're waiting for one. We'll keep him bent over so long, maybe he'll get tired or angry."

I went back behind the plate and got ready, and the pitcher just stood there looking down at me. Stan waited and waited. After a while, without turning his head, he said to me: "I've got all night, Campy. He's got to throw the ball sometime."

How can you fool a guy like that?

Next to Musial, I'd rate Willie Mays and Henry Aaron as the best hitters I've ever seen in the big leagues. Duke Snider should have rated with these three, but he couldn't hit left-handers. Maybe that's not his fault, because the Dodgers saw so few left-handers.

No manager in his right mind would throw a southpaw against a lineup that had such powerful right-handed hitters as Gil Hodges, Carl Furillo, Jackie Robinson and me. When he did, the guy didn't last long.

Snider, being a left-handed hitter, should have led the league in batting every year. He should have hit .982. The guy was born under a lucky star. Imagine being a southpaw swinger and batting against nothing but right-handers for ten years? The Duke hardly ever saw a lefty. Alston took him out when they'd have a lefty pitching against us. And when you saw him swinging against one, you knew why. The guy who really tied him up in knots was Harvey Haddix, who pitched that no-hitter for twelve innings, only to get beat. Alpha Brazle would get Snider out, too; but I don't remember ever getting a hit smaller than a double off him. Other lefties who were "cousins" of mine were Ken Raffensberger and Johnny Antonelli.

The guy who can be the greatest all-around player of them all is Willie Mays. That goes for everybody, past and present. I remember Willie when he was just a kid and the way he has developed is something out of this world. I honestly believe Willie doesn't know how good he really is. And I doubt if some of the other teams know. The Dodgers certainly don't. He keeps belting their brains out, and they keep right on pitching to him. I used to tell my pitchers not to pitch to him, but they didn't always listen. I see where they're still challenging him. They just don't never learn. There's only one thing to do with Willie when he's up there with somebody in scoring position and first base open. Walk him and work on the next batter. I don't care who the next batter is. He's not going to hurt you as much as Mays, even with the bases full.

I miss Willie. I used to get a kick watching him play. He's the most exciting player I've ever watched — whether he's hitting, fielding or running the bases. He's got that certain thing called color. People just roar when they see him walk out on the field. He's just as liable to do anything. The only player who matched him in excitement on the ballfield was Jackie Robinson.

It's difficult to compare Willie and Jackie. They're two different types. Jackie could think so much faster than anybody I ever played with or against. He was so outstanding. He was always two steps and one thought ahead of the next fellow. And he had tremendous ability to go with it. Willie has tremendous ability, too. If he could think like Jackie, he'd be a league all by himself.

I sincerely believe Willie will be the majors' next .400 hitter. There isn't anything he can't do. He can run; he can steal bases; he gets base hits; he takes base hits away from you; and he throws better than anybody. You name it and he'll do it. The only player today who compares with Willie in all-around ability is Mickey Mantle. I think Mantle has more power than anybody in baseball. Mays can hit a long ball, too; but not as far as Mantle. I never saw anyone with the power Mantle has, unless it was Josh Gibson. I was amazed when I walked into the Washington ball park once and saw a sign which said: "Mantle hit over this." You just couldn't believe that any human being could hit a ball that far. I don't care how hard the wind was blowing. You just don't hit a ball that far.

I think Mays can run as fast as Mantle; and defensively, Willie is far out in front. He hardly ever misplays a ball. He's so fast and gets such a good jump on the ball, he reaches balls that no other outfielder could get near to. The only fault I might find with Willie is that he charges ground balls too fast.

Another thing, Willie runs too much. He led the league in stolen bases the last two or three years. And he'll probably do it again. But he's foolish. Every time he steals a base, he takes a chance. I told him that. Willie is now out in San Francisco, but he still makes his winter home in New York. Every once in a while during the winter, he visits me in my liquor store in Harlem. We go down in the basement and we talk baseball.

I told Willie, "You know every time you steal a base you're gambling on your career. Look what happened to Monte Irvin. He tried to steal a base and he ended his career with a broken ankle."

I used to talk and talk. I'd tell him, "Look, Willie, you don't get paid for stealing bases. You get paid for hitting the ball over the fence." You know what Willie answers? Noth-

286

ing. He just sits there and doesn't say a word. Finally, I'd give up. What's the use? He's not going to change. He just plays one way. He don't know any other way.

Willie had the advantage of breaking in under Leo Durocher. He was really Leo's boy. I don't know another person who knows as much about baseball as Durocher. I played under Leo only a short time but I liked the way he managed. He keeps a ball club hopping all the time. Charlie Dressen managed just like Durocher. I enjoyed playing under him, too. They like to gamble and they'll do just the opposite of what you'd expect. If I was a manager, that's the kind of baseball I'd play.

Burt Shotton and Walter Alston, my other managers in the big leagues, played very conservative baseball. They played the game according to the book, as they say. They knew how to get things across without hurting anyone's feelings. They are the gentlemanly type. Durocher and Dressen, on the other hand, will do anything to win.

One fellow I think could make a great manager is Pee Wee Reese. He's not only one of the smartest men in the game, but one of the finest persons I've ever known. Pee Wee did more for me on the team than just about anyone I can name. He was my friend right from the start. When I was on the "This Is Your Life" television program, he presented me with a silver tray autographed by all the guys I played with. Pee Wee has been the kind of guy who, if I ever was really upset by anything, could smooth me out, and do it quietly.

Clyde Sukeforth, who scouted me for Mr. Rickey, helped me a lot at Nashua. Walter Alston also helped. He made me feel at ease right at the start and he gave me the confidence I needed when he let me manage the team that time he was put out of a game. But the guy who helped me more than anybody else, the guy to whom I owe more than I can ever pay back, is that little Southern gentleman, the Kentucky colonel, Harold "Pee Wee" Reese. God bless him!

TWENTY-NINE

I'VE HAD A STRUGGLE ALL MY LIFE. I'M A COL-ored man. I know there are lots of things that I can do and things that I cannot do without stirring up some people. But a few years ago there were many more things that I could not do than is the case today. I'm willing to wait. I believe in not pushing things; in giving the other fellow a chance. A man's got to do things the way he sees them. No other way.

One reason why I've never had any trouble with white folks — well, hardly ever — is that I've always tried to treat people like I've wanted to be treated. I try to think before I say anything to anyone. I don't want to hurt anyone's feelings because I don't want them to hurt my feelings.

Just how far this has carried me I can best illustrate by something that began in Vero Beach, Florida, and ended in Los Angeles, California; something that gave me the biggest thrill of my life; something that proved to me what I always believed — that this is a wonderful world with a lot of wonderful people in it.

It all began on March 5, 1959, while I was with the Dodgers at Vero Beach. I was having breakfast in the club dining room when Mr. O'Malley came in and whispered something to me.

"Roy, I'd like you to be in the press room at four o'clock today. Remember four o'clock. It's important."

That's all. He didn't say what it was about or why he wanted me to be there. He left without saying another word.

I had no idea what it was all about, but I spent the next

288

few hours trying to figure it out. I thought, of course, it had something to do with the team. I had been working with Johnny Roseboro, teaching him the little extra tricks of catching. The Dodgers had a lot of young pitchers in camp, and I thought maybe they wanted me to work with them. I couldn't imagine anything else.

Anyway, at five minutes to four, I wheeled myself into the press room. The room was filled with reporters. Mr. O'Malley was at the head of the press table. Seated around him were Manager Alston; my old buddy Pee Wee Reese, now a coach; Carl Erskine, who was the team's player representative; and Red Patterson, the club's publicity man.

As soon as I arrived, Mr. O'Malley arose, walked over to me and handed me a sheet of paper.

"Roy," he said, "read this, and if it's all right with you I'll make the announcement."

It was just one paragraph, but I had to read it twice to make sure I was reading it right. Even when I finished reading it a second time, I still couldn't believe it. I never was so touched before. Tears came to my eyes. Finally I looked up at Mr. O'Malley and asked, "What am I supposed to say?"

"Just say if it's all right with you," he said.

"Certainly it's all right with me," I said, "and I also want to say thank you with all my heart. This is wonderful, just wonderful."

Mr. O'Malley then read the statement.

"The Los Angeles Dodgers and New York Yankees have agreed to play a home-and-home exhibition series, the first game to be played at the Los Angeles Coliseum this May 7, the second game to be played at Yankee Stadium in 1960. The games will be played in honor of Roy Campanella, with a portion of the Dodgers' proceeds from the games going to Roy."

This was really something. All obstacles had already been pushed aside. Erskine had gotten approval from all the Dodger players. The Yankees, who were scheduled to play a game in Kansas City the night before, had agreed to fly on to the Coast for the game. Ford Frick, the Commissioner of Baseball, had given his blessing, and Warren Giles, the National League President, had given the Dodgers permission to play the game that night even though they were to play the Giants that same afternoon in San Francisco. Giles's approval was needed because of the rule which states that no team can play in two different parks the same day.

I had never been quite so excited by anything. And it couldn't have come at a better time for me. It was during the time my son David was involved with the courts, and I really was down. This gave me a tremendous lift.

I left for Los Angeles on Saturday, April 11. Jim Williamson, my attendant, was with me. We took off from Idlewild airport in an American Airline jet. It was the first time I had ever flown in a jet and I was a little worried. I knew that the jets fly at a high altitude and I had been told that people in my condition might black out when the plane reaches around 25,000 feet. We flew as high as 30,000 feet and I didn't come near blacking out. I had been advised to drink a glass of water each half hour. I did just that, and I had no trouble at all.

I sat in the front end of the plane, closest to the door. I was pushed up the ramp into the plane in a special eighteen-inch-wide wheel chair; and once in the plane, I was placed in the first regular seat on the right — with only the regular passenger seat strap to help support me. It was a very pleasant five and a quarter hours' flight, and it would have taken less time, but we had to buck a 100-mile headwind a good part of the way.

We ran into a little difficulty when the plane landed in
290

Los Angeles. They had no such special chair as they had at Idlewild and the captain and his crew were embarrassed. The problem was solved for them while they were trying to decide what to do. Several friends of mine were waiting at the airport for me. One of them was Tank Younger, the professional football star. A 250-pound fullback with the Pittsburgh Steelers, Tank grabbed me under the armpits, lifted me like a baby and carried me out of the plane. Then when they brought out my chair, he sat me in it as gently as you please.

Mr. O'Malley had reserved a double suite for me at the Sheraton West Hotel. It was off the lobby overlooking the swimming pool. It was really elegant and very convenient, too. I didn't have to worry about an elevator. Also, the Rush Chevrolet people let me have a brand-new station wagon during my stay in Los Angeles. The car was equipped with special seat belts, identical to those in my car.

I wasn't in the hotel more than an hour when they called a press conference. I was asked the usual questions: How was my trip? How did I like being in California? What did I think about the Dodgers' chances in the pennant race? How did I feel about the short left field fence in the Coliseum? Did I intend to make my home in Los Angeles?

I stayed exactly a month in Los Angeles and I attended every home game the Dodgers played. I must have been a good luck charm for my old buddies because they won the series from each team they played as long as I was there.

I was really kept busy in L. A. Just two days after I got there, I was guest of honor, along with Stan Musial of the Cardinals, at a dinner in the Beverly Hilton Hotel given by the Southern California Baseball Writers Association.

Stan and I were honored as the only players in history ever to win the National League Most Valuable Player award three times.

It was a wonderful night for me. Mr. O'Malley sat at my right on the dais and Dinah Shore at my left. To Dinah's left was Frank Sinatra. A lot of celebrities from the entertainment and political fields were there. Art Linkletter was master of ceremonies. Among the entertainers were Joe E. Brown and Joe Garagiola. Joe is the former major league catcher who caught on in radio and television and made good with a bang. Sinatra sang and so did Dinah. All the players from the Dodgers and St. Louis Cardinals attended. Stan and I were presented with silver trays. Yes, it was quite a night for me, but the biggest kick I got was being able to feed myself and eat like any other person there. The only time I needed help was when I wanted a drink of water. Mr. O'Malley had to hold the glass for me.

That was Monday, April 13. The next night was the Dodgers' home opening and the Cardinals were the opposition.

I was invited to throw out the first ball. The writers were a little worried that I wouldn't be able to throw the ball, but I had a surprise in store for them. What nobody knew was that I had been practicing flipping the ball underhand in the back yard of my home in Glen Cove. I played catch with Roy, Jr., and I got so I could even catch the ball when Roy tossed it to me.

I arrived at the park early Tuesday evening. Kenny Washington, a former great all-around UCLA athlete who played high school and college football with Jackie Robinson, drove me to the Coliseum, only a half hour's drive from the hotel. I spent some time chatting with the boys in the clubhouse. Then, about a half hour before the game was scheduled to start, Pee Wee Reese wheeled me down a special runway out onto the field, in back of the screen, behind home plate. The pre-game ceremonies had already begun. The tremendous crowd — I learned later there were over 68,000 people in the park — stood up and cheered when I was introduced. It was a wonderful feeling.

Pee Wee was my attendant throughout the entire ceremonies. Everytime I looked around, he was wheeling me some place. Finally, it was time for the game to begin. The umpire gave Pee Wee the ball, but he was a bit embarrassed about handing it over to me.

"Campy," he said nervously, "you sure you can throw it?"

I grinned. "Just give me the ball, old buddy," I said, "and I'll show you."

He put the ball in my hands and I flipped it to him with both hands, sort of like a quarterback making a shovel pass to one of his backs.

"Now throw it to me," I said.

Pee Wee hesitated, then tossed the ball underhand to me. I caught the ball against my chest with my arms and let it roll down into my hands. The photographers made us repeat this game of catch several times while they snapped pictures like mad. Finally, after the field was cleared of all but the players, I flipped the ball to Johnny Podres, and the Dodger pitcher walked out to the mound to pitch against the Cardinals' lead-off batter, Don Blasingame. I watched the entire game from my spot on the field near the Dodger dugout. They put a little screen in front of me for protection from foul balls. I had that same spot for every game.

Like I said, I kept busy all the time I was in Los Angeles. I didn't want to stay cooped up in the hotel. All the games, except those on Sunday, were played at night, and during the day I was asked to make appearances at hospitals, schools and other institutions. I also was invited to a number of luncheons and civic affairs. And I found time to visit with friends I had known back East.

One of the nicest things that happened to me out there was seeing my friend, tutor and first manager at Baltimore, Biz

293

Mackey. Biz now lives in Los Angeles. When I learned where he was living, I wasted no time contacting him and invited him to have dinner with me. I hadn't seen him in fifteen years. Later, he was my guest at the special Yankee-Dodger exhibition game played in my honor. Tickets for that game were as scarce as hen's teeth and we had Biz sit with Ruthe in our special box.

Yes, Ruthe and the kids came out for the game. The Dodgers left Thursday, April 24, on a road trip. Their first stop was St. Louis. Ruthe and the children arrived that afternoon, and I was driven out to the airport to meet them. Besides Ruthe, there were Roy, Jr., Tony, and Princess. David, who couldn't afford to take time off from his school studies, went to stay with his grandmother in the Bronx. The kids were awfully excited. They had heard quite a bit about California and were anxious to see the movie sets in Hollywood and meet the movie stars. The place they wanted most to visit, though, was Disneyland.

When Ruthe lifted Princess up and put her in my lap, she hugged me and kissed me and then whispered in my ear:

"Daddy, when will you take us to Disneyland?"

It was nice having Ruthe with me, especially in view of the fact that April 30 was our anniversary. We celebrated it quietly with a bottle of wine, preferring to be by ourselves that night. I couldn't help but think back to a year ago at this time. It was a little different then. I was still lying flat on my back, unable to do anything for myself and wondering whether I ever would. Now I can do practically everything but walk. That night I read the Bible and said a little prayer before I went to bed, thanking God for all the things He had done for me.

Hardly a day went by that I didn't give some kind of a talk either in a school or in a hospital. One day George Vico, who used to play with Detroit and Cleveland in the American

294

League, asked me would I make an appearance at a hospital for crippled children. The hospital lacked a whirlpool tank needed for polio-stricken youngsters, and couldn't afford to buy one. George said if I would make an appearance, he felt certain that enough tickets would be sold to get the money necessary to buy the tank. I assured him it would be a privilege to visit with these youngsters. It worked out fine. The hospital got the money for the whirlpool tank.

The next day was May 7, and what a hectic day — and night — that was. It began with a luncheon in my honor tendered by the California Sportscasters Association. I was made an official member of the association and I was presented with a special sportscasters jacket. Tommy Harmon, the former Michigan University football star, as president of the association, made the presentation.

"Campy," he said, "now you never have to worry about not being seen, because the color of this jacket is the brightest red we could find."

I sat on the dais next to Ted Husing who in his time was one of the really great sports announcers. Ted had an operation for a brain tumor several years ago, and although he lost his eyesight for a while he is making a brave comeback. It was inspiring just to talk with this man. His faith, wonderful disposition and courage were really something to behold. He told me something that interested me very much. For some reason or another, I never was told before that Ted Husing had been a patient at Rusk Institute, too. And strangely enough, he occupied the same room I did, 107.

I was really touched that afternoon. Buzzie Bavasi, the Dodgers' vice president, made quite a speech. It brought tears to my eyes. Quite a few people, he said, were under the impression that the exhibition game between the Yankees and Dodgers that night was purely a charity game for Roy Campanella.

"That's the furthest thing from the truth," Bavasi said. "I want you all to know that this is not a charity game. We're not helping Campy because he needs help. This is a game to honor Roy. This is the Dodgers' way of saying thanks to Campy for everything he has done for the organization through the years, for all the pennants he has helped us win, for all the customers he has brought in to our games, for all the fans he has brought not only to the Dodgers but to all baseball. I feel I know Roy Campanella better than anyone else in baseball. He started his career in organized ball with me in Nashua. He's one of the reasons why I've moved up. I'd like to say right now that as long as there is a Dodger organization, there will always be a place in it for Roy Campanella."

Is it any wonder that I had tears in my eyes?

None of the Dodger players attended the luncheon, for the simple reason that the team was up in San Francisco playing the Giants. The Yankees arrived in town that afternoon. They had flown in from Kansas City where they had played a regular season game the night before. Del Webb, co-owner of the Yankees, and Warren Giles, President of the National League, visited with me at my hotel suite later that afternoon and we had a pleasant chat. Del recalled an incident in the 1955 World Series between the Dodgers and Yankees that caused him a lot of embarrassment. It took place in Ebbets Field. A Yankee batter raised a high foul popup between third and home plate. I hustled out there as fast as I could, but the wind kept carrying the ball into the boxes. I leaned over for the ball, but it came down and hit Webb, who was occupying a box seat behind third base, right on the head. It was more embarrassing than painful.

The Dodgers hadn't arrived yet, when I got to the Coliseum for the game, so I went out on the field to watch the Yankees work out. I passed the time renewing acquaintances with the Yankee players and writers until the Dodgers arrived.

296

The ceremonies began at seven o'clock, an hour before game time. Pee Wee wheeled me out between the pitcher's mound and second base. It was a beautiful night. I looked out into the stands. They were jam-packed. I had never seen so many people in one place. I felt humble. It was only an exhibition game. In the standings, it meant nothing. Yet there wasn't an empty seat. I found out later that 93,103 were in the park, and another 15,000 had been turned away. It was the only time in history that the Coliseum had ever been sold out for a night attraction. It was also the largest crowd ever to see an organized baseball game anywhere. Baseball's previous high attendance, 86,288, was in the fifth game of the 1948 World Series at Cleveland between the Indians and the Boston Braves.

My heart was filled. I felt the people of Los Angeles were paying me a great honor, an honor I hardly deserved. After all, I was no more than a name to most of these people. I had never played a game of baseball in their city. I wasn't even a Dodger any more. Thousands upon thousands of them had never seen me play anywhere. Yet they cheered me as if I had just hit the home run that won the pennant for the Los Angeles Dodgers.

First, each member of the Yankees and Dodgers lined up along the first and third base lines. Each player, coach and manager was presented with a silver plaque and a sterling silver baseball on a mahogany stand with the inscription *Roy Campanella Night   May 7, 1959*. There was a copy of my signature on each plaque, and in addition each player found his own name engraved on his trophy. Even the umpires got one.

After Ruthe and the children were introduced over the public address system, the announcer started talking about me. Pee Wee, who stood at my side throughout the entire ceremonies, took off his L. A. cap and put it on my head. I

297

cried without shame as this tremendous throng — all 93,103 of them — stood up in tribute and shouted a welcome that sounded like the roll of thunder.

It's impossible to describe how I felt just then. All I know is that I found it difficult to speak.

"I thank God that I'm living to be here," I said slowly into the microphone. "I want to thank each and every one of you from the bottom of my heart. This is something I shall never forget as long as I live . . . It's a wonderful tribute. I thank God I'm alive to see it. Thanks a million."

I couldn't say any more. I wanted to but I couldn't find the right words. I wanted to pour out my heart to these wonderful people. I wanted to thank Mr. Del Webb and Mr. Dan Topping and all the Yankees for coming way out halfway across the country to play a game in my honor. I wanted to thank Mr. O'Malley and Buzzie Bavasi and all my old Dodger buddies. I wanted to thank the whole world just for being alive. I wanted to say a lot of things but I couldn't. It's hard to speak when you're crying.

I thought it was all over when Pee Wee pushed me back behind the screen near the Dodger dugout and the game got under way. But it was only the beginning. In between the fifth and sixth innings, time was called and Pee Wee pushed me out again between second base and the pitcher's mound. Then all the lights in the Coliseum were put out. At a given signal by the public address announcer, the people in the park lighted matches. The sight was electrifying. The Coliseum suddenly burst into a mass of blinking stars. It was a gesture, for my benefit, in the form of a birthday cake. I've never seen anything like it.

The sight reminded me of the time in Ebbets Field a few years back when the Dodger fans gave Pee Wee a night. They had put out the lights in Ebbets Field, too, with Pee Wee standing at home plate with me right beside him.

"Remember, Pee Wee," I said now, "on your night in Ebbets Field? 'Campy, come with me and stand next to me,' you said. 'I don't want to stand up there all by myself.' Well, buddy, it's your turn now to stand with me."

When the crowd was announced at 93,000, I couldn't help but note that it was my uniform number in reverse, 39.

Yes, it was a night to remember.

I got up bright and early the next day and was driven to the Hollywood Park race track where they had named the sixth race "The Campanella Purse." It was a $20,000 added handicap and the winner was Silky Sullivan. As usual, he was dead last at the halfway mark, but came all the way to win. Mervyn LeRoy, the track president, had Silky led over to me in the winner's circle and the photographers snapped pictures all over the place. I was presented with a sterling silver plaque and Silky's owner gave me the winner's wreath of flowers for Ruthe.

The day was Friday, May 8. Ruthe took the kids to Disneyland the following day while I stayed in the hotel. The full week's activity had really exhausted me. Monday was packing day and Tuesday we paid a visit to the ball park to say goodbye to the fellows, and that evening we took a plane for home.

It was good to be home, but for the first time ever, I didn't get that feeling of complete happiness at being home. Ruthe felt the same way and even the kids kept asking when we would go to California again. The truth is we all fell in love with Los Angeles. The weather was so perfect and I felt so much better out there. I like the outdoors, and the climate in Southern California permits one to be outside most of the time.

While we were in California, Ruthe looked at some property and made several inquiries regarding a ranch type house. We also asked about my rehabilitation treatments, and we learned that the UCLA Medical Center is scheduled to open a rehabilitation wing very soon. So if we moved out to California, my rehabilitation program could continue. Besides, Mr. O'Malley is anxious for me to live on the Coast. The Dodgers have plans to hold winter baseball clinics around Los Angeles and invite their promising players out there for advanced training. They want Pete Reiser, a former Dodger star who now manages one of their farm teams, and myself to run this instructional camp. That means I'd have to spend most of my time in California.

It's not going to be easy leaving my lovely Glen Cove home on the beautiful Long Island Sound where I used to go fishing from my back yard and where my yacht the *Princess* was tied for years. It's not going to be easy to forget this rambling house where I had so much pleasure . . . and some heartaches too. It won't be easy being away from the many wonderful friends I made. But I'm sure I'll make new friends. And I'll be back in baseball which is my life. I don't believe I'd have made it if I hadn't had that determination to get into baseball.

People have been so wonderful to me, especially since my accident. Of the thousands and thousands of letters I have received, not one has been vicious. I have met thousands of persons since the accident. They say some people are really bad. I haven't run into one yet.

THIRTY

THE INSTITUTE OF PHYSICAL MEDICINE AND Rehabilitation in New York City — until recently at least — was a receiving station for broken necks. Nobody else wanted them. But if it is a community center for broken necks it's also a meeting place for great hearts. And the man who boosts the spirit and drive of today's not-so-helpless cripple into tomorrow's productive human is Dr. Howard A. Rusk.

Dr. Rusk must be seen, yes, and heard, to be believed. Take it from Campy, he's doctor, salesman and evangelist all rolled into one. As I've said before, up through the early stages of World War II, anybody who got what I got was simply stored away to die. Usually it didn't take long. Due to Dr. Rusk and to the great improvement in antibiotics, that's no longer true. Working along with antibiotics, Dr. Rusk, in the last fifteen years, has brought the hopeless cripple back to the walking wounded. That in itself is a chapter of human history that would make a book all by itself. Today, this man and his work are known not only in this country but all over the world!

Until January 28, 1958, I was a ballplayer whose aim, then at least, was to catch one more full season with the Dodgers. After that, well, maybe I could turn to coaching. Baseball was my world. In many ways that still goes. Today I'm still an ex-ballplayer whose life centers around the game, but I know that I'm something else too. Because, where before I might have been a fellow with a fair understanding of life, today I understand a great deal more about many more things . . . especially this wonderful thing called the human spirit. And so, while this accident made me a cripple, it also made me a better human. And please don't chalk that up to saying "Campy's preaching." I ain't.

Beginning from the time of my accident, and for the best part of a year, I knew what it is to be real sick. Fearful sick. And I was a long ways from being out of the woods, so to speak, for some time after I was moved to the Institute. I was scared and I hurt all over and, like I said, there were times when I dreaded facing the possibility that I was broken so bad I might not be able to support my family or myself any longer. That was the worst fear. But I didn't want to show

301

this fear to Dr. Rusk or the wonderful man that he assigned to my case, Dr. Edward Lowman.

One day when Ruthe was sitting there and trying to keep my mind off myself, she said, "Campy, Dr. Lowman talked to me today about you."

"Yeah?" I replied, not hardly listening. "What did he have to say?"

"He says that he has yet to see you depressed . . . really depressed. That worries him. He says that if a patient doesn't show his sorry thoughts, but keeps them bottled up inside, it can be a bad sign. He wanted to know if you ever break down a little and let go when we're alone, here."

"What did you tell him?" I asked.

"I told him the truth. I said, 'Yes, Doctor, Campy's had quite a few bad sessions when we've been alone. He still does.' Dr. Lowman was pleased to hear that."

Several days later, Dr. Rusk stopped by my room. After we'd talked about anything and everything except my condition, he said, "Campy, I know what you're thinking, and I think I know what you're asking yourself. You're asking the old question: Why must I suffer? It's possible that the answer to that is in the work of the potter. You see, Campy, great ceramics are not made by putting clay in the sun. They only come from the white heat of the kiln. In the firing process, some pieces are broken. But those that survive the heat are transformed from clay into objects of art."

It wasn't until several weeks later, after I began to take my place in the hospital community, that I began to understand Dr. Rusk's words better. Quadriplegics or paraplegics, we've all suffered — not only in body but in mind. We've been through the white heat of that kiln. But due to that torture — and it is torture — I think that maybe we have a bond of understanding that goes below any surface stuff. So, in a sense then, we have not wasted our pain.

One day, while I was rolling through the halls of the Institute in my chair, I heard Dr. Rusk talking to someone in his office. To this day I don't know whether that person was a man or a woman, a reporter or a businessman, or even a patient. But I did hear him tell that person: ". . . People have such strength and potential, and more when they're paralyzed. Once they get over that hump, successfully pass through that first bad depression, they are better, spiritually, than ever before! These quadriplegics and paraplegics have such spirit as a well person can never understand."

Dr. Rusk was referring to me and thousands more like me. But it took me a lot of time to understand and appreciate the truth behind that statement. Today, however, I know those aren't just words.

For any cripple, part of learning how to live again is tied up with learning the workings of the body, and how to get the most use out of whatever muscles and nerves are left. Nature has given us all such tremendous power to recuperate and, as Dr. Rusk, Dr. Lowman and the therapists put it, powers of "overcompensation." The average "well" person uses only 25 per cent of his physical makeup in daily living. But the blind man uses 100 per cent of his sense of touch and hearing. That is how he sees! That white cane he carries serves as his ears and eyes. His ears become so sensitive that he can tell whether the echo is off a wall, a line of trees, or from an open space.

There was a time when I didn't give much of a thought to a blind man's cane except to think how bad off he is.

But now I know that the blind man's sense of hearing, touch and smell make up for his lack of sight. His other senses are in a kind of overdrive. It's almost impossible for anyone who isn't blind to learn to read Braille. That's because his sense of touch is not sensitive enough. And according to Dr. Rusk, if that blind man is put to work in a photographic dark

303

room, before long he will turn out 30 per cent more work than the man with sight who is working alongside him!

That's what Dr. Rusk means by overcompensation. And he expects each one of us cripples to "beef up" whatever we still have until we get "muscles on muscles." Give a paraplegic a job that needs upper arm strength and hand movement, and chances are he'll outdo the ordinary worker because he "walks on his hands," as the saying goes.

If it took me some time to really grasp the reason behind all this, it wasn't for lack of good teachers. Aside from our therapists, it took others just like me to teach it. I'm supposed to have done a lot for crippled youngsters. Well, if the hundreds of letters that I received from crippled children and adults, too, mean what I think they do, then maybe I am becoming a sort of symbol. Let me just say, however, that people like Michael Friedman and Gilbert Provencher, Father Thomas Carroll, Ruth Purdom, Ben Mewbourne, Charles Poore, Ubaldo Nino, Ann Previti, Eleanor Moriarty, Jimmy Duffy — and others who were patients at Rusk's with me, did even more for me! However, most of those quads I got to know in the Institute were struck down in their teens and their early twenties. My professional life was practically finished when I got hit; theirs hadn't even started. It is these, especially the youngsters, who helped to inspire me.

All my life I have fought, in my own way, for equality, integration and understanding of minority groups. But from here on, I've taken on an even bigger job — fighting for the equality, integration, and understanding and acceptance of the severely handicapped.

We're a rugged breed, us quads. If we weren't we wouldn't be around today. Yes, we're a rugged breed; and, in many ways, we've been blessed with a savvy and spirit that isn't given to everybody.

Today, if I am a "life member" of this rugged breed, I've

also got a lot of people on my team. Thanks to the unseen army of medical men and women all over the world now striving to learn . . . well, some day maybe, I'll get out of this chair and walk again with my youngsters! So far, there's no way medical science knows to make a severed or a badly damaged spinal cord heal and function. But I've got to keep that hope! And I intend to hold onto it. While a quad never wants total acceptance of his condition, he does want understanding of what's wrong with him. Cancer patients are in the same boat with us . . . maybe more so. They also have hope that one day — maybe tomorrow, maybe next week, maybe next year — another human, or a team of humans, will come through with a cure for their disease.

And let me say that this refusal of total or full acceptance of his disability all hooks up with one thing — *Faith,* an almost divine faith.

Down in the reception room of the Institute of Physical Medicine and Rehabilitation, over on the East River at 400 East 34th Street in New York City, there is a bronze plaque that's riveted to the wall. During the months of coming back to the Institute for treatment — two and three times a week — I rolled through that reception room many times, coming and going. But I never quite made the time to pull over to one side and read the words on that plaque that were written, it's said, by an unknown Confederate soldier. Then one afternoon last May, after I'd come home from that big night in Los Angeles, I did. I read it, and then I read it again. When I finished it the second time I was near to bursting — not in despair, but with an inner glow that had me straining to grip the arms of my wheel chair.

Here it is:

A CREED FOR THOSE WHO HAVE SUFFERED

I asked God for strength, that I might achieve
I was made weak, that I might learn humbly to obey . . .

I asked for health, that I might do greater things
I was given infirmity, that I might do better things . . .

I asked for riches, that I might be happy
I was given poverty that I might be wise . . .

I asked for power that I might have the praise of men
I was given weakness, that I might feel the need of God . . .

I asked for all things that I might enjoy life
I was given life, that I might enjoy all things . . .

I got nothing I asked for — but everything I had hoped for

Almost despite myself, my unspoken prayers were answered
I am among men, most richly blessed!

No one could add anything to that.

T's